THE
Mystery
OF
Music
Second Edition

Kenneth Keaton

Florida Atlantic University

Kendall Hunt
publishing company

Cover image © Shutterstock, Inc.

Kendall Hunt
publishing company

www.kendallhunt.com
Send all inquiries to:
4050 Westmark Drive
Dubuque, IA 52004-1840

contents

introduction

To the Student

"The most beautiful experience is the mysterious. It is the fundamental emotion which stands at the cradle of True Art and True Science."
Albert Einstein

The art of music is central to the human experience. Music is as old as humanity, and it has been part of every human culture, no matter how primitive or advanced. While it might be presumptuous to assume that *Homo sapiens* is the only species which expresses itself through art and music—whales and dolphins certainly seem to communicate in sounds which might be something like our music or poetry—there is something uniquely *human* in our desire to reach beyond the necessities of mere existence and to proclaim our humanity through art.

Music expresses everything about us. Through music we celebrate joy and we mourn our sorrows, we convey our affirmation of life and beauty, and we express our horror at tragedy or our outrage at injustice. Love, hate, action, contemplation, sensuality, spirituality—the whole range of the human experience can be communicated through music. Humanity has always used the arts to express the inexpressible, to speak of that which is strongly felt but cannot be put into a concrete framework. Certain aspects of our existence can only be expressed through the sounds of music.

Music is a part of every person's life. We are all passionate about *some* kind of music, whether rock or rap, jazz or country, Jimmy Buffett or Johannes Brahms. Music speaks to the heart of our humanity and can be understood by anyone. Why, then, is it necessary to have a college class to help in the understanding of something that is so universally loved?

People seem to be most strongly attached to the music that is most common in their experience. People love what they know (a statement that is more accurate than the one which is more commonly heard: I know what I like). They tend to be bored by—and sometimes intimidated by—music that is unfamiliar. We tend to judge a musical experience by how close it comes to our own expectations; if the music does not sound like what we expect, we turn it off. But to understand any new experience, we need to have some idea what that new experience really is. A fan of hip-hop needs to know *something* about jazz before he or she can come to understand it and to love it, and vice versa. This is certainly the case when one hears music of the past, created originally for a different era than our own, yet continues to be performed and enjoyed, sometimes centuries later.

Many types of music are associated primarily with a particular group in society. Appalachian folk music, country music, or reggae, reflect particular segments of the population. Rock 'n' roll, in all its variety, reflects a specific generation or, at this point, several generations, each tuned in to a particular portion of rock history.

This book, however, is concerned with what is usually termed "Classical Music." The term is actually somewhat inaccurate; strictly speaking, the term "Classical" refers only to a fairly brief period of history, during the late 18th and very early 19th century. The designation "Western Art Music" is a more accurate, if less elegant, description of this body of music. What that refers to is nothing less than the finest musical expression of European and American civilization from the last thousand years!

A work becomes a classic when it touches something deeply human in its audience. At this point, the work attains a type of immortality; it outlives its creator, the audience for which it was created, even its national origins. Such a work, in a very real sense, belongs to everyone in Western civilization, regardless of origin or background.

Only a few works possess this sort of quality. The writer Theodore Sturgeon has postulated Sturgeon's Law, which can be politely paraphrased as deeming that 90 percent of everything is garbage. Some might put the figure even higher. In any case, music (or anything) that goes beyond that 90 percent group has this attribute. We can call it a transhistorical quality, or the ability of a work of art to transcend its specific era and to speak to all humanity, regardless of the separation by time or geography. Such music becomes the treasure of everyone.

This book, then, is designed to celebrate that universal artistic heritage. It is intended to concentrate exclusively on the heritage of Western Art Music, not because other types of music are not worthy of study, but because of the time limitations of a one-semester course. Popular music, jazz, and non-Western art musics deserve more than just a cursory mention in a text such as this. Instead, we will study the greatest western art music that has been created over the last 10 centuries, all written and performed by some of the most fascinating and colorful figures of all history. Keep your ears open—you are about to discover a wealth of riches!

THE LANGUAGE OF MUSIC

Music is often described as a universal language—justly so, for no recorded human culture has ever existed without music. Yet, it is a language with many dialects, and no one person understands all those dialects naturally. Music of different cultures, of different eras, or different generations, can all sound strange or foreign if we are not familiar with it. To become familiar with other dialects of music, we need to spend some time studying the materials of music, common to one degree or another with all forms of music. For this reason, we begin our study with a consideration of the elements which make up the language of music, in aural and written form.

Part of the reason for this portion of our study is to establish a common language for discussion of music. Just as the study of a spoken language must deal with parts of speech, tenses, and syntax, the understanding of musical language must consider aspects such as pitch, harmony, and form. Beyond this, however, we study aspects of the structure of music because that structure affects how we perceive music: how it touches us emotionally and sensually. A richer comprehension of the elements of music will actually clarify and intensify that emotional effect.

What Is Music?

The most reasonable place to begin is with the definition of music, except that music is not as easy to define as one might think. It is particularly difficult in the music of our 20th century, which is largely characterized by a challenging of traditional definitions of music and a replacement of those definitions with all sorts of new ideas.

Leaving aside for now the radical ideas of the 20th-century avant-garde, we can at least agree that music involves the use of sound for communication. Music is distinguished from spoken language in that it makes a conscious manipulation of certain qualities of sound to achieve this communication. Musical sounds, for the most part, use four specific qualities of sound, each manipulated in various ways, to convey emotions, moods, and even images. These four qualities are **pitch**, **duration**, **intensity**, and **timbre**.

Pitch

All sound originates from vibration. If, for instance, the instructor's chair is pushed over, when it strikes the ground, it sets off a wave of vibrations that pass through the air and are picked up by our eardrums. The vibrations are passed through a series of small bones in the inner ear, where the mechanical energy of the sound wave is transformed into electrical energy by nerve endings and sent to our brains, where it is perceived as sound. Sound must travel through some transmitting medium. It travels more strongly and rapidly through water, as any SCUBA diver can confirm. And sound will *not* travel through a vacuum. So, when Star Trek's *Enterprise* (of either generation) passes through the vacuum of space, the whooshing sound heard during the introductions to the television shows could not possibly be heard.

When that vibration is at a constant rate, rather than a randomly fluctuating one, the sound has a perceptible **pitch**. As the rate becomes faster or slower, the pitch changes. We generally refer to faster pitches as higher and slower pitches as lower when discussing their relation to each other.

Duration

All musical sounds have a measurable **duration** because all such sounds exist in time. A note may exist only for a brief moment, or it may sustain itself for a long period, but it will have a measurable beginning and ending. Theoretically, a sound could last for days or even longer if it were created and sustained electronically, though such a sound would be of little use for creating music that would communicate anything.

Intensity

Just as the frequency of a musical sound determines its pitch, the amplitude of a sound determines its **intensity**, or its loudness or softness. Our perception of the intensity of a note varies widely according to a number of factors. A particular instrument or voice may be very powerful or rather slight; even certain types of instruments tend to be strong, while others are softer. Even the environment in which we hear music affects our perception of its intensity. The acoustic properties of a concert hall, an outdoor amphitheater, a night club, or even a living room or the interior of a car are all quite different, and the intensity of sound will be perceived distinctly in each separate place.

Timbre

Musical sounds can be produced that match in pitch, duration, and intensity, but are still quite different from each other, because of the fourth quality: **timbre** or **tone color**. This complex quality is created by the nature of the material that produces the vibrating sound.

Let us imagine a sound created with the same pitch (say, middle C; see subsequent discussion), duration, and intensity created from three different sources, such as a piano, a classical guitar, and a singing voice. The piano will create its sound by the vibration of a set of three metal strings, all tuned to the same pitch so they sound as a single note. The strings are set in motion by being struck by a felt-covered hammer, activated by depressing a key on the keyboard. The vibration of the strings is then transferred into an iron frame to which the strings are attached. This amplifies the sound. It is further amplified and projected by the wooden housing of the instrument, and the sound is projected out to the ears of the listener.

If the same sound is produced by a classical guitar, the timbre is quite different. The guitar also uses a tightly stretched vibrating string to create its sound, but it only uses a single string, made of nylon. It is set into motion by a finger pushing the string aside and releasing it. The vibration of the string is transferred through the bridge into the top of the instrument, which is made of a soft wood that will vibrate easily and therefore amplify the sound. The vibration of the top is further intensified by the sides and back of the instrument, which are made of a hard wood that will reflect the sound, finally projecting it to the ears of the listener.

Though they are distinct, the sounds of the piano and the guitar are related, as they both originate from vibrating strings. But the same note produced by a human voice is startlingly different. Here, the vibration is produced by human tissue, the vocal chords of the larynx. The folds of tissue are stretched to a particular tension and are set in motion by air passing over them from the lungs, producing a particular pitch, duration, intensity, and timbre. The sound will also vary among human voices, male or female, depending on the natural thickness of the vocal chords of any individual.

Another interesting difference between the sounds of the piano and guitar and that of the voice is the quality of sustain. A note from a singer can sustain at the same level of intensity, or even get louder, while a note sounded by a guitar or a piano will immediately begin to decay. These two instruments can only give the illusion of getting louder in a passage by playing each individual note in a group more strongly.

The Linear Aspects of Music

Any single musical tone will have distinct qualities of pitch, duration, intensity, and timbre. In a piece of music, those qualities are manipulated to form expressive and coherent musical segments, just as sequences of words of language form sentences and paragraphs. As we examine the ways in which these qualities can be arranged to create music, we will also discuss the means by which music is notated, in such a fashion that any trained musician can read it and recreate it at will. It is not necessary to be a fluent music reader in order to appreciate musical expression, but some knowledge of what these mysterious symbols indicate will certainly enhance your understanding and enjoyment of music.

Pitch

Sequences of pitches can do virtually anything. They can ascend, descend, or center around a single note; the distance between two pitches in a sequence can be very close or it can skip widely. Pitches are notated on a graph-like device called a **staff**, which consists of five parallel lines. Individual notes are indicated by an oval shape and are read from left to right; the pitch of a note is indicated by the position of the note on the staff, either on a line or on one of the spaces between the lines. The notes are named by the letters of the alphabet, from A to G, after which the sequence begins again with the same letter (those duplicate notes have a special acoustical relationship: the upper note is vibrating exactly twice as fast as the lower note with the same letter name). The exact note to which a line or space on the staff corresponds is indicated by a symbol at the beginning of the staff called a **clef**. For instance, if a staff begins with a **treble clef** (also called a **G-clef**—notice how the symbol curls around the second line of the staff, which is the note G), the pitches on the staff are as follows:

example 1

Pitches on the treble clef

This is actually not a very wide range of pitches; hardly enough to make much music. One can extend the staff by adding what are called **ledger lines**, which are simply extensions of the staff up or down. Just as the notes on the staff ascend or descend line to space to line, so do the notes on the ledger lines.

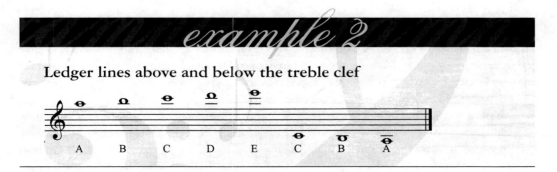

example 2

Ledger lines above and below the treble clef

This method can cover pitches as far as is needed, but is especially difficult to read when there are more than a few ledger lines. There are, however, other clefs, the most common of which is the **bass clef**, used to notate lower pitches. This is also called the **F-clef**—again, notice how the symbol curls around the second line from the top, which is the note F in bass clef.

Pitches on the bass clef

F   G   A   B   C   D   E   F   G   A

Notice that the first ledger line below the treble clef and the first ledger line above the bass clef is the note C. It is in fact, the same C, called **middle C**, between the treble clef and the bass clef. One can actually combine the two, by a bracket, creating what is called a **grand staff**, also called a **great staff**.

Pitches on the grand staff

C D E F G A B C D E F G

F G A B C D E F G A B C

Now we have quite a range of pitches. Not surprisingly, the grand staff is used for the notation of the wide range of pitches needed on keyboard instruments such as the piano and organ.

Duration

The relationship of notes of various durations is called **rhythm**. Most (though not all) music defines its rhythms by their relationship to a central recurring pulse, the **beat**. If you have ever danced to a piece of music, tapped your foot, or swayed with the music, you have responded to the beat. The speed of the beat is usually steady, though it can vary for expressive effect. The speed of the beat is known as the **tempo**.

In most music, that beat is organized into regular groupings, distinguished by sequences of strong and weak beats. This grouping is called the **meter** of a piece. The meter can be organized into groups of two, known as **duple** meter: **strong**, weak, **strong**, weak. It can also be organized into groups of three, known as **triple** meter: **strong**, weak, weak, **strong**, weak, weak.

Meter can become quite complex; some meters can be irregular, or asymmetrical. Commonly, we have what is called compound meter, with two different levels of metric subdivision. But all meters are, to one degree or another, an extension of duple or triple meter, as two and three are both prime numbers.

The relative duration of notes within a piece is indicated by the **shape** of the note symbol. Notice we say the "relative" duration: the exact duration is a factor of the tempo of the piece, but because rhythm is normally made of notes of a variety of different durations, some means of distinguishing those durations had to be developed. Generally, note duration varies by a factor of two—a whole note (a single empty note head) divides into two half notes (the note head with a stem attached, going up or down), which divides into four quarter notes (like the half note but the note head is solid), etc. There are also ways to divide note durations by three, or by other groupings, but division by two is the norm.

Eighth notes have a flag attached to the stem, or if there are two or more eighth notes, they can be attached by a beam across the opposite ends of the stems. Two flags (or two beams) make the note a sixteenth note, three a thirty-second note, and so on. Theoretically, the process can continue indefinitely, though it is rare to find more than three flags or beams. In Charles Ives' *Concord Sonata* for piano, there are two 1028th notes, with eight beams, but this is an example of extreme hyperbole, as it would be virtually impossible to execute those figures accurately.

In addition to note durations, there is also a way to indicate silences in music. This is necessary because the beat is always present, even though there may be no notes to be played at a particular point in the piece; some means is necessary to fill in those places where the beat continues but no notes are sounded. The symbols for silence are called **rests**, and they correspond to note values of similar rhythmic duration.

example 5

Rhythmic symbols, notes, and rests (to the 16th)

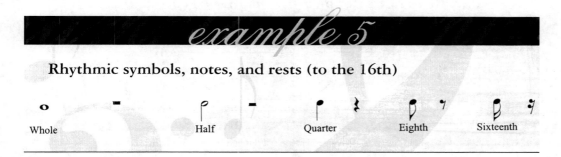

Whole   Half   Quarter   Eighth   Sixteenth

The meter of a piece is indicated by the division of the staff into sections, called **measures** or **bars**, by vertical lines, cleverly called **measure lines** or **bar lines**. The amount of beats found in each measure is indicated by a pair of numbers at the beginning of the piece, just after the clef. These numbers, called the **meter signature** or **time signature**, indicate two different points of information. The top number indicates the number of beats in a measure, and the bottom number indicates the kind of note that gets one beat. The top number can therefore be anything, though it is not usually more than 12, but the bottom number *must* be a 1, a 2, a 4, an 8, a 16—in other words, it must correspond to a type of note (whole, half, quarter, eighth, sixteenth, etc.) that actually exists. To make matters somewhat simpler, in most music, the lower number will be either a four or an eight. Two is uncommon; and 1, 16, or 32 are quite rare.

Notice in the following examples that in, for instance, 4/4 time (often indicated with a C, for **common time**), one need not have four quarter notes per measure, but one must have the *equivalent* of four quarter notes or rests in each measure.

4/4 time: four beats per measure, quarter note gets one beat

3/8 time: three beats per measure, eighth note gets one beat

3/2 time: three beats per measure, half note gets one beat

The tempo is indicated by any of several words from the Italian language. Italian terms are especially common in music terminology because Italy was the dominant European musical culture when much of music notation and practice was being standardized.

Standard terms to indicate tempo

Prestissimo	Extremely fast
Presto	Very fast
Vivace	Lively
Allegro	Fast
Allegretto	Moderately fast
Moderato	Moderate
Andantino	A brisk walking speed
Andante	Walking
Adagio	Slow
Largo	Broadly
Grave	Extremely slow

The alert student will notice that these are hardly exact terms; in fact, in the literal Italian meanings, they seem to have little to do with tempo. *Andante* means "walking," but how fast does one walk? *Allegro* actually means "happy." How fast is happy? Does it depend on how happy one is? *Allegretto* is simply a diminutive of *Allegro*, presumably meaning "little happy." In fact, these indications convey more of a sense of mood than a literal tempo.

Perhaps this is because there really is not a single proper way to play any particular piece of music. Even when composers use a specific tempo indication, they often give a range of appropriate speeds rather than a single recommendation.

That specific indication is only available through the use of a 19th-century invention, the **metronome**. This device consists of a swinging pendulum with a moveable weight, which ticks from side to side at a specific rate per minute; the closer the weight is to the central axis of the pendulum, the faster the ticking becomes.

A composer might indicate a tempo of 120 beats per minute as follows: mm = 120. The letters stand for "Maelzel's metronome," after the inventor of the apparatus, Johann Nepomuk Maelzel (1772–1838). Maelzel was an eccentric inventor, a friend of Beethoven, who is currently known only for this device, though he gained some fame during his lifetime with various other inventions, such as his mechanical chess player. This fame turned to infamy when it was revealed that he had hidden a midget chess player within the mechanical mechanism.

The metronome is well-known to student musicians, nearly all of whom grow to loathe this unforgiving little box; however, it is an indispensable tool for any performer. Most musicians now use electronic versions of the metronome.

The metronome. © JupiterImages, Inc.

Melody

A series of pitches and rhythms that convey a coherent musical idea is known as a **melody**. Melodies are characterized almost as much by their rhythms as by their pitches. If one were to take the pitches of *The Star-Spangled Banner* and play them in a different rhythm, one can perhaps recognize the identity of the piece, but only with difficulty.

Melodies are characterized as either **conjunct** or **disjunct**. Disjunct melodies have wide spaces between many of their notes—*The Star-Spangled Banner* is a good example of such a melody, as anyone has discovered who has tried to sing it. Conjunct melodies are constructed in such a fashion that their notes are all fairly close to each other, moving without many leaps. A good example of this is the melody known to Americans as *My Country 'tis of Thee* and to the British as *God Save the Queen*.

Melodies, like spoken language, are constructed in a series of **phrases**. This is one of the most difficult concepts in music to define precisely. The composer Arnold Schoenberg said simply that a phrase is the amount of music that can be sung in a single breath (this could actually be said of spoken language also). A more specific definition, perhaps, would be the smallest section of a melody which makes sense on its own. Notice, the melody of *My Country 'tis of Thee/God Save the Queen* is divided neatly into two phrases, separated by the long note that ends the first phrase.

Another term related to melody is **theme**. The theme of a piece is its most important melody (or one of its most important melodies). If we ask an acquaintance if he or she knows a particular song or piece, we will often identify the music by singing its theme—not the whole piece, but one particularly memorable melody.

Intensity

The levels of intensity within a piece are referred to as its **dynamics**. Even more so than with tempo, the dynamics of a piece are qualities in which relative values are more important than absolute ones. No one has ever tried to establish specific decibel levels to indicate the loudness or softness of a passage. Dynamics will vary according to the player him- or herself, the player's instrument (both the type of instrument and its relative quality), the type and size of ensemble, the type of music, and the environment in which the music is being made.

Like tempo, dynamic indications are derived from Italian. Only two terms, with modifiers, are in use: *piano* and *forte*.

example 10

Dynamic level indications and their abbreviations

Pianissimo/pp	very soft
Piano/p	soft
Mezzo piano/mp	moderately soft
Mezzo forte/mf	moderately loud
Forte/f	loud
Fortissimo/ff	very loud

The levels can be extended as is desired: *ppp*, *pppp*, *fff*, *ffff*; again, extreme extensions seem to be more for hyperbole than for any realistic information.

Incidentally, the relationship between the dynamic indication *piano* and the musical instrument of the same name is an interesting one. The piano was invented around 1719 by the Italian instrument maker Bartolommeo Cristofori. It differed from its predecessor the harpsichord in that it was the first keyboard instrument which could make a significant difference in loudness or softness by the mere touch of the hands on the keyboard. Cristofori was brilliant as an instrument maker, but less so as an instrument namer; the best name he could come up with for his new child was the *pianoforte*, or the "soft-loud" (it is also known as the *fortepiano*, or the "loud-soft"). The instrument dropped the *forte* part of the name during the late 19th century.

These dynamic indications are all for static dynamic levels. For changing dynamics, the terms *crescendo* (getting gradually louder) or *decrescendo* or *diminuendo* (getting gradually softer) are used. Composers may write out the word at passages where such an effect is desired, or they may use symbols.

Symbol for Crescendo:

Symbol for Decrescendo/Diminuendo:

Timbre

Over the millennia of recorded history, many different types of instruments have come and gone, but humanity discovered from a very early time that certain media are ideal for the production of musical sounds. Though the instruments themselves have flourished and become obsolete, the *families* of instrument have been comparatively constant: **strings**, **woodwinds**, **brass**, **percussion**, and even **keyboard** instruments have existed since Greco-Roman civilizations. The only new family to come into being during our own century has been the **electronic** instruments.

The Voice

Of course, the oldest and most beautiful of all instruments, the model that all instrumental music seeks to emulate, is the human voice (it seems likely that the oldest profession is not that of the prostitute, but of either the singer or the farmer). The most important types of voices for the non-specialist to know are those six that define most singers. Three types describe female singers, from the brightest tone and highest range to the darkest and lowest: **soprano**, **mezzo-soprano**, and **contralto** (or simply **alto**). The other three describe male singers, also from the brightest tone and highest range to the darkest and lowest: **tenor**, **baritone**, and **bass**.

It is important to realize that the voices are distinguished much more by their tone quality, determined by the relative thickness of the vocal chords, than by their pitch range. Indeed, there is much overlapping of ranges, and at least one note, middle C, is common to both the soprano range and the bass range. Six (or more) singers can therefore sing that same middle C, and each sound different from the others.

There are many types of voices, often characterized by the singer's specific abilities rather than by the voice's general qualities. A **coloratura soprano**, for instance, has a very high range and an extremely flexible technique. A **spinto soprano** has a powerful, dramatic voice, as does a **heldentenor**. A **basso profundo** emphasizes the lower range of his voice, whereas a **basso cantante** emphasizes the upper notes.

The **countertenor** is a male singer who has developed the **falsetto** range of the voice to sing with a particularly strong, beautiful tone. The falsetto voice is an extension of the male voice into the range of a female alto or even a soprano; it was used particularly during the Middle Ages and Renaissance for sacred choral music in which it was forbidden to use female voices.

Strings

The stringed instruments all produce their sound from the vibrations of tightly stretched strings. Pitch is controlled by several factors. It can be changed by tightening or loosening the tension of the strings, usually from the gears or pegs to which the strings are attached. The diameter of the string is also a factor—a thick string will have a lower pitch at the same tension as a thin one. In addition, the pitch can be controlled by shortening the vibrating length of string by pressing the string into a fingerboard on the neck of the instrument. The shorter the vibrating string is, the higher its pitch will be.

The family of stringed instruments can be divided into two groups: those that produce their sounds by plucking a taught string and those that produce their sounds by drawing a bow across the string. The bow, usually made of wood, stretches several lengths of horse hair to a particular tension. The hairs are then coated with a sticky resin, which causes the string to vibrate as the bow is drawn across it. By skillful manipulation of the bow, an incredible variety of tone and articulation can be produced. The bowed string instruments are the closest of all instruments to the human voice in terms of the range of sounds which can be produced.

The **guitar** is the most typical of the **plucked string** family. The instrument has six strings, which are stretched over a neck and onto imbedded metal bars called **frets**. These enable the player to shorten the string length and to raise the pitch without muffling the sound with the flesh of the fingers—the string vibrates more clearly when in contact with the fret than with the finger. Other plucked string instruments include the **mandolin**, the **banjo**, the **ukulele**, and the **lute**.

The **harp** is the largest member of the plucked strings and is the only one without a fretted neck. Instead, the harp has a single string for each note, all attached to a large frame. The player sits behind the frame to play the instrument. The notes C and F are distinguishable by being a different color from the other notes; this keeps the player from getting lost among all the strings.

Modern members of the **bowed strings** have in common more than the use of the bow. All of the instruments have the same shape, differing only in size and range. They produce a similar sound quality

Figures 1.2–1.7 are members of the plucked string family

Guitar. © JupiterImages, Inc.

Harp. © JupiterImages, Inc.

Mandolin. © JupiterImages, Inc.

Figures 1.2–1.7 are members of the plucked string family

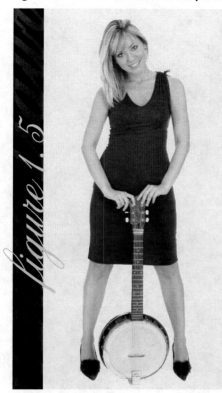

Banjo. © JupiterImages, Inc.

Lute. © Elizabeth Parodi, 2010. Used under license from Shutterstock, Inc.

Ukulele. © JupiterImages, Inc.

throughout their range, and it is no accident that this group dominates the modern orchestra, both in numbers and in sound.

The **violin** is the smallest of the bowed strings, with the highest range and the brightest tone. Like its larger sibling the **viola**, it is held under the chin of the player, supported by the left hand. The still larger **violoncello** (often just called the '**cello**) is too large to be held under the chin; the player sits behind the instrument, which is held between the legs, resting on a metal pin that runs from the bottom of the instrument to the floor. The largest member of the family is the **double bass** (also called the **contrabass** or the **bass violin**); this behemoth is too large even to sit behind. The player must stand or sit on a high stool and hold the instrument while upright.

Members of the bowed string family

Violin. © JupiterImages, Inc.

Viola. © JupiterImages, Inc.

Violoncello. © JupiterImages, Inc.

Double Bass. © Kuz'min Pavel, 2010. Used under license from Shutterstock, Inc.

Woodwinds

One of the main characteristics of the bowed string instruments is their homogeneity of sound quality—they blend perfectly over a wide range of pitch. The **woodwind** family is just the opposite. These instruments have a wide variety of sound qualities because there are no less than three means of sound production among them. Each of the instruments is constructed as a hollow tube, with holes at specific points along its body. The holes are covered with keys, or sometimes with the fingers. When all the holes are covered, the vibrating column of air is the longest; as a longer string has a lower pitch, the longer column of air in a wind instrument produces a lower pitch. The pitch is changed by uncovering holes in the instrument to shorten the column of vibrating air.

The source of the vibration is what distinguishes the woodwinds. In **single-reed** instruments, the vibration is caused by blowing into a mouthpiece that has a single reed, carved of cane, clamped into a wooden mouthpiece. The reed is carved thinly enough that as air is blown between it and the mouthpiece, it vibrates, and produces the instrument's sound.

There are only two kinds of single reed woodwinds: the **clarinet** and the **saxophone**. There are, however, many different versions of each of these instruments. The clarinet is made of wood—it has a beautiful, warm sound in its lower **register** (pitch range) and becomes piercing in the upper register. The saxophone is made of metal, though with a wooden mouthpiece, and has a much more brilliant sound. It, too, is made in several different ranges: soprano, alto, tenor, baritone, bass, and contrabass, among others.

Single-reed instruments

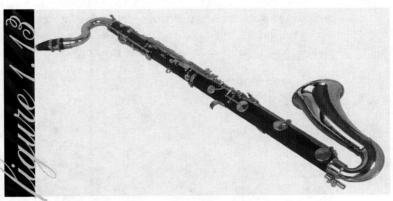

Bass clarinet. © JupiterImages, Inc.

Soprano saxophone. © JupiterImages, Inc.

Bb clarinet. © JupiterImages, Inc.

Tenor saxophone. © JupiterImages, Inc.

Alto saxophone. © JupiterImages, Inc.

Baritone saxophone. © JupiterImages, Inc.

The **double-reed** instruments have a mouthpiece made entirely from reeds: it consists of two thin cane reeds that are carved to precise dimensions and tied together. The player directs a thin stream of high-pressure air between the reeds to produce the sound. The highest of the double reed instruments is the **oboe**. An alto version of the oboe is called the **English horn**, though it is not English but French. The original name was *cor angle*, angled or bent horn, a reference to the angle of the mouthpiece. Somehow the name became corrupted to *cor anglais*, English horn, and that designation has remained.

The **bassoon** and the **contrabassoon** make up the lower end of the family. Unlike the single reed instruments, the double reeds are not made in several different ranges and types. However, during the Renaissance and Baroque periods, there were many different kinds of double reed instruments, each of which was made in several different ranges.

Double-reed instruments

Oboe. © Shutterstock, 2010. Used under license from Shutterstock, Inc.

English horn. © Shutterstock, 2010. Used under license from Shutterstock, Inc.

Bassoon. © mkm3, 2010. Used under license from Shutterstock, Inc.

A third type of woodwind is **reedless**. The **flute** and its smaller cousin the **piccolo** (from the Italian, *flauto piccolo*, or "little flute") make sounds by blowing across an open hole, in much the same way as sounds can be made by blowing across the mouth of a soft drink bottle. The flute (which also exists in alto and bass versions) is perhaps the most agile of all the woodwinds, with a pure, crystalline sound from its metal construction. Actually, all the woodwinds are agile instruments, and can be played very rapidly. What they lack in power, they make up in their wonderful range of tone qualities.

Flute. © JupiterImages, Inc.

Reedless woodwind instruments

Alto Flute. © mkm3, 2010. Used under license from Shutterstock, Inc.

Bass Flute. © mkm3, 2010. Used under license from Shutterstock, Inc.

Piccolo. © Shutterstock, 2010. Used under license from Shutterstock, Inc.

Brass

The **brass** instruments are just the opposite of the woodwinds—they are not nearly as agile, but they can be immensely powerful. Like the bowed strings, the brass instruments have a certain homogeneity of tone. The sound is produced by the vibration of the player's lips in a cup-shaped mouthpiece. The lips are pulled taut and are placed in the mouthpiece where they make a sound which is considered horribly insulting in most cultures, but when that sound passes through the length of the tubing of the instrument, it changes into tones of real beauty. Incidentally, the saxophone, an instrument made of brass, is not considered a brass instrument because it uses a different method of sound production.

Pitch on brass instruments changes by tightening or loosening the lips, or by increasing the amount of tubing in use to make the sounds: the longer the tubing, the lower the pitch. Most of the brass instruments add extra length to the vibrating column of air by depressing valves or keys, which will engage extra lengths of tubing to lower the pitch. The main exception to this method is the **trombone**, which lengthens its air column by a movable slide, operated by the player's right hand. Valve trombones do exist, but they have never been popular because the typical sound of the instrument relies so heavily on the action of the slide.

Other brass instruments include the **trumpet** and related instruments such as the **cornet** and **flugelhorn**. These are the highest in pitch range of the brass instruments. There is also the **French horn**, which grew out of the hunting horns of earlier eras. The bell of the French horn is at a right angle to the mouthpiece. The instrument naturally produces a rather harsh sound, and it is normally muted by placing the fist of the left hand directly into the bell; the resulting sound is particularly powerful and noble.

The **tuba** family is at the bottom end of the brass instruments; in addition to the standard orchestral tubas there are several other types, including the **baritone horn** or **euphonium**, the **Wagner tuba**, and the **Sousaphone**, which wraps around the shoulders of the player for use in a marching band.

Brass instruments

Trumpet. © Popkov, 2010. Used under license from Shutterstock, Inc.

Flugelhorn. © Horatiu Bota, 2010. Used under license from Shutterstock, Inc.

Brass instruments

Trombone. © Glenda M. Powers, 2010. Used under license from Shutterstock, Inc.

French horn. © Glenda M. Powers, 2010. Used under license from Shutterstock, Inc.

Euphonium. © mkm3, 2010. Used under license from Shutterstock, Inc.

Tuba. © Shutterstock, 2010. Used under license from Shutterstock, Inc.

Sousaphone. © vpix, 2010. Used under license from Shutterstock, Inc.

Percussion

The diverse instruments of the **percussion** family create their sounds by being struck, either with the hands, with wooden sticks, or with mallets tipped by various kinds of materials. The instruments can be divided into two types: melodic and non-melodic instruments.

Melodic percussion instruments actually produce pitches and can play melodies. This group includes the **timpani**, or **kettle drums**, which do in fact resemble a large copper kettle covered by a drum head. Unlike most of the drum family, the timpani (the plural of timpanum) are tunable, by tightening or loosening the drum head. By playing a set of three or more timpani, melodies can be produced on them.

Other melodic percussion instruments produce pitches on tuned metal bars (including instruments such as the **glockenspiel**, the **vibraphone**, and the **tubular bells**) or on tuned strips of wood (such as the **xylophone** and its larger cousin the **marimba**). The **steel drum**, popular in the Caribbean Islands, is another example of a melodic percussion instrument.

Melodic percussion instruments

Timpani. © Shutterstock, 2010. Used under license from Shutterstock, Inc.

Marimba. © Jorge R. Gonzalez, 2010. Used under license from Shutterstock, Inc.

Xylophone. © Viacheslav Zhukovskiy, 2010. Used under license from Shutterstock, Inc.

Vibraphone. © Susan Stevenson, 2010. Used under license from Shutterstock, Inc.

Non-melodic percussion instruments are unique among musical instruments in that they are not designed to play specific pitches, but only to create some sort of satisfying thump when struck. This group includes various sorts of **drums**, which are hollow cylinders across which some sort of membrane has been stretched. **Snare drums**, for instance, have wires called snares stretched across their lower face; these give a distinctive rattle when the opposite side is struck. Other types of drums include the **bass drum**, the **tom tom**, the **conga drum**, and the **tambourine**.

Non-melodic percussion instruments create sounds by vibration of the entire body of the instrument when struck. These instruments include the **cymbal** (*not* symbol: that's for poetry class), the **gong**, the **triangle**, the **wood block**, the **castanet**, and the **brake drum**. Yes, even an automobile brake drum has been used in composition—in fact, virtually any object that creates an interesting sound when struck can be, and has been, used as a non-melodic percussion instrument.

Non-melodic percussion instruments

Bass Drum. © Mark Herreid, 2010. Used under license from Shutterstock, Inc.

Snare Drum. © VolkOFF-ZS-BP, 2010. Used under license from Shutterstock, Inc.

Cymbal. © Timothy Geiss, 2010. Used under license from Shutterstock, Inc.

Gong. © Vladimir Kirienko, 2010. Used under license from Shutterstock, Inc.

Triangle. © mkm3, 2010. Used under license from Shutterstock, Inc.

Tambourine. © Skyline, 2010. Used under license from Shutterstock, Inc.

Keyboard instruments

Piano. © James Steidl, 2010. Used under license from Shutterstock, Inc.

Harpsichord. © Linda Bucklin, 2010. Used under license from Shutterstock, Inc.

Accordion. © Alexei Novikov, 2010. Used under license from Shutterstock, Inc.

An interesting example of non-melodic percussion music is the piece *Fur Music*, by Nelson Howe. The instrument for this piece is constructed by nailing various types of fur, fabric, and carpeting to an 18" by 30" piece of plywood. The piece is performed by the player scratching the various pieces of fabric in a prescribed rhythmic and dynamic pattern. It is, admittedly, subtle.

Keyboard

The **keyboard** instruments are not universally recognized as a separate family. Many sources, for instance, place the piano in the string family, while others include it among percussion instruments. Frankly, the keyboard instruments are not convenient to classify. The **piano**, for example, does make its sound from vibrating strings, but it is quite unlike any other stringed instrument, and, while it creates its sound by striking those strings, it also behaves quite unlike any of the melodic percussion instruments. In a similar fashion, it makes little sense to group the mighty **pipe organ** with the woodwind instruments. For convenience, then, we shall consider any instruments that control their notes from a keyboard as a separate family. In addition to the piano and organ, this family includes such instruments as the **harpsichord**, an early keyboard instrument whose mechanism plucks its strings rather than striking them to produce its sound; the **clavichord**, an extremely quiet instrument whose strings are struck by a metal tangent to create its subtle sounds; and the **celesta**, whose sounds are produced by metal bars within its frame.

Organ. © Craig Hanson, 2010. Used under license from Shutterstock, Inc.

Electronic

The newest addition to the families of instruments—indeed, the only addition since antiquity—are the **electronic instruments** of our own time. Many acoustic instruments, such as the electric guitar, have been altered to amplify and manipulate their naturally produced sounds, but true electronic instruments *produce* their sounds through electronic means. The earliest such instrument was the **telharmonium**, a huge (200 tons!) electronic keyboard first introduced in 1900. Later electronic devices include the **ondes Martenot**, a device that would control its pitch either by a keyboard or through a sliding metallic ribbon, producing a continuously variable pitch, and the **theramin**, which consists of a straight antenna wherein pitch and dynamics are controlled by the proximity of the player's hands to that charged antenna. Both instruments produce eerie, otherworldly sounds unavailable through acoustic means.

Recent electronic devices are grouped under the general name of **synthesizer**, though strictly speaking, all electronic instruments are synthesizers of some sort. The new technology of the synthesizer changes almost by the week—it is a challenge just to keep up with the technological capabilities, not to mention the artistic possibilities.

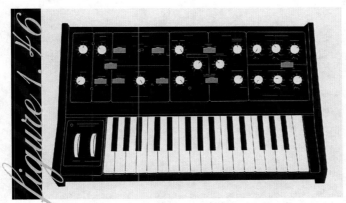

Electronic instruments: Moog Synthesizer. © Peter Albreksten, 2010.
Used under license from Shutterstock, Inc.

The Orchestra

The alert student, at this point, is perhaps wondering what all these instruments sound like. To experience those sounds, or at least a good sampling of them, let us hear a remarkable piece of music by an English composer of our own century, Benjamin Britten. The piece has the fancy title *Variations and Fugue on a Theme by Henry Purcell*. Before this course is over, you will know what variations are, what a fugue is, and who Henry Purcell was, but for now, let's just refer to the piece by its alternative title, *A Young Person's Guide to the Orchestra*.

An **orchestra** is a large group of various kinds of instruments and is mainly distinguished by the fact that the instruments are in groups, or sections. In other words, there are more than one of each type of instrument (music for a smaller ensemble, with only a single player to a part, is called **chamber music**). In Ex. 12, we can see a representation of the typical layout of a modern orchestra.

example 12

Diagram of the orchestra

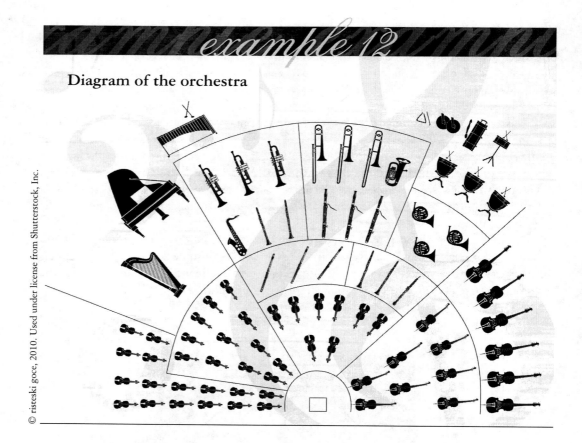

The conductor is at the front of the orchestra. A poster popular among musicians portrays a figure in a tuxedo holding a baton standing in front of a podium reading the directions before him: "Wave your arms in the air until the music stops, then turn around and bow." This is *not* the job of a conductor. A conductor has perhaps the hardest job in all of music: to control a set of nearly 100 headstrong musicians and to mold them into a single cooperative and coherent artistic entity. The conductor sets tempos, controls dynamics and entries, balances the overall structure, and establishes the very personality of what is being played. In rehearsals, a conductor has to be able to determine any problems in the overall mass of sound being produced and to correct them quickly and efficiently. He or she must have a solid working knowledge of each of the instruments and must have an incredibly precise ear. Orchestras are notoriously unforgiving to conductors whom they feel are inadequate, but powerfully loyal to those who gain their respect and confidence.

The closest instruments to the conductor, and the most numerous in the orchestra, are the bowed strings. There are *two* sections of violins, then violas, violoncellos, and double basses, spread from the left to the right of the conductor (an alternate method, favored by quite a few conductors, is to split up the violins, firsts on the far left, seconds on the far right, with the violas, 'cellos and double basses in between). The only plucked string instrument regularly in the orchestra is the harp, behind the first violins. The other plucked strings have too quiet a sound quality to be heard over the other instruments.

Immediately behind the strings are the woodwinds, with the saxophone conspicuous by its absence. The saxophone is rarely heard in the orchestra because it was invented after the instrumentation of the orchestra became standardized. It is occasionally heard, especially in works by French composers; this is not by accident, since Adolfe Sax, the instrument's inventor, spent most of his career in Paris. Behind the woodwinds are the brass instruments, with the percussionists, who tend to become rather rowdy, in the far left rear of the orchestra.

Britten's *A Young Person's Guide to the Orchestra*, as the title implies, is designed with an educational purpose: to acquaint the listener with the characteristic capabilities of the various sections and instruments of the orchestra. All too frequently, "educational" is synonymous with boring, but not with this piece: Britten's composition is one of the most ingenious orchestral pieces of all time, a remarkable combination of lyricism, wit, drama, and excitement. The piece is in what is called **variations** form, in that each section is some sort of development or extension of the original idea. Actually, the form is only loosely adhered to; it is only an excuse to pass through each section of the orchestra, and then each instrument, to give the listener a taste of the characteristic sound of all the members of the orchestra.

The final section is called a **fugue**. This form will be discussed at greater length later in the text, but for now one only need realize that a fugue is based on a single theme called a subject. It enters alone, then it is heard again from another instrument, then another, and another. As each new instrument enters, the others remain in play, until by the time we've passed through the orchestra, everyone is making an incredible cacophony.

Just at the point at which it seems the whole piece will degenerate into chaos, the brass family enters, together playing the original opening theme of the piece. It is a remarkable finale to a remarkable piece. Listen first without the written guide, and try to distinguish the sounds of each section and of each instrument.

A Closer Look

Benjamin Britten: *A Young Person's Guide to the Orchestra*

Opening theme for full orchestra
    Woodwind section
    String section
    Brass section
    Percussion section
    Full orchestra

Var. 1: flutes and piccolo
    Note the agility and the crystalline clarity of tone of these instruments.

Var. 2: oboes
    The double reed oboes can sound a bit like a duck when used by a bad player, but in the hands of a real artist, the sound is exceptionally expressive.

Var. 3: clarinets
    The clarinets are as agile as the flutes, but with a somewhat darker and warmer sound because they are made of wood rather than metal.

Var. 4: bassoons
    The bassoon can sound alternately comic or melancholy. Britten has somehow managed to capture both moods here.

Var. 5: Violins
    The most numerous instruments of the orchestra—note, at the end of their section, that they can also create sound by being plucked.

Var. 6: Violas

Var. 7: Violoncellos

Notice what the composer does with these two instruments: the sound of all the string instruments is very closely related, and Britten ends the violas in almost the same register as the 'cellos begin. It is difficult, intentionally, to tell the difference until the 'cellos drop down in pitch to where no viola has gone before.

Var. 8: Double Basses

Out of the depths come the lowest voices of the orchestra.

Var. 9: Harps

The only plucked strings of the orchestra are finally heard.

Var. 10: French horns

The brass family is introduced by the French horns, with their beautiful, noble, distant sound.

Var. 11: Trumpets

Here we have what sounds like two trumpets chasing each other.

Var. 12: Trombones and Tuba

The regal sounds of the trombone are joined, somewhat later, by the deep tones of the tuba.

Var. 13: The percussion section

The various percussion instruments enter very rapidly, with a repeated passage for the timpani and bass drum underlying the entire section. First we hear cymbals, then tambourine, triangle, snare drum, woodblock, xylophone, castanets, gong, whip, and finally all of the instruments together. The section concludes quietly with triangle and xylophone, before introducing the final . . .

Fugue: The closing fugue begins with the piccolo alone, followed in quick succession by the flutes, oboes, clarinets, bassoons, violins, violas, violoncellos, double basses, harps, French horns, trumpets, trombones and tubas, and every percussion instrument known to Western civilization. Finally, when the point of near chaos has been reached, the brass section brings back the original theme, and a triumphal conclusion is achieved at last.

Repetition and Contrast

In any successful piece of music, the composer will make an attempt to balance repeating and contrasting elements. Too much of either can be deadly for the audience. A piece that repeats its ideas without any surprises can be breathtakingly dull; by contrast, a work in which no idea is repeated will leave the listeners lost, without anything recognizable to follow.

A composer can use any elements of music to achieve this balance. To see how the linear qualities of sound—pitch, duration, intensity, and timbre—can be manipulated for expressive purpose, let us hear a work in which the composer has deliberately limited himself to altering only two of these aspects. The piece in question consists only of a single melody repeated throughout its 15-minute length. Pitch and duration, then, are kept constant. The composer introduces contrasting elements in dynamics and timbre. The work begins very quietly and gets gradually louder, bit by bit, until by the end of the piece the entire orchestra is playing at full volume. This piece has been described as the longest crescendo in the history of music.

In addition to changing the level of intensity, the composer also manipulates timbre. Each time a phrase of the melody is introduced, it is played by a different instrument or group of instruments, so it never sounds exactly the same at any point. In fact, this piece is also effective in getting to know the sounds of the instruments of the orchestra, though unlike Britten's *A Young Person's Guide to the Orchestra*, it was *not* designed with an educational purpose:

some of the instruments are used in unusual ways and do not produce what would be considered their typical sounds.

The piece in question is by French composer Maurice Ravel. It is based on a Spanish dance form known as a *bolero*, which is in a slow triple meter. Each beat is divided in two parts, and each of *those* parts is divided into three parts.

The rhythm of the bolero

The rhythm is played by the snare drum throughout the entire piece as other elements slowly develop (orchestral percussionists are *not* fond of this piece). It is scored for a full orchestra, including English horn and a pair of saxophones, a tenor, and a soprano. This is one of Ravel's most popular pieces; it entered the world of popular entertainment several years ago in the movie *10*, in which it was used as the music to which Bo Derek liked to copulate.

Vertical Aspects of Music

The alert student will have noticed in the final portions of Ravel's *Bolero* that something new was happening. When the strings finally came in with the melody, they played first all together, but when the theme came around again, some of the instruments played *other* sounds, at other pitches. The sound was varied, and enriched, by different sounds being played simultaneously.

This is a very different quality from what we have been discussing thus far, and now it is time to move away from the linear aspects of music and consider what happens when sounds occur together. The effect of simultaneous sounds is called **harmony**. Here we have an aspect in which music is quite different from spoken language. We can only comprehend one voice at a time in spoken language, but in music it is perfectly common to hear several things simultaneously. This multiplicity of events and layers does not make it more difficult to understand what is happening musically; in fact, it intensifies the experience.

Harmony

Before we can discuss harmony, we have to have some idea of what notes are to be used to create harmonies, and how two or more notes relate together. The quality produced by any two or more simultaneous sounds is determined by the ratio of the rates of vibration of the notes. Remember, musical pitch is determined by the rate of vibration of a note. If two notes are vibrating at exactly the same rate, the sound will be very stable—that is how a piano can have two or even three strings vibrating for any single note, and still produce a sound as if only a single note is vibrating.

The distance between any two notes is referred to as an **interval**. Musicians have names for any interval, but for the non-specialist, only a few are important to know. The first is the **octave**, which refers to the distance between a note and its duplicate eight notes away. For instance, the distance between middle C and the C notated on the third space of the treble clef is an octave. The two notes share more than a name. They share a special relationship of their rates of vibration: 2 to 1. The higher C is vibrating exactly twice as fast as middle C. As the ratio of their rates of vibration is 2 to 1, they produce a sound that is almost as stable as two notes of exactly the same pitch.

The smallest interval in general use is called the **half step**. It can be most easily seen on a piano keyboard, on which each key, black or white, is only a half step away from any adjacent key. We didn't even name some of these keys when discussing the notation of pitch—the white keys represent the letter names of the notes, while the black keys represent some of the half steps in between those notes. These notes "in the cracks" are labeled according to whether they are higher or lower than the natural note. If it is a half step higher, it is called **sharp**, represented by the symbol #. If it is lower, it is called **flat**, represented by the symbol ♭. Therefore, C-sharp and D-flat are two different ways of naming the same pitch. A third symbol, the natural ♮, cancels out a flat or a sharp.

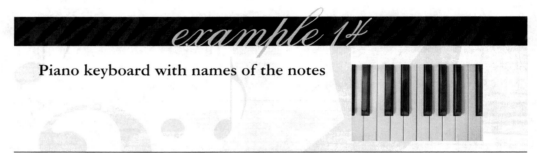

Piano keyboard with names of the notes

Piano keyboard: © MTrebbin, 2010. Used under license from Shutterstock, Inc.

Notation of C# and D♭

Notice that not all natural notes have a sharp or flat between them. Between E and F, and between B and C, there is only a half step. This arrangement of half steps and **whole steps** (the interval that consists of two half steps) is important in the creation of scales, which we shall discuss subsequently. The whole octave is divided up into a set of 12 half-steps.

The Overtone Series

Musical practice does not use all available pitches, but only a select portion of them—those 12 half steps in the octave. This is not a function of culture; it is common to all cultures, whether Native American, European, Asian, African, etc. The practice is common to all human cultures because it is not based on any single human culture but arises from a phenomenon of nature called the **overtone series**.

When any musical tone is heard, the ear hears one primary sound called the fundamental, but that is not the only sound being produced. Other partial sections of the vibrating sound exist, over one-half of its length, and one-third, one-fourth, one-fifth, and so on. (*Note*:

This effect can be heard fairly easily on a plucked string instrument such as a guitar, by touching the string lightly at one-half of its length—or one-third, one-fourth, etc.—to stop the fundamental vibration, only allowing the upper partials to vibrate. On piano, this can be demonstrated aurally, if not visually, by rapidly playing a low note while silently depressing the note an octave up—the upper note will continue to vibrate sympathetically after the lower has been muted.)

Only a few of these sounds are easily audible to the ear, but acoustic scientists have understood the principles since ancient times; when all the sounds in the overtone series have been accounted for, eliminating octave doubling, what we find is the 12 different notes in an octave.

This natural phenomenon, then, is the source for the sounds that make up the universal language of music. Some cultures use fewer tones in musical practice, some divide the half step into a quarter step in complex ornamentation, but *all* cultures use the 12-part division of the octave as the foundation for their musical language.

The Scale and Tonality

Music is based on a set of pitches called a **scale**, from which melodies and harmonies are constructed. The scale not only defines the notes that will be used in the piece, but it defines the note on which the piece will center. Traditional music is **tonal**, in that it tends to center on a single note, called the **tonic** note. Listen, for example, to someone play *My Country 'tis of Thee/God Save the Queen*, leaving out the last note. It is maddening . . . someone *must* finish that melody by playing that last note, which was also the beginning note. That note exerts a powerful gravity, and the piece is not complete until the piece arrives at its tonic note, also called the **key** of the piece.

The scale, then, defines the tonality or key of a piece, but there are various kinds of scales—for instance, the scale that includes all 12 notes in the octave is known as a **chromatic scale**.

example 16

The chromatic scale

It is rather rare for a piece to be based on a chromatic scale; in any case, that scale doesn't really define the key. More commonly, music is based on an eight-note scale (including the last octave duplication) called a **diatonic scale**. There are several types of diatonic scales, but all consist of eight notes (seven intervals—it takes two notes to make a single interval) that include five whole steps and two nonadjacent half steps. The most common diatonic scale can be made by playing the natural notes (white keys) of a piano keyboard from C to C. This makes what is called a **major scale**; because it begins and ends on the note C, it is more specifically called a C major scale. It consists of the following pattern of intervals: whole, whole, half, whole, whole, whole, half.

The C major scale

This pattern of two whole steps, a half step, three whole steps, and a half step will always make the diatonic scale called a major scale, no matter what note begins the scale. It is such a common sound that even most non-specialists can tell when a "wrong note" is heard in the scale. Try, for instance, listening to someone play the piano notes from G to G, on all the white notes, and listen for the note that sounds out of place.

G to G, all natural notes

It is that next-to-the-last note of the sequence that sounds out of place: the scale ends with *whole, half, whole*, instead of *whole, whole, half*. This, of course, can be corrected by raising that F with a sharp. *Now*, the final intervals are in the right order: whole, whole, half.

G to G, with F#

As you can imagine, you can start on any note and, by the addition of the appropriate flats and sharps, collectively called **accidentals**, create a major scale. This can be done by adding an accidental on any affected note, or it can be done by a musical shorthand called the **key signature**. This is a series of sharps *or* flats (never both) at the beginning of the piece, after the clef and before the meter signature, which alter the appropriate notes to define any particular major scale.

Key signature for G major

The sharps or flats always occur in a particular order, creating a rather elegant cycle, that covers all possible keys, but that particular aspect of music theory is beyond the level of this course. It is enough just to understand the general purpose of the key signature.

Incidentally, pieces do not always remain in the same key throughout their length. Often, the piece will change its key in a process called **modulation**. The modulation may be fairly brief, and only indicated by the temporary addition of the appropriate accidentals, or it may be longer, and there may be an actual change of the key signature.

The major scale is not the only kind of diatonic scale. Another common scale can be produced by playing the natural notes on the piano beginning and ending with A. This produces a **minor scale**. Minor scales are often designated by a lower case letter.

The a minor scale

Notice the pattern of intervals in this scale: whole, half, whole, whole, half, whole, whole. It is this structural difference that actually creates a different *mood* in these notes. The difference is often described as between happy (for the major scale) and sad (for the minor). While that is a bit of an oversimplification, it does give some indication of the qualities involved.

The primary difference between major and minor scales is the distance between the first and third notes of the respective scales (the last two intervals of the minor scale are unstable—there are in fact three different minor scales, distinguished by those changing upper intervals, but the beginning notes are always the same). In a major scale, the distance from first to third notes is two whole steps; in a minor scale, the distance is a whole step and a half step. This small difference in structure can actually change the entire emotional quality of a piece of music.

Chords

Now that we have some idea of the notes that we will be using to create music, we can talk about harmony. When two or more notes are sounded together, harmony or, more specifically, a **chord**, is produced. Traditional theory defines a chord as three or more notes, because the most common chord in traditional music is indeed a three-note chord called a **triad**.

A triad is produced from a particular diatonic scale by combining every other note from the scale until a three-note set is obtained. One can, for instance, combine the first, third, and fifth notes from a C major scale and get the following triad.

Triad on C, from a C major scale

In the same way, a triad can be constructed on any note of the scale. By combining the second, fourth, and sixth notes, a triad on D can be made, and so on. The set of triads made from a diatonic scale in this way is called the **diatonic triads**.

Diatonic triads in C major

If you have ever played guitar or piano to accompany popular songs, folk songs, or hymns, you have perhaps noticed that songs in a particular key often share the same group of accompanying chords. This is because those chords are all built from the scale of the key itself. The chords can be either major or minor (or, more rarely, of other qualities) in the same way that a scale can be major or minor: by the distance between the first and the second note of the triad (which would be the third note of the scale).

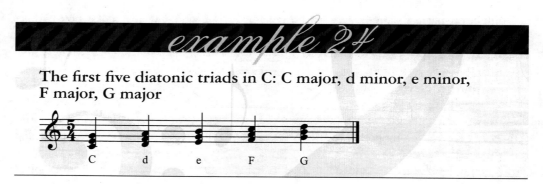

The first five diatonic triads in C: C major, d minor, e minor, F major, G major

Triads are not the only kind of chords. In fact, any set of notes played together constitute a chord. Chords, or harmony in general, are described as either **consonant** or as **dissonant**. Consonant harmonies have a stable, relaxed, pleasing sound, while dissonant harmonies are unstable, tense, and rather harsh in sound. The quality comes from the relationships of the pitches involved: the more closely related is the ratio of rates of vibration among the notes, the more consonant the sound will be. For an example, listen to the following four chords, which are increasingly dissonant.

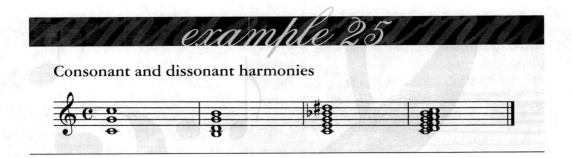

Consonant and dissonant harmonies

It is important to stress that dissonant harmonies are *not* simply unpleasant sounds that should be avoided. In fact, it is the balance between consonance and dissonance that makes music interesting. Dissonance creates a tension in music that must be resolved, and this whole process of harmonic tension and resolution, called **harmonic progression**, is at the very core of musical expression. There are, in fact, specific ways to resolve particular dissonances; music students spend quite a bit of time mastering these methods at the beginnings of their studies in music theory.

The effect is similar to events in a drama, or even a comedy. How many people, for instance, would attend a movie or a play in which nothing happened—where a group of people simply sat around eating breakfast, or some such thing. Obviously, audiences would wait years to avoid such a production. The *essence* of theater is the establishment of conflict and its ultimate resolution.

In music, the same process of tension and resolution is at work, and a piece that is entirely consonant, or entirely dissonant, is extremely rare. There is one specific type of structure, called the **cadence**, that is used in music as a sort of punctuation, to mark the ends of musical phrases just as a period will mark the end of a written sentence. Without getting into the actual structure of the various kinds of cadences, let it suffice to describe a cadence as a pause or a place of rest in a piece of music at which tense harmonies resolve to relaxed ones. Listen to the final phrase of *The Star-Spangled Banner*, particularly to the last two chords, and you will hear a good example of a cadence.

Texture

Musical texture refers to the interrelationships of melodic lines in a piece of music. There are three types of texture: **monophonic**, **homophonic**, and **polyphonic**. The linguistic connection is obvious: the final two syllables ("-phonic") refer to sound.

Monophonic ("one sound") texture consists of only a single melodic line, with no accompaniment. Real monophonic texture is actually rather rare—an example can be found in the mysterious chanting of the priests of the medieval Catholic Church, which can still occasionally be heard performed. Another rather ironic example can be heard in Janis Joplin's popular song, *Oh, Lord, Won't You Buy Me a Mercedes-Benz*, sung entirely without accompaniment.

Homophonic ("same sound") texture consists of a single melodic line with some sort of bass line or chordal accompaniment. Most of Ravel's *Bolero* is in homophonic texture.

Polyphonic ("many sounds") texture refers to music that consists of two or more melodic lines sung or played simultaneously. The final fugue in Britten's *A Young Person's Guide to the Orchestra* is a good example of this: after the piccolo entered with the main theme, each member of the rest of the orchestra entered in turn, all continuing to play with each new entry.

Many pieces will consist of a mixture of textures; Britten's piece, for instance, had elements of all three types at various points. Texture describes a fairly limited aspect of musical structure, but it is especially important when studying the various historical periods of music, which are partially distinguished by their use of musical texture.

Musical Form

The final aspect of the structure of music to be considered is the arrangement of contrasting and repeating materials in a piece, referred to as its **form**. Form in music can become incredibly complex, but here we will only consider the simplest types of forms.

One particular type of form is restricted solely to vocal music. It refers to a piece that consists of several different verses of text, each set to the same music. The form is called **strophic**, and it is commonly found in folk songs, hymns, popular songs, even in the national anthem (be honest, how many of you know the second and third verses to the *Star-Spangled Banner*?). It is, however, only found in vocal works, because the contrasting element in strophic form is in the text, not the music.

The other forms we will examine here can be found in vocal or instrumental music. The simplest type of form is a two-part form called **binary** form. It consists of two parts, which are designated by letters: **A B**. Binary form is especially common among the dance pieces of the Renaissance or the Baroque; the sections are often repeated, producing an arrangement of **AA BB**.

By returning to the opening idea after a contrasting one, we create a three-part form called **ternary**: **A B A**. As one of the simplest examples, think of the children's song *Twinkle, Twinkle Little Star*.

A further extension of ternary form would be to add a third idea, returning to the first after each new idea is introduced. This is known as **rondo** form. There are various types of rondo form, such as **A B A C A** or **A B A C A B A**. Each is distinguished by the return of the **A** section after each new idea is introduced. In most rondos, indeed in all of the more complex types of musical form, the sections are distinguished not only by the use of different themes but by the use of different keys.

The last form we will discuss here (the **fugue** and **sonata form** will be discussed in the sections on the Baroque and Classical periods, respectively) is one we have already encountered: **variations** form, sometimes called **theme and variations**. In this form, a theme is stated, and each subsequent section is an unfolding development of that idea. If this were to be outlined by letters, it would look something like this: **A A' A''** . . .

Composers often use variations form quite loosely. Britten's *Variations and Fugue on a Theme by Henry Purcell/A Young Person's Guide to the Orchestra* makes very little attempt to relate subsequent sections to the original theme. Other composers treat the form more conservatively, staying very close to the original theme. Listen to the following piece by the 18th-century composer Wolfgang Amadeus Mozart, a set of variations for piano on a French nursery tune, *Ah, vous dirai-je, Maman* ("Ah, I Tell You, Mama"). Notice how the variations shift types of activity between the right hand (which controls the higher notes) and the left hand (on the lower notes). Notice also that both the tempo and the meter do not vary until the final two variations—even here, however, one can hear the echoes of the original ternary form theme, which you should recognize as a piece with a more familiar English title.

A Closer Look

Mozart's *Variations on "Ah, vous dirai-je, Maman"*

Theme: Ternary form, with first section repeated (AABA)

Var. 1: Sixteenth notes in the right hand

Var. 2: Sixteenth notes in the left hand

Var. 3: Triplets (three notes to the beat) in the right hand

Var. 4: Triplets (three notes to the beat) in the left hand

Var. 5: Lighter, two notes at a time in each hand

Var. 6: Rapid motion, first in the left, then the right hand

Var. 7: Very brilliant passage, activity in the right hand

Var. 8: Modulation to a minor key

Var. 9: Back to a major key

Var. 10: Another very brilliant passage

Var. 11: Tempo slows greatly, mood becomes more lyric

Var. 12: Return to a fast tempo, now in triple meter

Structure and Perception
How the Elements of Music Affect Emotions and Perceptions

We have begun the study of the mystery of music by examining the elements of musical structure to begin to understand how a piece of music is put together. Certainly, all the strange terms we have learned serve the purpose of establishing a common language for discussion of music, but there is a more important reason for this first section. That reason is the connection between structure and perception: the fact that all the aspects of musical structure do indeed have an impact on how the piece communicates with us emotionally. Let us explore this by listening carefully to two works and then examining how the elements of their musical structure contribute to their emotional impact. The first piece is not "classical" music at all, but by a popular singing duo from the 1960s: Paul Simon and Art Garfunkel. First listen to the piece, and then we will consider the elements of timbre, rhythm, melody, harmony, form, texture, and dynamics.

A Closer Look
Simon and Garfunkel: *Scarborough Fair/Canticle*

Timbre: instruments used include guitar, bass guitar, harpsichord, glockenspiel. Four voices, both tenor.

Rhythm: triple meter, with a gentle character rather than driving

Melody: mostly conjunct

Harmony: primarily consonant

Form: modified strophic form

Texture: initially homophonic, then polyphonic

Dynamics: gradually increasing to a point of greatest intensity just before final verse, then concluding softly

Two things seem unusual in the timbres of the piece: the absence of any percussion instruments, except for the glockenspiel, and the *presence* of a harpsichord. The harpsichord is an obsolete keyboard instrument, popular during the 16th through the 18th centuries. What, then, is an ancient instrument doing in a late-1960s popular song? It seems to serve the purpose of bringing the imagination of the listener back in time—sounds associated with the distant past bring us back to that period. We view that time, perhaps with rose-colored glasses, as a simpler time, a more peaceful and tranquil era. The absence of the percussion in the piece likewise contributes to an overall sense of serenity.

The use of four voices from two human beings is achieved, of course, through the miracles of electronic overdubbing. Both voices would be considered tenors, though Art Garfunkel's voice is much lighter than that of Paul Simon. He is almost, though not quite, a countertenor.

The next three elements (rhythm, melody, and harmony) also contribute to the overall sense of sweetness and serenity. Triple meter has a more gentle, less driving quality about it; conjunct melodies likewise move smoothly, without a sense of nervous activity. The harmonies are mostly consonant; while some dissonances are used, the main emotional impact of the piece is not accomplished by harmonic tension.

The form of the piece is a modified strophic form—modified, in that each verse is somewhat different from the others, in the accompanying music and in the added counterline of the *Canticle*. Nevertheless, the piece maintains the basic simplicity of the form of a folk song.

The texture of the piece begins as homophonic, and then changes to polyphonic. After the first verse, the harpsichord enters, with a counter melody that persists through the rest of the piece. In the same verse, the *Canticle* enters, and this gets close to the heart of the piece. The tensions of the piece result from the juxtaposition of two different texts, each describing a different scenario. In *Scarborough Fair*, we hear a young man reminiscing about an old lover, fondly remembered; in the *Canticle*, we here another image entirely, of a young man going off to war. Through polyphonic texture, the two sentiments can be portrayed simultaneously, and the ironic contrast is much stronger.

The structure of the dynamics is also important. The contrast throughout is muted; passages tend to get louder through the addition of extra instruments and voices rather than from the increasing intensity of the players themselves. The dynamics reach a peak at the close of the next-to-the-last verse and then taper off for the final verse.

It is no accident that this particular place was chosen for the strongest dynamics, and the greatest activity and the most intense harmonic dissonances of the piece also occur here. At this point, the contrast of the young lover and the young soldier, ordered to kill and "to fight for a cause he'd long ago forgotten," is at its greatest. For the final verse, the *Canticle* is omitted, as is the electric bass guitar, and there is a return to the serenity of the peaceful past.

We must remember some history to appreciate the impact of this song properly. When it was released, the United States was at the height of the Vietnam War. Whatever one's thoughts may be on that conflict, it can be generally agreed that the dissention over U.S. involvement tore the country apart. This piece was a quiet protest over the futility of that war, or indeed of any war. It was perhaps more powerful because it was so quiet—in much the same way that one can command the attention of a crowd more effectively by a whisper than by a shout.

Each of the elements of musical structure contributes to the emotional impact of this piece. It is interesting to contemplate which element was most important in making that impact: timbre, rhythm, melody, harmony, form, texture, or dynamics—though, like so much in music, there really is no "correct" answer.

A Closer Look

Nikolai Rimsky-Korsakoff: *The Procession of the Nobles*

Timbre: full orchestra

Rhythm: triple meter, martial character

Melody: disjunct in opening section, conjunct in contrasting sections

Harmony: relatively more dissonance

Form: rondo (A B A C A)

Texture: mixture of monophonic, homophonic, and polyphonic

Dynamics: widely varying, mostly fairly loud

And now for something completely different: a brilliant work for full orchestra. The use of brass and percussion instruments in the opening fanfare sets a vivid mood for the piece, while bowed strings (and harp!) and woodwinds create a more lyric contrast to set off the recurring fanfares.

The piece is in fact a processional, from the opera *Mlada* by the 19th-century Russian composer Nikolai Rimsky-Korsakoff. It has the distinct character of a military march, and one has to listen carefully (particularly to the snare drum rolls at the beginning) to hear that the beat does recur in groups of three, rather than the duple meter of most marches. The composer even tries to throw the listener off in the first contrasting section, where he writes a part for harp playing groups of two chords against the triple rhythm.

The melody of the fanfares is quite disjunct, with a completely different character than that of *Scarborough Fair*. It conveys a sense of energy and of celebration rather than serenity. The dynamics likewise convey a sense of vigor and power. The nobles seem to be celebrating some great victory.

Though the piece seems quite complex, its form is a simple rondo, which enables the exciting brass fanfares to recur three times. The harmony is not particularly dissonant by most standards, though it does seem to use more dissonance than the last piece we heard. The texture mixes all three possibilities, from the monophonic opening to the polyphonic mixing of the various brass instruments in the rest of the fanfare, with some longer homophonic passages in the B and C sections. The very mixture of textures contributes to the festive mood of the music.

Again, it can be seen that each of the elements of musical structure contributed to the emotional impact of this piece. One could hardly imagine that the effect would be the same if the opening passage were played, say with clarinets. It is likewise interesting to contemplate which element was most important in creating *this* work: timbre, rhythm, melody, harmony, form, texture, or dynamics.

The Procession of the Nobles conveys a distinct image of some sort of national celebration, perhaps of some military victory—and many classes, hearing the piece without it being identified, have also imagined that the music represents some time in the distant past, possibly ancient Rome. Such images have nothing to do with real Roman music but are more the product of film scores of our own time. Epic movies of ancient civilizations often are scored by composers who were heavily influenced by the music of Rimsky-Korsakoff and other Romantic era composers.

Now that we have a foundation, with some knowledge of the basic elements of the musical language, it is time to move on to the next part of our study of the mystery of music. We will get some idea what the music of the past *really* sounded like, and we'll encounter some of the most remarkable creative work of the last thousand years of Western civilization!

Glossary

Alto: the darkest and lowest female voice

Arpeggio: a chord played by breaking the notes into separate parts, giving rhythmic interest to a static harmony

Banjo: member of the plucked string family, with four or five strings across a fretted neck, and a body composed of a membrane stretched across a round frame

Baritone: a male voice, darker than a tenor but brighter than a bass

Bass: the darkest and lowest male voice

Bass clef: a symbol placed at the beginning of a staff that indicates that the second line from the top is the note F (also called an F clef)

Bassoon: bass member of the double reed woodwind family; also in contrabass variety

Binary form: two-part form: AB; frequently each section is repeated: AABB

Brass family: wind instruments that make their sound by the vibration of the lips in a mouthpiece

Cadence: a stopping or resting point in a piece of music, where tense harmonies resolve to relaxed ones

'Cello: member of the bowed string family, the second lowest range, played held between the legs (also *violoncello*).

Chord: two or more notes sounding simultaneously

Chromatic scale: a scale that consists of all twelve half steps in the octave

Clarinet: member of the woodwind family, using a single reed, with a wooden body, typically ebony; also in alto and bass versions

Conjunct: describes a melody in which the pitches are mostly close to each other

Consonant: harmonies that sound pleasing or stable

Crescendo: a passage of music that gets gradually louder

Decrescendo: a passage of music that gets gradually softer (also *diminuendo*)

Diatonic scale: a scale that consists of eight notes, defining five whole notes and two half notes; the half notes are never adjacent

Disjunct: describes a melody in which the pitches often leap several notes away

Dissonant: harmonies that sound unstable, harsh, or unpleasant

Double bass: member of the bowed string family, the lowest range (also *contrabass, bass violin*)

Duple meter: a beat that is organized in groups of two

Duration: the length of time that a note sounds

Electronic family: instruments that generate their sounds by electronic rather than mechanical means

English horn: member of the woodwind family, using a double reed and a wooden body; larger and darker than an oboe, with a bent (angled) mouthpiece that, when misread, gave it the "English" designation

Flat: a symbol that lowers the pitch of a note by one-half step

Flute: member of the woodwind family, making its sound without a reed, but by blowing across an open mouthpiece; also in alto and bass versions, and a smaller, higher pitched version called the piccolo (properly, *flauto piccolo,* little flute)

Form: the arrangement of contrasting and repeating musical materials

Forte: loud

French horn: member of the brass family, with the bell at a right angle to the mouthpiece; played with the left hand inserted into the bell

Grand staff: a combination of a top staff in the treble clef and a bottom staff in the bass clef; used mainly for keyboard instruments

Guitar: member of the plucked string family, with six strings across a fretted neck, and a wooden body (in acoustic versions)

Harp: member of the plucked string family, with one string for each note of a diatonic scale over several octaves, stretched across a large wooden frame

Homophonic texture: music that consists of a single melody with accompaniment; this might be a bass line, a chord, or an arpeggio

Intensity: the loudness or softness of a single musical sound

Interval: the distance between any two notes

Key: the note that is the center of a piece in tonal harmony

Key signature: a set of flats or sharps (never both) placed after the clef and the meter signature that indicates what note serves as the key of the piece of music

Keyboard family: instruments that control pitches from a keyboard

Major scale: a diatonic scale that is constructed with the following intervals: whole-whole-half-whole-whole-whole-half; the distance between the first and third notes is two whole notes

Mandolin: member of the plucked string family, with four courses (pairs) of strings each tuned in unison, stretched across a fretted neck

Measure: a space on a staff, indicated by two perpendicular lines, that contains a specific amount of notes of a set duration; typically, all the measures in a given section will contain the same amount of notes

Melody: a set of notes (pitches and durations) that makes a coherent musical statement

Meter signature: two numbers, placed at the beginning of a piece just after the clef, that define the organization of the recurring beat; the top number tells the number of beats per measure, and the bottom number tells what kind of note gets one beat (also called the *time signature*)

Metronome: a device that can tick at a specific number of beats per minute; may be mechanical or electronic

Mezzo-soprano: a female voice, darker than a soprano but brighter than an alto

Minor scale: a diatonic scale that is constructed in various intervals, but the distance between the first and third notes is always a step and a half

Monophonic texture: music that consists of a single melody with no accompaniment or counter melody

Note: a single musical sound

Oboe: member of the woodwind family, using a double reed and a wooden body

Octave: the interval between a note and its duplicate eight notes away

Percussion family: instruments that make their sound when struck; may be melodic or non-melodic, depending on whether or not they can make an identifiable pitch

Phrase: the smallest segment of a melody that makes a complete thought

Piano: soft (the instrument, originally *pianoforte,* is so named because it can play loud or soft, at the control of the player)

Pitch: the sound of a single musical tone based on its rate of vibration

Polyphonic texture: music that consists of two or more melodies sounded simultaneously

Rest: an indication of silence for a specific duration

Rhythm: the arrangement of notes of varying durations in a piece of music

Rondo: a musical form in which the main theme returns after each new them is introduced: e.g., ABACA

Saxophone: member of the woodwind family, using a single reed and a metal body; comes in soprano, alto, tenor, baritone, bass, and contrabass sizes

Sharp: a symbol that raises the pitch of a note by one-half step

Soprano: highest and brightest female voice

Staff: a grid of five parallel lines, and the spaces between them; the position of a note on the staff indicates its pitch

String family: instruments that make their sound with a vibrating string, activated by a bow, or by plucking with hand or plectrum

Strophic form: musical form that consists of the same music set for two or more verses of text; peculiar to vocal music

Syncopation: an accent on a note not normally accented

Tempo: the speed of the beat of a piece of music

Tenor: highest and brightest male voice

Ternary form: three-part form: ABA

Theme: the main melody of a piece of music

Theme and variations: a musical form in which each section is based on, but different from, the original theme: A A' A" A'" . . .

Timbre: the character of a single musical sound, derived from the source of the vibration (also called *tone* or *tone color*)

Tonality: the tendency of a piece of music to center on a single tone

Treble clef: a symbol placed at the beginning of a staff that indicates that the second line from the bottom is the note G (also called a G clef)

Triad: the most common chord in Western music, consisting of three notes from a diatonic scale, every other note until three is reached (i.e., notes 1-3-5, 2-4-6, 3-5-7, etc.)

Triple meter: a beat that is organized in groups of three

Trombone: member of the brass family, with a moveable slide rather than valves to change the pitch

Trumpet: member of the brass family, highest pitched, with valves that can lower pitch when depressed by engaging a longer length of tubing

Tuba: the bass member of the brass family; comes in various versions, from the smaller baritone horn and euphonium and the regular orchestral tuba to the Sousaphone, which wraps around the players shoulders to be carried in a marching band

Viola: member of the bowed string family, the second highest range

Violin: member of the bowed string family, the highest range

Woodwinds: instruments that make their sounds from the vibration of a reed, two reeds, or vibrations made by blowing across the edge of an open mouthpiece

Tear-Out No. 1

1. What is the texture of this piece?
   Remember, this is texture, so your choices are monophonic, homophonic, polyphonic, or some mix of these.

2. How would you describe the harmonies of this piece?
   And this is harmony, which will be described as either consonant or dissonant.

3. What instrumental family or families are playing?
   The families are strings, woodwinds, brass, percussion, keyboard, and/or electronic.

4. Is the meter duple or triple?
   Though there are pieces that combine the two, this is not one of them.

5. What happens to the dynamics of the piece?
   Do you hear a crescendo, a decrescendo, or are the dynamic levels constant?

Listening Exam

The Middle Ages (450–1450 C.E.)
The Dark Ages Between Civilizations

Nearly all music appreciation books start the historical part of the study with the Middle Ages. That may seem an odd choice—wasn't there music before this period? And what does the name mean, anyway: "Middle" Ages? Middle of what?

To answer the first question first, of course there was music before the Middle Ages. But we know comparatively little about it, because there was no way to record it. Music is an experience, one that occurs in space and time. For the last 100 or so years, we've been able to capture a musical experience and preserve it electronically, by making some sort of recording. The earliest version was a wax cylinder developed by Thomas Edison: the sound vibrations were etched into the cylinder, rotating across its length in a tight spiral. Over time, the medium changed; cylinders became discs, direct etching was replaced by magnetic tape, analog was replaced by digital, records replaced by encoded compact discs, then mp3, mp4, and whatever has been developed between when this is written and you read it. But before that, music had to be experienced live, with actual human beings performing it. Sometimes, the music was improvised, or memorized, but since around 900 C.E., at least in the West, there was a written notation developed that would indicate what sounds were to be produced to make the music. We start our study with the music of the Middle Ages because that is the first time there is a large body of music that survives in written form, the first material we have available for study. Music has been a part of all human civilizations, but all that had no way of being recorded has been lost to history.

Music in Ancient Greece and Rome

The earliest civilization that can be considered specifically Western is that of ancient Greece. Greek culture provides the model for much of our modern Western world, including the beginnings of democracy, of humanism, and a philosophy that seeks to understand our world through logical observation, rather than seeing life clouded in an incomprehensible mystery.

Only about six complete pieces of music still exist, along with around 30 fragments of pieces and several treatises that discuss music, from the seven-century period of the height of Greek civilization. Imagine, if you will, trying to understand the nature of the music of our own time if, since the end of the 13th century, only six complete pieces had survived. It would only give the most shadowy images of how important music is in our world. And because the early church, when it displaced the Roman Empire, intentionally destroyed much of the remnants of the pagan world, there is no continuity of musical practice that survives from this time.

We do know that music was considered of great importance to the Greeks. It pervaded all public aspects of life and all social classes. No one was considered a fully educated person unless he had been trained in two areas: music and gymnastics. Music prepared the mind and the spirit, gymnastics the body. The Greek Olympic Games included music and poetry in addition to athletic competition.

The Greek philosophers all included music as a central part of their visions of a utopian society—though not all music. They taught, according to the **Doctrine of *Ethos***, that music greatly affects the moral behavior of the listener (our word *ethics* comes from this term).

chapter two

Interestingly, both Plato and Aristotle believed that young people should be forbidden to listen to certain types of music because it was believed that it would corrupt their morals. The current concern over the harmful effects of certain types of popular music, which has led to warning labels on records in addition to more serious types of censorship, has been around for millennia.

Music in Greek Religion: Apollo and Dionysus

The Greeks believed that music had a divine origin, and worshipped **Apollo** as the god of music. In fact, the Greek pantheon of deities included many who were associated with music, and most included some type of music in their worship. The nine **muses**, goddesses who were to oversee the creative activities of humanity, included three who inspired aspects of music: Terpsichore, Euterpe, and Polymnia. Indeed, the term *music* is derived both from the muses and from **Musaeus**, a legendary Thracian musician associated with the origins of music.

The principal god of music, **Apollo**, stood for order and sobriety, clarity and logic, serenity and contemplation. His temple was inscribed with wisdom of the Delphic oracle: *Nothing in excess*. Apollo was the ideal god for a civilization founded on philosophy, which means "the love of wisdom."

However, the cool morality of Apollonian ideals seemed to have no room for passion and ecstasy, aspects of humanity that may be controlled but can never be denied. A new religion swept Greece sometime after the 9th century B.C.E., the worship of **Dionysus**, god of wine. Dionysian ideals were the opposite of the Apollonian—"Nothing in Excess" became instead everything in excess. The power of intoxication was celebrated rather than reason and order. Worship included drunkenness, feasting, wild dancing, and orgiastic sexuality.

In every other culture that has seen such an excess, an extreme reaction was produced that promoted asceticism and a revolt against the flesh. In Greece, however, the culture seems to have realized that ecstasy and serenity, order and abandon, are not necessarily opposites. Clearly, restraint is meaningless without something to be restrained.

Eventually, the worship of Dionysus was reformed and the wine god was accepted with the other deities. According to legend, the reconciliation was accomplished by **Orpheus**, the greatest musician of Greek mythology.

The Orphic reconciliation is particularly important because it laid the foundation for nearly all of Western musical development. As far back as the ancient Greeks, it was realized that all artistic expression, whether music, dance, literature, or visual arts, must establish a balance between the **Apollonian** and the **Dionysian**. Passion and order are not contradictory, but are mutually dependent. Passion without order becomes unintelligible; logical structure with no emotion to express becomes sterile. For any work of art to communicate effectively, there must exist a balance of structure and content, of order and emotion. When discussing *aesthetics*, the study of artistic beauty, the Apollonian ideals of order, serenity, and restraint are often called **classic**. The Dionysian ideals of freedom and passion are called **romantic**.

When studying the development of music, we will see throughout history a swinging pendulum between these two poles. A particular era may emphasize one or the other, though the two will always be in some degree of balance. Music, indeed any type of art, cannot exist without elements of both the Apollonian and the Dionysian, the classic and the romantic.

The Middle Ages (450–1450 C.E.)

Now to the second question: the middle of what? The Middle Ages (which you will also hear referred to as the Medieval Period) are, in fact, in the middle of—or, more accurately, between—two great Western Civilizations: Ancient Greece and Rome and the Renaissance. The very name "Renaissance" means "rebirth"—it was a conscious recreation of the humanist thought, and resulting culture, of Greco-Roman civilization.

The Catholic Church

Rome, at her peak, dominated much of the known (to Rome) world. And civilizations at such pinnacles often find that it is impossible to sustain—at least, none has done so in the world's history to date. Roman civilization deteriorated, their hold over their territories decayed, and eventually the empire fell.

It was replaced by the emerging Catholic Church, which had been the state religion since Caesar Constantine converted in 312 C.E. Even the governing hierarchy of the Church mirrored that of Rome, with the Pope replacing Caesar, Cardinals replacing Senators, and Bishops replacing local governors.

Catholic doctrine at that time taught that day-to-day life was, if not unreal, at least unimportant in comparison to the life after death, the life of the spirit. That belief led, at least in part, to a civilization unconcerned with such things as progress, science, research, and discovery. The concern was for the spiritual; fleshly concerns and desires were suspect, if not outright sinful (the belief of some that it was sinful to expose the naked body, even to one's self, led some to refer to the era as "a thousand years without a bath").

And, indeed, that was largely what happened during the time. Progress was slow, if it existed at all. Little of importance was discovered in the sciences, and superstition was pervasive. Political entities were mostly unstable, with no single nationality dominant. Civilization consisted largely of three levels: the aristocracy who were the land owners, the serfs who were the servants who worked the land for the owners, and the clergy.

Of the three levels, only the clergy was normally literate. Priests, monks, and other church representatives needed to be able to read to know the Bible and other sacred writings. Aristocrats may have been learned, but opportunities were few, and society relied much more heavily on memory and testimony for the enforcement of laws and agreements.

Dates

Historians love dates. They can help make some sense of past events and of the development of individuals and institutions. But they can be misleading, especially when one applies them to eras of art or music history. Most authorities agree on the various eras of music history, each identified by certain common characteristics. But even if we accept the dates of 450–1450 C.E. for the Middle Ages, that doesn't mean that in the precise year 1450, people in Europe said "enough of this . . . I don't know about you, but I'm ready for a Renaissance." Changes were gradual. Some began well before the usual target date, and others took a long time before becoming standard modes of operation. There will be overlap, and there will be creative figures who anticipated changes early, and others who maintained the old ways well after most had left them behind. The general outlines are important, but not precise.

The Catholic Church was the dominant force during the Middle Ages, and the primary unifying element in Europe. Customs varied widely, as did language—two communities a few miles apart might speak dialects that were mutually unintelligible. But all, or at least most, of Europe was united in following the same religion. Jewish communities existed, particularly in the larger cities, and pockets of pagan practice persisted, especially in rural areas. But on any given Sunday, whether a person was in Spain, what is now Italy, Austria, Denmark, or England, the worship service was the same experience. It was even in the same language: Latin.

Arched cloister in a monastery. © Rodion, 2010. Used under license from Shutterstock, Inc.

Nowhere was the practice of Catholicism more intense than in the **monasteries** and **convents**. These were communities where believers—ordained priests and nuns—separated themselves from secular life and devoted their lives to their faith. The communities were often quite autonomous: farming for food, keeping livestock for meat and milk, even making their own wine, and such activities took up much of daily life. But the real purpose of this existence was religious, and every day the monks or nuns devoted themselves to the study of scripture, prayer, worship, and contemplation.

Worship was not weekly, but daily, every few hours. Eight times each day, the monks or sisters would meet in the sanctuary to celebrate the **Hours of Divine Office**, often called the **Offices**. **Matins** was held at midnight, **Lauds** just before dawn, **Prime** at sunup, Terce at midmorning, **Sext** at noon, **None** in mid-afternoon, **Vespers** at sunset, and **Compline** before sleep. These worship sessions included prayer, scripture readings, . . . and music.

The main worship was the **Mass**, the symbolic recreation of the Passover Feast Jesus celebrated with his disciples just before his crucifixion: the Last Supper, now celebrated as Holy Communion. The structure and text of the mass changed as appropriate for the season, but certain aspects were constant.

The Catholic Church has an annual season, corresponding to certain events in the life of Jesus and the development of the early church. Texts appropriate for Easter may not be so for Pentecost or Christmas. Those sections of the Mass that changed according to the season were called the **Proper**—that is, words proper for the season.

But other sections of text were included regardless of the season. These were the **Ordinary**—words ordinarily included whenever a Mass was celebrated. The Ordinary consisted of six sections:

- *Kyrie:* Lord, have mercy, Christ have mercy.
- *Gloria:* Glory to God in the highest, and peace on earth to men of good will. We praise You; we bless You; we worship You; we glorify You. We give thanks to You for Your great glory. Lord God, Heavenly King, God the Father Almighty. Lord Jesus Christ, only begotten Son. Lord God, Lamb of God, Son of the Father. You that take away the sins of the world, have mercy upon us, receive our prayer. For You only are holy, You only are Lord, You only are the most high, Jesus Christ. Together with the Holy Ghost in the glory of God the Father. Amen.
- *Credo:* I believe in one God; the Father almighty, maker of heaven and earth, and of all things visible and invisible. And in one Lord Jesus Christ, the only begotten Son of God, begotten of the Father before all worlds; God of God, light of light, true God of true God, begotten not made; being of one substance with the Father, by Whom all things

were made. Who for us men and for our salvation descended from heaven; and was incarnate by the Holy Ghost, of the Virgin Mary, and was made man. He was crucified also for us, suffered under Pontius Pilate, and was buried. And on the third day He rose again according to the Scriptures, and ascended into heaven. He sits at the right hand of the Father; and He shall come again with glory to judge the living and the dead; and His kingdom shall have no end. I believe in the Holy Ghost, the Lord and giver of life, Who proceeds from the Father and the Son, Who with the Father and the Son together is worshipped and glorified; as it was told by the Prophets. And I believe in one holy catholic and apostolic Church. I acknowledge one baptism for the remission of sins. And I await the resurrection of the dead and the life of the world to come. Amen.

- *Sanctus/Benedictus:* Holy, Holy, Holy, Lord God of Hosts. Heaven and earth are full of Thy glory. Hosanna in the highest. Blessed is He that comes in the name of the Lord.
- *Agnus Dei:* Lamb of God, Who takes away the sins of the world, have mercy upon us. Grant us peace.
- *Ite missa est:* Go, the Mass is ended.

The Music of the Church

Now, for those of you who feel this has somehow morphed into a comparative religion class, let's remember: nearly all of these texts were set to music. All the eight daily Offices, the Mass Proper, and many musical versions of the Ordinary were sometimes spoken, but often sung. And all it was recorded in the earliest versions of musical notation. Together, it is the earliest large body of music that survives in Western civilization, and its existence is why we start the study of music in the Middle Ages.

The Mass Ordinary, after a time, became the words that were set when someone composed a Mass, and are still used that way (though the *Ite missa est* is rarely included). The text is not terribly poetic. It's not even in the same language—the opening *Kyrie* is Greek, the rest in Latin (and the Sanctus lifted directly from Jewish Liturgy, the thrice repeated *Kadosh, Kadosh, Kadosh*/Sanctus, Sanctus, Sanctus/Holy, Holy, Holy). But it has been set to music more often than any other set of words in history. It is a testament to the origins of our culture.

And there is a great deal of music here. Each of the Offices included music, and the music varied for each of the eight hours and across the year. The Mass Proper varied according to the season, and there were many musical settings of the Ordinary. The music was called **chant**, or sometimes **plainchant** or **Gregorian chant**.

"Gregorian" is a reference to Pope Gregory the Great, who reigned as Pope between 590 and 604 C.E. By tradition (which may be at odds with actual fact), Gregory is credited with creating the chants and is sometimes pictured with a dove on his shoulder, singing into his ear. This was the Holy Spirit, dictating the music to him.

More likely, Gregory put in motion the work to organize existing chants (there were several variants in differing geographical locations) into an annual cycle—an impressive if not miraculous task. He also established the *Schola cantorum* in Rome (School of Singers) to train musically gifted priests to sing the more difficult chants.

Once a system of notation had been developed, the Church collected them into the *Antiphonale*, the most important chants for the Offices; the *Graduale*, the most important chants for the Mass; and the *Liber usualis*, with a selection from both (Pope Gregory's Greatest Hits, as it were).

The music was varied, but all of it had certain things in common. Plain chant was:

- Monophonic
- Rhythmically free, without any recurring pattern of beats
- Modal

This last quality, modal, refers to the scales that were used for plainchant—these were not the major and minor scales we use today, but were related to them. In fact, the various modes can be constructed by taking a major scale and beginning on a note other than the first. For instance, if you took the notes of a C major scale, but started and ended on D, you would have what is called Dorian mode. Starting on E creates Phrygian mode, on F is Lydian, and on G Mixolydian.

Their use could be quite complicated, beyond the scope of this course, but the important thing to understand is that plainchant does not sound like we expect music to sound. Each of these qualities is different from the way we usually hear music. The scales are not what we're used to hearing. We rarely hear monophonic music, totally without any accompaniment. And most of what we listen to today is organized into a steady beat with repeating patterns of two or three beats.

One enterprising scholar in my class once answered a question to name three characteristics of plainchant by saying it was monophonic, modal, and boring. To the last, I could only ask "to whom?"

Remember, when you hear plainchant, that it is music that was not designed for an audience—unless you think of God Himself as the audience. This was mostly sung within the monastery, with the purpose of expressing faith and worship of the Divine. It quite deliberately lacks qualities that would make it interesting for a concert audience.

Hildegard of Bingen

Sometimes you will read that plainchant was always sung by male singers. This is true as far as the public liturgy is concerned, but nuns within their convents also used the music designated for the Offices and Mass (the Church forbade women to be heard in public worship).

One figure from the era was particularly important—she is often called the earliest known woman composer, but she is actually one of the earliest known composers of either gender (most of the surviving chant does not acknowledge the composer). Her name is Hildegard.

Hildegard of Bingen lived from 1098 to 1179 C.E. in what is now Germany. The reference to Bingen is the location of the convent she established and led toward the end of her life. She was a remarkable woman. In an era noteworthy for repression of women, she was not only director of a convent, but a public figure, one who travelled and preached. She was also not only a composer, but a poet, a painter, a biographer, and an author of medical texts. The Church made several attempts to silence her, but she managed to continue her work by claiming to be "just a poor little woman, simple and unlearned." At one point, she embarked on a series of journeys through what is now Germany, preaching and teaching. At that time, both activities were officially forbidden to women, but she had been recognized as seer/prophetess by Pope Eugenius III, and her reputation as "The Sybil of the Rhine" induced the Church to support her.

Hildegard of Bingen. © Zvonimir Atletic, 2010. Used under license from Shutterstock, Inc.

Hildegard had visions since she was a child. Her images are full of the emotional intensity (and sublimated eroticism) that found its predecessors in such writings as the Song of Songs, and believed that the melodies which she used to set her music were given to her by the Holy Spirit.

I saw a great star, most splendid and beautiful, and with it a great multitude of falling stars which with the star followed southwards . . . And suddenly they were all annihilated, being turned into black coals . . . and cast into the abyss so that I could see them no more.

Neurologist (and music lover) Oliver Sachs has pointed out that these visions are consistent with a type of migraine headache—a woefully unpoetic, if probably accurate, explanation.

Though you will often hear her called St. Hildegard, and though Popes Gregory IX, Innocent IV, Clement V, and John XXII worked to have her canonized, she was never formally a saint. She is listed in the *Roman Martyrology*, and the Church named September 17, her birthday, as her feast day.

example

Hildegard: *O quam mirabilis*

Secular Music: Troubadors, Trouveres, Trovatori, and Minnesingers

While the Catholic Church dominated the Middle Ages, there was a secular life, and music from that survives, though far less than that of the Church. The music of the common people can only be guessed, as that which does survive does so in written form, from a class of aristocratic poet-musicians of the age.

These went by different names depending on their region. In southern France, they were called *Troubadors*; in Northern France, *Trouveres* (or, if a woman, *Trobairitz*). In Italy, they were called *Trovatori*, and in Germany *Minnesingers* (the German prefix *minne* refers to romantic love). The style of these musicians varied in ways that specialists can recognize, but the music had certain things in common:

- It was sung in the vernacular (the common language, rather than the universal Latin of the Church).
- It was sometimes more rhythmic, rather than the unmetered style of plainchant.
- Like plainchant, it was modal.

Another way in which the secular music differed is that it was sometimes accompanied by some instrument like a lute (a relative of the guitar) or a small harp. Often, an aristocrat was accompanied by a servant known as a *jongleur*, or *menestral*. These figures were not only of the lower classes, they had something of a cursed status—the Church denied them the sacraments and a holy burial on death. But they provided entertainment, such as dancing or juggling, and played the instruments while their aristocratic masters sang (some authorities believe they may have set the texts to music, rather than the poet, though none is credited with this).

Sometimes the poetry would be devoted to retelling current events, or perhaps praising a more powerful host, but mostly it is of the tradition known as **Chivalric**, or **Courtly Love**. The codes of Chivalry (from the French *cheval*, or horse—these writers were sufficiently wealthy that they could own a horse) are familiar from

A troubadour © zmajdoo, 2010. Used under license from Shutterstock, Inc.

modern movies depicting the time. They were real, however, and dealt with the honorable way to live, even to the extent of how to treat a defeated enemy. And they also dealt with love, which was a tricky business in such a repressive age. The repression of all things sensual is likely the reason why so many of the poems depict a passion that is unrequited, even impossible. The Lady cannot be physically touched, only treasured, and used as inspiration for bold deeds, like invading other countries and taking the land away from those who actually owned it.

For an example of this, let's again turn to a woman, the *Trobairitz* Beatritz, Comtessa di Diá, who complains at having loved not wisely, but too well.

Beatritz, Comtessa di Diá: *Estat ai en greu cossirier*

Instrumental music in the Middle Ages wasn't really rare, but because it was practiced by mostly uneducated musicians, mostly memorized and improvised, very little has survived in notated form. From approximately a thousand years, only about 50 pieces have survived, mostly dance music known as *estampie*. The music is also mostly monophonic and modal, though it is dance music, and can be quite sprightly and rhythmic. Passages are often repeated, and sometimes one encounters a sort of form described as *heterophonic*, in which the same melody might be heard in different octaves, and with some added ornamentations, like trills and turns. And as you might expect, almost all of the works are anonymous. If the musician isn't even recognized by the Church, he is not likely to be recognized as an artistic creator by society.

Something New under the Sun: The Beginnings of Harmony

Harmony is such an ever present characteristic of Western music that it is hard to imagine a world without it. But it hasn't been around forever. All the music we've considered so far has been monophonic—no harmony, no accompaniment except a drone, no harmonic progression. All that had to be discovered and developed.

The first appearance of harmony was called *organum*, and the earliest form of that was called *parallel organum*—parallel because the second, added, melody was always parallel in rhythm and interval. To a standard plainchant melody, a second line was sung, always a specific interval away (a perfect fourth or fifth, further types of intervals we didn't cover in earlier sections, but important because they produce particularly stable sounds).

Parallel Organum

This was first recorded in the late 10th century, and that's all, for about 200 years. That's astonishingly slow, even in medieval terms. Finally, someone figured out that you could get an interesting effect if the melody added to the chant moved in parallel rhythms, but different intervals. This was called *free organum*.

Free Organum

By the 12th century, a style had developed that allowed the second line to escape any parallel construction—the extra melody might have two, three, or any number of notes against the original plainchant note. This was called *florid* or *melismatic organum*. From this point, the **Notre Dame School** arose.

The Notre Dame School

When we refer to a "school" in this context, we don't mean an educational institution, but a group of composers who were related chronologically, stylistically, and geographically. The Notre Dame School was active in the late 12th and early 13th centuries, in or near Paris, France, and all had a similar style.

Most surviving music from this group is unattributed. Composers were not especially honored at the time, so many pieces are anonymous. Only two names have survived, **Leoninus** from the late 12th century, and his successor (and perhaps his student) **Perotinus**. We're going to hear excerpts from their settings of the same text, *Viderunt omnes* ("They all saw"). The setting from Leoninus is for two voices, from his collection *Magnus Liber Organi* (The Great Book of Organum). Perotinus' setting is the first known music for four voices. With this setting, we will only hear the first word.

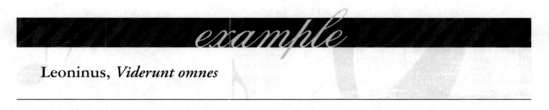

Leoninus, *Viderunt omnes*

Perotinus, *Viderunt omnes*

Most people won't find this music particularly attractive, unless the sheer strangeness attracts. There seems to be no purpose to the harmonies, which move without much direction between consonant and dissonant sounds.

But, remember, this is some of the earliest attempts at harmony. Its audience had no prior experience or expectations of what harmony would sound like, and composers took literally centuries to come to an agreement as to how to deal with multiple sounds.

There is a saying, attributed to India, that there is nothing new under the sun—humanity simply repeats itself in differing contexts. But *this* was new. Brand new. Nothing had been done with simultaneous sounds before.

Imagine, if you will, that you were living at this time, and you have come to Paris from some distant city. You attend Mass in the Cathedral of Notre Dame, then just recently completed. You have never heard anything but monophonic music, and suddenly you hear the sounds of Perotinus' four voice chorus bouncing around the sanctuary. It must have been an incredible experience!

The Ars Nova and Guillaume de Machaut

Ars nova means "new art," and refers to the music of 14th-century France. The term was coined by composer Phillipe de Vitry to distinguish the greater rhythmic, harmonic, and polyphonic complexity of the music of this era from what Vitry called the *Ars Antigua* of the 13th century.

The Church itself was not particularly enthusiastic about the new developments in music, and complained, somewhat justly, that the new polyphony was making the Latin text difficult to understand. In response to that criticism, the works of the ars nova are overwhelmingly secular in content.

The age of the 14th century was marked by political, religious, economic, military, and social upheaval. The papacy was divided. At some points, the entire population of Europe was excommunicated by one Pope or the other. The century saw the beginnings of humanism, the beginnings of the separation of church and state, a questioning of the authority of the church, and, of course, the Black Death.

The most important figure of this age, indeed, of all the Middle Ages in music, was Guillaume de Machaut (c. 1300–1377 C.E.). Machaut is, to a greater degree than any other musician, recognized as both poet and musician. He was an ordained priest, but spent life in the service of John of Luxembourg, King of Bohemia. In his 60s, he carried on a rather involved affair with Peronelle d'Armentiers, the 19-year-old daughter of an aristocrat and a bit of a Medieval groupie, with a taste for men of arts and letters.

Machaut was the first recorded composer to organize his own collected output. Most of his output is secular, though the most important piece is sacred: the *Notre Dame Mass*. It was probably composed in 1364, possibly for the coronation of King Charles V, though this is not confirmed. And the *Notre Dame Mass* has nothing to do with the Notre Dame School. The French simply means "our Lady," a reference to the Virgin Mary, so whenever you find French Catholics, you'll find references to *Notre Dame*.

Machaut: *Notre Dame Mass: Gloria*

This music is certainly more recognizable to the modern ear. It has a more purposeful use of harmony, more sense of structure—note how it builds to the final "Amen" climax—yet something is missing. That something is a sense of the pure, sensual beauty, absent in the Middle Ages largely because the church-dominated society considered sensuality something akin to sinful. But something new was about to be born . . . or, more precisely, reborn.

Glossary

Apollonian: in ancient Greece, the cult of Apollo taught the virtue of balance, restraint, order and logic, with the motto, "nothing in excess"; in the arts, those values are also referred to as Classical

Ars antigua: the "ancient art," describing the music of late 12th and 13th century France

Ars nova: the "new art," describing the music of 14th century France

Dionysian: in ancient Greece, the cult of Dionysus prized emotion, exploration, freedom of expression; in the arts, those values are also referred to as Romantic

Doctrine of ethos: in ancient Greece, the idea that music has an effect on behavior (the root of the work *ethics*)

Mass: the primary liturgy of the Roman Catholic Church, centering on the celebration of the Eucharist

Minnesinger: secular itinerant poet-musician in Medieval Germany

Offices: more properly, the *Hours of Divine Office*; a series of eight liturgical ceremonies held around the clock in monasteries, which included prayer, scripture reading, and singing of plainchant

Ordinary: the sections of the Mass text that were included every time the Mass was celebrated: *Kyrie, Gloria, Credo, Sanctus,* and *Agnus Dei*; after Machaut, a composer setting the Mass would set these sections, not the entire Mass text

Plainchant: monophonic, modal, rhythmically free vocal music used in the liturgy of the Medieval Roman Catholic Church; also just *chant*, or *Gregorian Chant*

Proper: the sections of the Mass text that changed according to the season, as was proper or appropriate for the season

Troubadour: secular itinerant poet-musicians in Medieval southern France

Trouvere: secular itinerant poet-musicians in Medieval northern France

THE RENAISSANCE (1450–1600)

Humanity Awakens

"The world is coming to its senses, as if from a long sleep."
Erasmus

The transformation of society in Western Europe was sufficiently dramatic that it is known as a renaissance, or rebirth. It was also, like all such historic shifts, gradual; however, it was fueled by several developments.

The **Renaissance** was a rebirth of the last great civilization Western Europe knew: the Greco-Roman era. More specifically, the humanist ideals of Ancient Greece saw a revival. There was a movement away from the medieval notion that humanity was essentially depraved and that salvation lies only in the spiritual life. Now, humanity was also important, worthy of contemplation, of development, and of exploration.

Several things made this possible. The breakdown of the authority of the Church that began during the 14th century was an important start. Public, and private, criticism of a corrupt clergy eventually led to an increased separation of church and state authority, and the Church saw her ability to control all aspects of life eroded.

One of the most important qualities for a humanist society to flourish is the ability to have access to information. Without education, it is impossible to be free of fear and superstition; faith can be stronger if it is not blind. But this was difficult during the Middle Ages. Books had to be written out by hand, one at a time. Because of this process, books were very expensive; one would have to be very wealthy to own more than a few.

All this changed in about 1440, when Johannes Gutenberg invented a device for printing using a press with movable type. Though the initial set-up was still a difficult process, once it was completed, one could print as many copies as were desired. The difference this made in the availability of information and the spread of literacy was profound.

You will notice also that we keep referring to Western Europe. Actually, the East never went through a dark period comparable to that of the West. The Eastern Church centered in Constantinople (formerly Byzantium, now known as Istanbul) maintained high rates of literacy and the connection with pagan Greco-Roman culture was never intentionally severed. When Constantinople fell to the Turks in 1453, scholars who had been a part of the Eastern Church fled to Rome and brought with them their knowledge of ancient Greece.

Likewise, southern Spain had been occupied for some centuries by Moors from northern Africa. That Islamic culture supported and tolerated a large Christian and Jewish population (as People of the Book, worshippers of the same God if somewhat out of date with the most recent prophet). That culture was expelled in 1492, in what is known as the *Reconquista*. What was left behind included such treasures as the Library at Toledo, filled with treasures from Ancient Greece and Rome. The few remaining Muslims and Jews who managed to escape persecution often did so because of their abilities as translators of the Arabic texts—the texts were not originally Arabic, but were themselves translations from Greek or Latin.

chapter three

The Italian Renaissance

In keeping with the new emphasis on humanity as human, and not only as a spiritual metaphor, the visual arts started to develop startling differences. Chief among these was an expanded sense of perspective and realism. Whereas medieval art often seemed two-dimensional and cartoonish, the art of the Renaissance did not shrink from portraying humans as living, fleshly beings. The idea of sensual beauty was welcomed, not distrusted.

In addition, the patronage of all the arts began to shift from the church to the court. Those courts vied with each other to see who could bring the finest artists, architects, and musicians to grace their palaces. Italy, in particular, was the center of all this—so much so that the period is sometimes called the Italian Renaissance. Dominant families ruled city-states: the Medicis in Florence, the Sforzas in Milan, the Gonzagas in Mantua, and the Pope in Rome (who, by this time, was as much a political leader as a spiritual one). Everyone seemed to be trying to "keep up with the Medicis," and civilization is richer for that.

The Basilica of San Lorenzo in Florence, built for the Medicis, begun by Brunellesci, completed by Michelangelo. © JupiterImages, Inc.

The Origins of Renaissance Music

While Italy was the undisputed center for visual arts, the earliest music that can be described as "Renaissance" was from England, in the works of John Dunstable (1385–1453). His contemporaries described his music as possessing a quality they referred to as "the English Sweetness," referring to a sweetness of harmony. The music of the Middle Ages can be described by a number of adjectives, but "sweetness" is really not among them. Dunstable was active both in England and on the continent (England had possessions in Northern France at this time). He left about 60 compositions; though chronologically closer to the dates of the Middle Ages, his music is clearly in a new style.

That new style had as its primary emphasis a homogenous blend of equal sounds. By now, the sensual beauty of harmony was both understood and enjoyed. Specific sets of rules to govern composition were established, and composers began to try to match the emotions of the text to the sounds of the music.

The Burgundian School

These composers were all associated with the court of the Duke of Burgundy, officially the vassal of the King of France, but in practice, equal in power. The Burgundian court ruled over what is now northeastern France and portions of Belgium, the Netherlands, Luxembourg, and the Lorraine. Duke Philip the Good ruled over a resplendent court from 1419–1467. He was a great patron of music and kept a chapel of 15–27 singers and some instrumentalists. These musicians were of international origin (French, German, English, and Portuguese). The most important composer of this group was Guillaume Dufay (c. 1400–1474). Dufay was not a regular member of that court, but his music was played there and is the finest of the period.

example

Dufay: *Lamentatio Sanctae Matris Ecclesiae Constantinopolitanae*

This piece is still a transitional work between Middle Ages and the Renaissance. In particular, the use of instruments in sacred music was avoided—if the goal was a homogenous blend of equal sounds, this was best done with an unaccompanied vocal ensemble. The term *a cappella* refers to this unaccompanied texture. It means "as the chapel," which means the Pope's chapel. That would seem to be a reliable means of determining appropriate Catholic practice.

The Burgundian School worked with three types of music: the **Mass** and **motet** (in sacred music) and the **Chanson** (for secular music). The latter term is simply French for "song" and is one of many terms for secular vocal music. The *mass*, at this point, means a musically unified setting of the Ordinary of the Mass. A *motet* is any unaccompanied sacred vocal music on a text other than that of the Ordinary of the Mass. It might be a portion of the Proper, some scripture, or religious poetry. Notice that the motet is distinguished from the Mass in its source of text, not its musical style. The music would sound the same.

The Franco-Flemish School

The Franco-Flemish School succeeded the Burgundians and was the first group of composers whose style was fully that of the Renaissance, without any transitional characteristics. They were centered in the same area as the Burgundians but were no longer associated specifically with the court of Burgundy. Musicians from this region came to dominate Renaissance music, indeed to define it, for the first two-thirds of the period. It became a point of pride for the great Italian courts to hire a Franco-Flemish musician for their chief musician, known as the *maestro di capella*, or Master of the Chapel (in French, *maitre de chapelle*; in German, *Kapellmeister*).

The great figure of this school was **Josquin des Prez** (c. 1440–1521). Born in Hainault (now a part of Belgium), he spent most of his career in Italy: for the Sforzas in Milan, for the Papal chapel in Rome, for Louis XII in France, and finally as *maestro di capella* for the Duke of Ferrara.

Josquin was held in the highest regard by his contemporaries, called the "best composer of our time" and the "Father of Music." Martin Luther was especially fond of Josquin: "He alone is master of the notes; they must do as he wills. As for the others, they must do as the notes will."

Josquin standardized several aspects of the Renaissance style. He established the standard texture for sacred vocal music: a polyphonic setting of four voices (though he often wrote for more, or occasionally for fewer). He also perfected the use of *imitation*, a device which would repeat, at a different pitch, a melody that had been heard in another voice. Often, several voices would overlap in this technique, and each new phrase of text might begin another sequence.

His music is more fully expressive of the text than any composer had achieved before. His music features a strong and detailed reflection of the sense of the words, based on chromaticism, melismatic ornamentation, and contrasts of rhythm and texture. He used a device called **tone painting**, or **text painting**, in which the music directly reflects the sense of the text. A passage about ascending into heaven, for instance, might be set to a rising scale.

example

Absolon, fili mi—motet

Absolom, my son, my son Absolom
Would that I had died for you, my son Absolom
Let me live no longer, but descend into Hell, weeping.

Note Josquin's use of imitation, and use of tone painting: on "descend into Hell, weeping," the melodies *and* harmonies descend around the cycle of fifths from Bb to Gb (beyond Eb was rare), as the basses end on a note of cavernous depths.

The origin of this motet is rather bizarre. The work was commissioned for Pope Alexander VI, who was in mourning over the death of his favorite son, Juan Borgia (the Pope, also Juan Borgia, had 12 sons (yes, at this time priests and popes were supposed to practice celibacy)). Juan was his third and was his favorite because he had been fathered through the Pope's daughter Lucretia (herself infamous for her habit of poisoning her rivals). The son was found two days after his death. His throat had been cut, and his hands were bound behind him. A stone was attached to his neck, and he was submerged in a river. His purse was untouched, so the death was probably a political assassination. Despite the circumstances of the commission, the work is one of Josquin's most hauntingly beautiful compositions.

Josquin's masses have the same musical style as his motets, but most of them are based on some sort of borrowed melody. That melody, called the *cantus firmus* ("fixed song"), was the basis for the initial statements of counterpoint that wove through the work. The borrowed music may be a plainchant, as in this case, or it could be a popular *chanson*—indeed, one of the most popular melodies to base a mass on was a tune called *L'homme arme*, or the Armed Man. Hardly an idea that seems appropriate for worship, but the sense, even from the Church, was that once the words were removed, the remaining melody was neither secular nor sacred, and could be freely used in a mass. Listen first to the plainchant on which Josquin's *Missa pange lingua* is based, and then you'll hear the same melodies in the opening section, the *Kyrie*.

Plainchant: *Pange lingua gloriosa*

Josquin: *Missa pange lingua: Kyrie*

The Reformation

The example of Pope Alexander VI's offspring is not an isolated example of the corruption of the Church, and several movements were begun with the aim of reforming corrupt practices such as the selling of Indulgences, through which it was possible to purchase permission to sin with the appropriate amount of money. Several movements arose with the aim of reforming the Church; most of them ended after the execution of their leaders.

The Reformation is generally understood to begin with Martin Luther's attempts to reform the abuses the Catholic Church had fallen into. When Luther nailed his 95 theses to the door of the church in Wittenburg, he had no intention of starting a new religion. He nevertheless found that unsolicited advice on how to improve oneself is usually as welcome as most communicable diseases. He found himself excommunicated. Moravian reformer Jan Hus, for instance, was burned at the stake, though his movement survives even today as the Moravian Church.

As Luther's movement gained momentum, similar movements sprang up in other countries under other leaders. All had in common the rejection of the authority of the Pope and the use of scripture and liturgy in vernacular. The effective result of the Reformation was the breaking of monopoly of power that the Catholic Church had enjoyed for some thousand years. Even the remaining Catholic countries had the threat that they could join the Protestant camp if Rome became too meddlesome. Europe was now divided, in effect, into a Protestant north and a Catholic south.

The Counter-Reformation

It soon became evident that the growing tide of reformation would not be stopped simply by excommunicating and executing the leaders of the movement. Growing consensus also realized that there was a real need for change in the Church, to return to its rightful purpose and practice. The **Council of Trent** was convened to this end. It was held between 1545 and 1563; the first ten years were spent in preparations for the actual meeting.

The Council eventually solidified standardized dogma and the requirements for the priesthood. It also addressed many of the abuses that had caused the Church's followers to lose their trust in the Church leaders, while at the same time increasing Church authority and power.

You will notice that there was nothing among those decisions about music. But music was under consideration—specifically, a set of reactionary delegates wanted to get rid of all this new-fangled harmony and go back to only using plainchant. Ultimately, the Council did *not* mandate the abandoning of polyphony, nor the use of a secular melody for a *cantus firmus*. Composers were, however, admonished to be aware of the purely spiritual nature of liturgical music, to avoid all that was "impure or lascivious" so that "the House of God may rightly be called a house of prayer." The composer credited with answering this call most perfectly was **Giovanni Pierluigi da Palestrina** (c. 1525–1594).

Palestrina takes the name by which he is known from his hometown. He is generally considered to embody the modal contrapuntal ideal. His style is sober, conservative, and objective. He avoids most dissonance and sensuality, and his works are harmonically pure. One of the most important features of his music is a nearly absolute clarity of text setting, despite his reliance on what is essentially the same style as that of the Franco-Flemish School.

His entire life was spent in Rome in the service of the Catholic Church; he served in the Papal court, at St. John Lateran Church, at Santa Maria Maggiore Church, and in the Roman Seminary. He was not a priest but was very devout. His compositions are almost entirely sacred: 102 Masses, 450 motets, 56 "spiritual madrigals," and 83 secular madrigals. These latter are early works, and are not particularly interesting; later in life, Palestrina said he "blushed and grieved" to have written such carnal works.

Pope Julius III (formerly Archduke of Palestrina Giovanni del Monte) initially hired Palestrina for the Papal Chapel in Rome in 1551. After his death in 1555, he was succeeded by Marcello Cervini, who reigned as Pope Marcellus for three weeks before his death. During that time, on Good Friday of 1555, Marcellus personally rebuked the Papal Choir for careless singing: "Whatever was performed . . . must be sung in a fitting manner, with properly modulated voices, so that everything could be heard and understood properly."

Palestrina took these words from an especially beloved Pope to heart. Marcellus' successor, Pope Paul IV, barred Palestrina and many members of the choir because they were married. Members of the choir were not required to be priests, but they were required to be celibate, a rule that had not been enforced for many years. Palestrina took a post in St. John Lateran Church in Rome and began what was to be his most famous work, which he dedicated to Pope Marcellus.

The *Missa Papae Marcelli* (Pope Marcellus Mass) has a bit of legend associated with it. It is supposed to have been written in specific response to the edicts of the Council of Trent. Specifically, this work was written to demonstrate that it was possible for a polyphonic work to be textually intelligible. Palestrina's reputation thus became that of the "Savior of Polyphony" by demonstrating that contrapuntal music—polyphony—was compatible with the new style of the Counter-Reformation.

The legend is somewhat in doubt—actually many of Palestrina's works could have produced the same results, as textual clarity is a hallmark of his style. Palestrina's personal attachment to Pope Marcellus seems to be more at the heart of the work. Regardless, the work does exemplify the style of the Counter-Reformation perfectly. It is one of only six of Palestrina's Masses that is "free"—not based on a borrowed *cantus firmus*.

example

Palestrina: *Missa Papae Marcelli: Credo*

Listen to how Palestrina solves the problem of clarity of text setting in a polyphonic texture. The *Mass* is set in six voices, but he only rarely writes for all six at a time. Most of the phrases of text are not overlapping, but set in block harmony, with only subtle movement within. He achieves variety of sound by breaking the six voices—soprano, alto, two tenors, and two basses—into an ever-changing set of mini-groups. Perhaps he'll first set for SAT1B1, then for SAT2, then for T1T2B1B2, then for SA . . . and so forth.

He only needs to do this in the two sections of the *Mass* with a large amount of text, the *Gloria* and the *Credo*. The other sections are brief enough that he can overlap the melodies without any problems of intelligibility.

Secular Vocal Music

After 1540, with the dissolution of the Hapsburg Empire, there was a breaking from the dominance of the Franco-Flemish style and a rise of a new set of stylistic trends that reflected the various nationalities of their origins. This trend can best be seen in the secular music of the period—sacred music has always been a more conservative area, and the Franco-Flemish style remained dominant until the beginning of the Baroque period. There was a general simplification of styles. The type of music varied in name according to its area—in France, the *chanson*; in Italy, the *madrigal*; in England, there was another version of the *madrigal*, and also the *ballett* and the *lute song*. However, they all had certain things in common. They were:

- Sung in the vernacular;
- Sung by a chamber choir, one singer to a part;
- Usually *a cappella*;
- Usually more rhythmic than sacred music; and
- Set to sentimental or erotic poetry.

The French Chanson

Let's start in France, with an example of a *chanson* that is an exception to at least one characteristic above. Clement Jannequin's *La guerre* (*The Battle*) is a musical depiction of the Battle of Marignon, compete with battle sounds, though all done with the voice. It is also rather longer than the usual chanson.

example

Clement Jannequin (c. 1485–1558) *La guerre*

Monteverdi and the Italian Madrigal

The madrigal is similar to a motet but is more vivid and varied. It used tone painting extensively and had a sentimental or erotic text. It was staggeringly popular, a kind of rock 'n' roll of the 16th century. More than 2000 collections were published between 1530 and 1630. Madrigals were sung at all sorts of courtly social gatherings and at meetings of academies that discussed literary, artistic, or scientific matters. Not surprisingly, its popularity coincided with the golden age of Italian poetry, just as the German Lied in the 19th century coincided with the zenith of German Romantic poetry. It was a truly international style, with versions in Italian, French, English, and German.

The madrigal found its greatest expression in the works of **Claudio Monteverdi (1567–1643)**. You will notice that his dates span both the end of the Renaissance and the beginning of the Baroque; indeed, he was an important transitional figure. As a Renaissance composer, he brought the madrigal to a level of perfection, and ultimately turned his works into a series of quasidramatic scenes. These were the foundation for the new form of opera, the form that was to define the Baroque.

His mature madrigals were attacked by theorists of his day as unnatural and incorrect. His defense was that his work was defining a new practice of music, not superior to the first practice but different from it in that text dominated the music, rather than the opposite, as had previously been the case. Ultimately, his sensitivity to the drama of his text made him, during the Baroque, one of history's greatest opera composers. The bulk of his career was spent in two cities: Mantua, from 1590 to 1613, for Duke Gonzaga; and Venice, from 1613 to 1643, where he was the music director of St. Mark's Cathedral.

example

Monteverdi: *Zefiro torna*

Elizabeth I. © JupiterImages, Inc.

Elizabethan England

Queen Elizabeth I ruled over England from 1558 to 1603, during one of the country's most glorious periods. England was at the peak of her economic, military, and artistic power. The Spanish Armada had been defeated, and England quite literally ruled the seas. The alliance with the Anglican Reformation movement gave political autonomy from Rome. It was the age of Shakespeare, Bacon, and Marley. It was also the age of Byrd, Dowland, Morley, and Weelkes.

In 1558, a collection of Italian madrigals in an English translation was published in England, called *Musica transalpina*, and set off a veritable craze for the madrigal. The English madrigal differs from its Italian model in that it tends to pay greater attention to purely musical qualities rather than dramatic ones. It is as if the English madrigalist is primarily a musician, while the Italian madrigalist is primarily a dramatist. The style approaches tonality more than modality, and only rarely uses dissonant effects. The effect is more natural and less jarring. There was an emphasis on a variety of approach. To quote Thomas Morley:

"*You must in your music be wavering like the wind, sometimes wanton, sometimes drooping, sometimes grave and staid, other while effeminate . . . and the more variety you show the better you will please.*"

In 1601, Thomas Morley (1557–1602), composer and holder of the royal monopoly on music publishing, printed a collection of 25 madrigals written in praise of Queen Elizabeth. The collection was called **The Triumphs of Oriana**; as was customary during the Renaissance, the collection presents the figure of the Queen in the guise of Oriana, a figure from classical mythology. Each of the works ends with the phrase, "Then sang the nymphs and shepherds of Diana, Long live fair Oriana."

example

Thomas Weelkes (c. 1575–1623)
As Vesta was from Latmos Hill Descending

As Vesta was from Latmos hill descending,
she spied a maiden Queen the same ascending,
Attended on by all the shepherds' swain,
to whom Diana's darlings came running down amain,
First two by two, then three by three together,
Leaving their goddess all alone hasted thither;
And mingling with the shepherds of her train,
with mirthful tunes her presence entertain.
Then sang the shepherds and nymphs of Diana,
Long live fair Oriana! (Kamien)

Weelkes was one of the finest of the English Madrigalists. He had some trouble holding a regular job because of chronic alcoholism. This example is filled with examples of tone painting. The references to ascending or descending the hill are set to rising or falling scales, appropriately. The words "First two by two" are set for two singers, "then three by three" for three, "together" for the whole ensemble, and "all alone" for a single voice.

A lighter type of madrigal was also popular, called the **ballett**, or **fa-la**. It was constructed of alternating rhymed couplets of text, set in homophonic texture, and polyphonic sections of nonsense syllables (fa la la la la, etc.).

example

Morley, *Now is the Month of Maying*

A third type of piece, the **lute song**, or **ayre**, enjoyed a huge amount of popularity from 1585 until 1620, and then virtually disappeared from practice. The leading composer was **John Dowland** (1562–1626). Dowland was the finest lutenist and lute composer of his day, and a fine singer besides. He was a moody and temperamental character and never rose to the height of his profession despite his acknowledged talent. The fact that he kept converting to Catholicism and moving to Denmark did not help. His output includes a substantial quantity of solos for lute and four books of lute songs, often arranged as madrigals for chorus—though they were conceived as solos.

example

Dowland, *Sorrow, Stay*

Sorrow stay, lend true repentant tears,
To a woeful wretched wight,
Hence, despair with thy tormenting fears:
O do not my poor heart affright.
Pity, help now or never,
Mark me not to endless pain,
Alas I am condemned ever,
No hope, no help there doth remain,
But down, down, down, down I fall,
Down and arise I never shall.

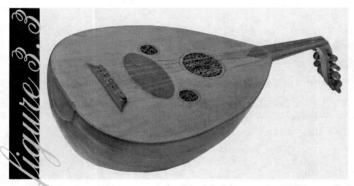

A lute. © JupiterImages, Inc.

A harpsichord. © Linda Bucklin, 2010. Used under license from Shutterstock, Inc.

Instrumental Music of the Renaissance

Thus far in the study of music history, instrumental music has been conspicuous by its comparative absence. In fact, most instrumental music prior to the middle of the Renaissance occurred in instrumental doubling (or replacing) of vocal parts, in dance music, or in courtly fanfares. Much of it was passed on orally or improvised; it was not notated and therefore not preserved.

The early part of the 16th century was marked by a rise in the importance of notated instrumental music. The status of instrumental musicians rose along with the rise in importance of the music. At least some of this change can be credited to the development of music printing. Collections of instrumental music, books on the technical methods of playing instruments, and books on the construction of instruments began to occur with increasing frequency.

The ideal sound of the Renaissance was considered to be a harmonious blend of sounds of equal tone colors. Not surprisingly, instruments of the day were conceived to match this ideal by construction in families, from soprano to bass. Thus, they could be grouped together in ensembles, known as consorts, with a perfectly blended sound throughout the register. The sound of Renaissance instruments was softer than modern instruments—and often had a somewhat nasal quality to the sound.

Instruments of the day were the distant ancestors of modern instruments. They were from the same families (strings, woodwinds, brass, percussion, keyboard) we now know, but in more ancient forms.

Stringed instruments included both plucked and bowed versions. Plucked instruments included by the *lute*, easily the most popular solo instrument of the period. Related instruments include the *cittern*, *pandora*, *theorbo*, and the *vihuela da mano* (the last a Spanish version of the lute that has a guitar-shaped body and a flat back, but is strung and tuned like a lute).

The *vihuela de mano*, as the name implies, was played by the hands. The vihuela de arco was a similar instrument played by a bow. It ultimately developed into the *viola da gamba*. These instruments were similar to the 'cello, but were fretted with six strings each. Many sources describe the viola da gamba family as the ancestors of the violin family, but in fact they developed concurrently. The violins displaced the violas da gamba during the 17th century.

Woodwind instruments included reedless instruments, such as the *recorder* family, and double reeds, including *krummhorns*, *kortholts*, *shawms*, and *rackets* (there were, oddly, no single reed instruments). Brass instruments included *natural trumpets*, *trombones*, *sackbuts*, and the *cornetto* (the cornetto was made of wood, but played like a modern brass instrument: through the vibration of the player's lips in the carved mouthpiece).

Keyboard instruments include the *clavichord*, the *harpsichord*, and related instruments such as the *virginal* and the *spinet*. The large *church organ* was developed toward the end of the period, but a more popular instrument was the *portative organ*, a table-top instrument played with one hand while the other pumped a set of bellows to produce the sound.

figure 3.5

A recorder. © JupiterImages, Inc.

The lute was by far the most important solo instrument of the period. Over 3,000 solos for the lute were published in England alone between 1585 and 1620. Dowland's works are quite the finest of the lot. Most of his pieces are dance pieces and/or arrangements of vocal pieces, but his finest pieces are his **fantasias**, improvisatory and contrapuntal pieces of remarkable invention.

example

Dowland: *Fantasy*

Though there were many different forms of instrumental music (the *fantasy* was one such type, freely constructed with an improvisational character), the majority of music that survives was dance music. There were many kinds of dances, each with a specific rhythm, tempo, and movements. The dances may be played on a lute or harpsichord, but were more often accompanied by a chamber ensemble.

Renaissance ensembles were known as **consorts**. They could by **whole** (all composed of the same type of instrument) or **mixed** (with various types). Interestingly, the music normally consisted of a set of four or more parts with no indication of what instrument was to play each part. The concept of idiomatic instrumental music was actually a product of a later age, the middle Baroque.

example

Michael Praetorius' (1571–1621) *Terpsichore* excerpts: *Courante, Gavotte, Spagnoletta, Bouree, Ballet, Volta*

Praetorius was a German composer who was best known for his church music, but he left a set of about 50 instrumental settings of dance music, collectively named *Terpsichore* after the Muse of Dance (in Greek mythology, there was a set of deities called Muses who oversaw the creative arts). Typically for the time, the score makes no indication what instrument is to play what part. As long as the music is in the instrument's range and character, any combination could be used. A good modern performance will change the instrumentations for each section to provide variety.

The Elizabethan **Broken Consort** is a specific type of mixed consort, a set of six instruments: Treble viola da gamba, treble recorder, bass viola da gamba, lute, pandora, and cittern.

Terpsichore. © ananas, 2010. Used under license from Shutterstock, Inc.

example

Allison's *The Bachelar's Delight*, from Morley's *First Book of Consort Lessons*

The lead roles are taken by the lute and the treble viola da gamba. The piece is in four sections, each repeated; you will hear that the repeats are not literal, but the themes are more elaborate, more of a variation of what was heard first. This practice was known as divisions and was common in Elizabethan music. Incidentally, the title does not mean what you think it means. It refers to another composer, Daniel Bachelar.

The Broken Consort is the earliest example of a large body of music composed for a specific instrumental ensemble. That honor is often given to another work, the *Sonat pian' e forte* by Giovanni Gabrieli, but Morley's collection predates that work, and the compositions were being performed some years before they were collected in his anthology. That does not, in the least, lessen Gabrieli's importance as a leading figure in the transition to the next era, the Baroque.

Glossary

Ballet: English secular vocal music of the Renaissance, consisting of rhymed couplets of text alternating with passages of nonsense syllables: e.g., "Fa la la" (also known as a Fa-La)

Broken consort: a specific type of mixed consort, consisting of lute, treble viola da gamba, treble recorder, bass viola da gamba, pandora and cittern; the earliest example of music for a specific instrumentation

Cantus firmus: in the Renaissance, a borrowed melody used as the compositional foundation for a Mass; may be a secular or sacred source (from Latin, "fixed song")

Chanson: Renaissance secular vocal music in France; a polyphonic setting of a secular poem

Consort: a Renaissance instrumental ensemble; may be *whole* (consisting of one type of instrument, such as recorders or violas da gamba) or *mixed* (consisting of instruments of different types)

Imitation: in Renaissance polyphony, the repeating of a melody in another voice at a different pitch level

Lute song: English Renaissance secular vocal music, set for a single singer accompanied by a lute

Madrigal: Renaissance secular vocal music, originating in Italy and frequently imported, especially to England; a polyphonic setting of a secular vernacular poem

Motet: during the Renaissance, a polyphonic setting of a sacred Latin text other than that of the Ordinary of the Mass

Tone painting: the use of musical devices to reflect the meaning of the text: e.g., setting the words "he ascended into heaven" with a rising scale (also known as *text painting*)

References

Delahoyde, Michael. n.d. *Renaissance Music*. Available at: http://www.wsu.edu/~delahoyd/renaissance/renaissance_music.html.

Kamien, Roger. *Music: An Appreciation*, 3rd ed. New York: The McGraw-Hill Companies, 1998.

Morley, Thomas. *A Plain & Easy Introduction to Practical Music*, ed. Alan Harmon. New York: W.W. Norton, 1973.

The King's Singers. n.d. *Madrigal History Tour*.

THE EARLY AND MIDDLE BAROQUE (1600–1700)
The Extravagance of Opera

The Origins of the Baroque

The dates for the Baroque period in music are 1600–1750, from the development of the new musical form of opera to the death of the greatest composer of the time, Johann Sebastian Bach. The term, which was borrowed from the visual arts, likely comes from the Portuguese *barroco*, which refers to an irregularly-shaped pearl.

Not all pearls are perfectly round. They are formed when a mollusk (typically an oyster, but most mollusks can produce pearls) gets a grain of sand lodged in its tissue and secretes a substance that will become mother-of-pearl around the sand to make it less irritating. The shape depends on where the pearl is formed in the mollusk. Perfectly round pearls are prized, but the distorted ones are less valuable. The term, in this context, is actually derogatory—it is insulting to refer to something as "baroque."

So, this is a bit of a mystery. Why name an artistic era after something believed to be flawed? The answer is that the Baroque did not name itself. It was named by the succeeding generation of artists, and that generation was, naturally, rebelling against the music it was replacing. That era thought Baroque art and music was excessive: so grandiose and theatrical that it had become ridiculous; so heavily ornamented that it had become fussy.

Time brings perspective. Most scholars no longer believe that the art or music of a given era is superior to that which preceded it; rather, it is only different. We now recognize that the Baroque in music was a time that valued emotional intensity, vivid contrast, and complex ornamentation. In short, it was a Dionysian age, the natural swing between two Apollonian eras, the Renaissance and the Classical Period.

It was an exciting time. The philosopher Erasmus had described the Renaissance as a time when humankind was awakening, as if from a long sleep. By the time of the Baroque, humankind had hit the ground running. Europe was experiencing a great wave of change. Explorations in, and exploitation of, the New World brought immense riches into Europe, and countries like England and the Netherlands that had strong merchant and banking institutions saw an increasingly strong middle class emerging.

This was the golden age of science. Antony van Leeuwenhoek invented the microscope, and an entire world of previously unknown life was discovered. Galileo Galilei (whose father Vincenzo was a musician and a member of the Florentine Camerata, which we will discuss shortly) invented the telescope and laid the foundation of modern astronomy. Sir Isaac Newton developed the mathematical discipline of calculus, and established the foundations of modern physics. In England, William Harvey discovered the principles of blood circulation, without which modern medicine would not have been possible. The Scientific Method, the standard for all subsequent scientific knowledge, was developed during this period.

chapter four

The Venetian School

Western music during the Middle Ages and the first two-thirds of the Renaissance was dominated by France, but by the late 1500s, Italy was beginning to be a significant rival. Italy, of course, was not a unified nation until the mid-19th century; at this time, it was a group of city-states, each independently governed but connected by varying dialects of the Italian language.

Venice was a prominent political center and first Italian world capital of music. It was one of Europe's few genuine republics: a representative government with members of both the aristocracy and the middle class. The citizens were quite proud of this fact, and there were 14 major celebrations of the "Serene Republic" annually. These celebrations were both civic and religious and were held in the piazza in front of patron saint's cathedral, St. Mark's.

San Marco Square, with Cathedral. © adam.golabek, 2010. Used under license from Shutterstock, Inc.

The *Catedral San Marco* has some of the finest acoustics in Europe and is characterized by a large pipe organ and two choir lofts on opposite sides of the sanctuary. The composers who are associated with the **Venetian School** exploited this in the form of polychoral works, compositions that were written for two or more choirs, along with other groups of instruments and the organ. The most important figure is **Giovanni Gabrieli** (1555–1612).

Scholars are divided as to whether Gabrieli represents the end of the Renaissance or the beginning of the Baroque. Let's listen to one of his polychoral motets and see what it has in common with the pure Renaissance style of composers like des Prez, Palestrina, or Byrd.

example

Gabrieli Motet: *In Ecclesiis*

The first, obvious difference is the use of instruments. Now, Gabrieli was organist for St. Mark's, so it is hardly unusual for him to include an organ accompaniment. But a brass choir? Remember, the ideal sound of the Renaissance was a homogenous blend of equal sounds. That's why *a capella* choral writing was so common. This music is not based on a blend, but on **contrasting** sounds. If the sound system in your class is a good quality, you will even hear the two choirs, and the vocal soloist, in different channels.

Another quality you hear is a difference of emotional display. Renaissance sacred music is often contemplative, quiet, otherworldly: an attempt to bring the singer/listener closer to the divine. This piece is almost theatrical, a shout to the congregation as well as to God. Each statement of *Alleluia* (from the Hebrew, *Hillel Yahweh*, "praise the Lord") gets bigger, and bigger, until the final cry of "GLORY!"

This piece, and most of Gabrieli's music, has two qualities that are at the core of the Baroque: contrast and the overt display of emotion. There are other aspects that have not been developed yet, or were in transition, but these are strong enough to identify the music as part of something new, something that would be called Baroque.

General Characteristics of the Baroque

The Concertato Principle: That emphasis on contrast actually has a name: the Concertato Principle. Simply put, it is the use of contrast as a structural principle. The Baroque loved contrast, whether timbre, tempo, tonality, or even mood. The only thing that the period avoided was contrasting moods within the same piece, and that will be profoundly important in the next era.

The Doctrine of Affections: The other aspect, emotion, also has a name: the Doctrine of Affections. According to this principle, the primary duty and purpose of art was to portray the emotions as vividly and as intensely as possible. Scientists at the time thought emotions (indeed, health in general) resulted from the balance of chemicals in the body. They believed in four humors: *sanguine*, *melancholic*, *phlegmatic*, and *choleric*. A sanguine person is outgoing, energetic, and optimistic. One who is melancholic is prone to depression and withdrawal; this type may also be contemplative. A phlegmatic person is quiet, uninvolved, and unconcerned. Finally, the choleric character is the authoritarian, a leader through strength and arrogance.

Music—indeed, all the arts—was concerned with the balance of these emotional states, both individually and in combinations. Composers developed particular devices to portray these states; rapidly repeated notes, for instance, indicated anger. But you don't need to know these codes to understand this music. It is intense, vivid, and colorful by design.

The Rise of Modern Instruments: The Baroque also saw the rise of modern instruments—at least, the direct ancestors of modern instruments. The Baroque oboe was different from the modern oboe, but at least they called it an oboe. And one group of instruments achieved near perfection during the Baroque: the **violin family**.

Violins, violas, and violoncellos were made during the Renaissance, but they were considered low-class instruments. The instrument of choice for aristocratic entertainment was the viola da gamba. But the violin family had a wider range of dynamics and timbre, qualities that better fit the emerging Baroque style and need for increased intensity. Several instrument makers—in most cases, several generations within the same family—were active in and around the Italian city of Cremona, and their names are synonymous with great instruments: Antonio **Stradavari**, Giulio **Guarnieri**, and Nicolo **Amati**.

These instruments still are the most sought-after, and costly, violins in the world. No one fully understands what makes them sound so magnificent—sweet tone, great power, wide range of timbres—though modern scientists have long studied them. Makers have dupli-

Stradivarius violin. © emin kuliyev, 2010. Used under license from Shutterstock, Inc.

cated the chemistry of the varnish used to cover them, have studied the grain of the wood, and measured precisely the dimensions of the sides and back as they were originally carved. One maker in Texas was soaking the wood in seawater for several years before construction. His instruments are excellent, though one must assume, even if this was Stradavarius' method, that the chemical content of the 20th-century Gulf of Mexico differs from that of the 17th-century Mediterranean Sea. The only thing that cannot be duplicated is three centuries of aging.

The Beginnings of the Orchestra: Prior to the Baroque, instrumental ensembles were chamber groups, with one player per part. Singers in choirs had long known that several singers to a given part make a different sound than a single player; there are subtle pitch differences that together make a softer blend of sound. It wasn't until the 1600s that musicians began to extend this practice to instrumental ensembles—larger groups with more than one player to a part called orchestras. Admittedly, the Baroque orchestra was modest in comparison to what later developed—usually no more than strings and a *basso continuo* (see subsequent discussion)—but the beginning was here.

Terraced Dynamics: Baroque dynamics followed a particular practice known as terraced dynamics. Dynamic levels, loud or soft, tended to move between each other immediately rather than gradually—a *piano* would rise immediately to a *forte*, rather than using a gradual crescendo. The emotional impact of this was perhaps the main reason, but not the whole story. After all, a good crescendo can be a highly intense experience. One might suspect that this practice arose because the instruments themselves lacked a wide dynamic range, so contrast was often achieved by alternating between a large group of instruments and a smaller, quieter one.

Further, the two main solo instruments of the period were incapable of anything but terraced dynamics. The lute was the favored instrument of the Renaissance, but its soft and subtle voice was inadequate for the emotional intensity needed for this new music. It was replaced by keyboard instruments: the **harpsichord** in the court and the **organ** in church. The largest harpsichords had two keyboards, each with a particular tone and dynamic level, and one could only get those two sets of sounds—or perhaps a third by linking both together.

The organ had far more range. Organs may have up to four keyboards, and the keys are linked to sets of pipes. The pipes are of different materials—metal alloys, various types of wood—and of different bores (the internal shape of the pipes), and each full set could play each of the notes of the keyboard or the bass. The banks of pipes (the finer the organ, the more varieties of pipes) were controlled by switches beside the keyboard called stops. The expression "to pull out all the stops" is from organists, meaning to employ all available resources. So, there were far more possibilities of sounds from an organ than from a harpsichord, but these changes of tone, and dynamics, could not be made gradually. You had to pull out (or push in) a stop, and the sound would then be on a new terrace and new level.

Tonal Harmony: Baroque music was written in a new harmonic system known as **tonal harmony**. Medieval and Renaissance harmony was **modal**, based on diatonic scales that were different from (though related to) the scales we call **major** and **minor**. The late Renaissance saw increasing use of those scales, and by the middle of the Baroque, they were used almost exclusively. The system is called **tonal harmony**. It took over music because harmonic progression can be defined more strongly because of the half-steps that end each of these scales, and that strength fit the needs of the time. This also means that pieces were identified by their **key**: Bach's *Mass in B minor*, Corelli's *Concerto grosso in C*. These designations only became common after tonal harmony had become dominant.

Basso continuo: With the development of tonal harmony came a need to establish harmonic progression effectively and definitively. This was done by the *basso continuo*, a continuing bass line that was heard in all Baroque music that had more than one instrument (the lack of a *basso continuo* is one of the few things that makes Gabrieli's music identify with the Renaissance rather than the Baroque).

The *basso continuo* consists of at least two instruments: a bass instrument, like a 'cello or a bassoon, playing the bass line; and a chordal instrument, like a harpsichord, organ, harp, or lute, doubling that line and providing harmony implied by it. The bass line had numbers underneath the notes that indicated (in widely-understood shorthand notation known as a *figured bass*) what harmonies were to be produced. Most modern performers just combine a harpsichord and 'cello and end it at that, but the musicians of the time used a wide variety of combinations. This was, after all, a time that loved contrast.

The Beginnings of Opera

The beginning of the Baroque period is usually given as 1600, coinciding with the development of the musical *genre* we know as opera. It seems rather appropriate that this era, which is defined by its theatricality, begins with the invention of the most important type of musical theater. Conveniently for historians, the first surviving opera (the name is taken from the Italian phrase *opera di musica*—works of music) was given its premiere on October 6, 1600. The medium itself has its origins in a mistake.

That last statement needs some elaboration. At the end of the 16th century, in the city of Florence in what is now Italy, a group of musicians, poets, artists, and other intellectuals met regularly in the home of Count Bardi, one of the city's leading aristocrats. The group is now known as the *Florentine Camerata*—the Italian word *camerata* refers to a society, club, or fellowship. Such groups were rather common during the late Renaissance; this group, toward the end of the century, began contemplating a recreation of Greek drama.

Of course, the Renaissance itself was a "rebirth" of Greek Civilization, so it was only a matter of time before someone got around to recreating drama. In its examination of Greek drama, the *Camerata* found that there was a chorus in these works, and they made the assumption that the Greek "chorus" was like a contemporary chorus—in other words, that it was set to music and sung.

This is the mistake alluded to above. In Greek drama, the chorus stood outside of the action and was not actually characterized, but instead narrated the play, commenting on the significance of what was happening. Modern scholars are not precisely sure how the chorus was presented in Greek drama. We do know that music played a part in the performances, because there are existing paintings of plays in action that include instrumentalists on stage, playing along with the actors. In addition, accounts of performances from ancient Greece seem to describe the actors' delivery as being highly inflected, something of a cross between speaking and singing. Despite this, it is unlikely that the chorus was completely sung like a modern chorus.

The *Camerata*, however, made the assumption that not only the chorus, but the entire production was set to music and sung. Therefore, to recreate Greek drama, they would have to develop an art form that was essentially a sung play, a drama set entirely to music. Unfortunately, there were no extant musical styles in the late 1500s that were appropriate for this task. Most late Renaissance vocal works, sacred or secular, were choral pieces—beautifully expressive, but not effective for conveying the thoughts, feelings, and actions of a single individual, because the identity of the individual is lost in a choral ensemble. Perhaps the closest medium for such a task was the lute song from Elizabethan England, but that tended to be much more lyric than dramatic.

The challenge, then, for the *Camerata* was to create a new kind of music that could convey the actions and feelings of an individual in a dramatic context. In time, they developed a new type of music that was proudly announced as the recreation of Greek song. They called the music **monody**, because it featured a single, expressive melody accompanied by the simplest of harmonic accompaniment on lute, keyboard, or some *basso continuo* combination. Eventually, the style came to be known as **recitative**. You can see the roots of the English word "recite" in that term: it refers to a type of vocal delivery that imitates and intensifies the natural inflections of human speech.

Listen to any successful public speaker and you will hear certain inflections used to intensify the meaning of his or her speech. These inflections are actually musical. Pitch will rise or fall, there will be a sense of dynamic variety as some words or phrases are spoken more loudly or softly, and there is often even a sense of rhythm in a speech, if not quite meter. Recitative imitates and intensifies these qualities—it is usually delivered in a rhythmically free, nonmetric quality. The first surviving opera was written with a substantial use of this new style of recitative. It was entitled ***Euridice***, by **Jacopo Peri** (1565–1633), with additional material by **Giulio Caccini** (c. 1545–1618).

The Legend of Orpheus and Eurydice

Orpheus was the son of Apollo, the god of music. He was reputed to be the greatest musician of all time; a singer and a lyre player whose music was so beautiful, skillful, and powerful that he could tame wild animals and cause the very stones to melt. Eurydice was his beloved wife, but shortly after their wedding, she was bitten by a poisonous snake, died, and was brought to Hades, the land of the dead.

Had Orpheus been wholly mortal, he could only lament the death of his wife; but, being partially divine (his mother was a mortal woman), he made an astonishing decision. He would go into Hades, the land of the Dead, and by the power of his music, he would bring his wife back to life again. He would convince the ferryman Charon to carry him across the River Styx, and he would tame Cerberus, the three-headed beast which guarded the entry to Hades. He would go before the very throne of the god of the dead himself, and by the beauty and strength of his song, he would convince the dreaded deity to allow his wife to return to the world of the living.

Figure 4.3

Orpheus taming wild animals, ancient Roman mosaic. © steve estvanik, 2010. Used under license from Shutterstock, Inc.

All this Orpheus accomplished—for the first time, one who had passed into death from life was allowed to return. He was left, however, with one provision: as he led his wife back to the sunlight, he could not turn around and look to see that she was still following him. Well, human nature was as perverse then as it is now, and Orpheus could not resist temptation. Just when he was almost to the surface of the earth, he turned to see his beloved spouse, just in time to see her fading from view, and returning to the dead.

At this point, according to the original myth, Orpheus collapsed, weeping uncontrollably, and was then torn to bits by a mob of intoxicated nymphs celebrating the rites of Dionysus—all presumably on Spring Break.

The myth of Orpheus was a natural choice for the first opera. What better way to recreate Greek drama, set entirely to music, than to choose the tale of the greatest musician of all time? Indeed, it has been a favorite topic for centuries; there have been many operatic settings of the myth of Orpheus and Eurydice—though most of the settings changed the original ending of the myth to something a bit happier.

Peri and Caccini's *Euridice* made quite an impact, but artistically it was not completely convincing, mostly because it relied so heavily on recitative. Recitative is a deeply expressive sort of music, but tends to become monotonous if relied on too heavily; Florentine audiences complained frequently of the "tedium of the recitative." Perhaps opera would never have caught on were it not for the genius of **Claudio Monteverdi** (1567–1643).

In 1607, Monteverdi composed his first opera, on the same subject. It was entitled *La Favola d'Orfeo* (The Fable of Orpheus). At the time, Monteverdi was working in Mantua; he was not a part of the Florentine Camerata and was consequently not bound by their theories. He realized that if one is to take a drama and set it to music, so that it is sung rather than spoken, then the music needs to bring qualities to the drama that it would not have otherwise.

Actually, the concept of the connection between music and drama is hardly unusual. In modern life, it is rare to see a movie that does not have a soundtrack of some sort. From the days of ancient Greece to the present, music has frequently been used to enhance the emotions of drama; however, the concept of a drama *entirely* set to music involves quite a range of ideas and devices to succeed.

Monteverdi realized that, expressive as it was, recitative alone was inadequate to create the musical setting of a drama. He began introducing other types of writing to give a sense of variety to the musical drama. **Recitative** is essentially a declamatory, nonmetric style of music wedded very closely to its text. *Orfeo* also includes other passages for solo singers called **arias**. These are more rhythmic and more melodically interesting. Eventually, their greater musical interest brought the arias to a position of much greater importance than recitative.

Monteverdi also used **ensembles**, which featured interaction among various characters: duets for two characters, trios for three, quartets for four, and so on. He used a **chorus**, particularly when he wanted to portray a group that had no individual identity, such as a chorus of shepherds or a chorus of soldiers.

In addition to these types of vocal writing, Monteverdi used instrumental interludes in *Orfeo*. Indeed, the orchestra that accompanied *Orfeo* was extremely large for its day, with some 40 players, including a large variety of continuo instruments. One such interlude, the **overture**, occurred at the beginning of the opera and served to set the mood for what was to follow. Other interludes occurred in between scenes to facilitate movement of characters or perhaps to accompany dancing.

Now we see something quite extraordinary taking shape. Within just a few years of its beginnings, the medium of opera has grown to something very much like its modern, mature form. That form is nothing less than a great synthesis of all types of artistic expression known to humanity. It includes various types of vocal and instrumental music, of course, but it also can include dance as well as the visual arts in the form of the backgrounds and costumes for the performance. Literature is included in the setting of the text, which contains elements of both poetry and drama. The term **libretto** refers to the text of an opera (or any large vocal work). It is a diminutive of the Italian word for book, *libro*, because the libretto was occasionally published separately in a "little book." Even architecture is a part of opera, in the form of the buildings in which the opera is performed—some of the greatest architectural monuments in the world are opera houses: the Sydney Opera House in Australia, *La Fenice* in Venice, the Metropolitan in New York, and the Bayreuth *Festspielhaus* in Germany.

To the uninitiated, the very concept of opera is rather strange—the idea of a drama set to music, sung instead of spoken, and frequently sung in a foreign language at that, is less than appealing on the surface. Yet, opera fans, those who know what the medium is really about, are some of the most intensely dedicated of all music lovers. The reason, simply put, is that opera represents the meeting of all artistic expression in one grand work. When it works, when the elements of music, drama, art, literature, and dance all mesh properly, the result is indescribable.

In a survey course such as this, it is difficult, if not impossible to experience the full excitement and fascination of this medium. Short of a special field trip to a live performance, one can only become exposed to brief recorded excerpts from an opera. Obviously, much is missing in such an experience: the sets and costumes, the acting and character development, and the very plot that builds up to important climaxes are all bypassed in the interests of time. Even a full videotaped performance lacks the atmosphere, the sense of event, of a live performance. By all means, if you get the opportunity to take in a live performance of a complete opera, make the effort to attend. You won't be sorry.

The Language Question

One of the ongoing, and perhaps irreconcilable, questions concerning opera is that of language. Should an opera be performed in the language in which it was written, or should it be translated into the vernacular of its audience? In other words, if an American audience is listening to Monteverdi, or to Verdi, should the works be sung in Italian or in English? Particularly for the first-time operagoer, the prospect of hearing an evening of singing in a language which is not one's own is terribly intimidating.

Many different solutions have been tried over the years. Early in the 20th century, it was not uncommon for singers to sing in the vernacular of their audience or even in their own native language. Some of the cast in one performance of Mozart's *Don Giovanni* sung in Italian (the language in which the original was written), some in German, and one in Hungarian!

Such an operatic Tower of Babel arose more for the convenience of the singers than for the purpose of enhancing communication with the audience. If we assume that the latter is the primary goal of a musical performance, it might superficially seem that the obvious choice for language would be to sing in the vernacular of the audience.

The problem of that solution is that it fails to account for the musical qualities of language. Any language, whether English, German, Italian, French, or Mandarin Chinese, will have qualities of vowel sounds, of inflections, of patterns of accents, and lengths of syllables that have a recognizable, and indeed a musical, quality. A composer setting a French text will not treat the words in the same fashion as he or she would if the text were in German or English. Consequently, to translate such a text into another language often destroys the truly musical flow of the original setting.

It is also quite arguable whether such a translation actually makes a text more comprehensible. The English language, in particular, is *very* difficult to sing in with a truly clear diction (be honest, now, how many of you *really* know the words to *Louie, Louie?*). Many people who are intimidated by the foreign language operas are initially delighted when they get a chance to hear a work done in English, only to find, to their chagrin, that they can understand only a fraction of what is being sung.

Currently in the United States, most major companies perform operas in their original language. A plot synopsis is given in the program book for listeners unfamiliar with the story of the opera being performed, but generally it is assumed that the listener has some prior knowledge of the work before coming. This is not really an unfair assumption—virtually any public concert caters to an audience familiar with its medium, whether that be jazz, rock, rap, country, or reggae. Classical audiences consist mainly of people at least marginally familiar with the works being played. The problem in opera, then, is how to make a work comprehensible to a novice, who may know something of the musical styles being performed, but who is intimidated by the language barrier.

Since the early 1980s, many companies have adopted a system that enables performances to be understood fully without sacrificing the beauty and natural inflections of the setting of the original language. During the performance, a translated text is projected onto a narrow screen at the top or bottom of the stage. The effect is similar to subtitles in a foreign-language movie (indeed, most opera performances on video use subtitles in the same fashion). In a live performance, they are usually called **surtitles** or **supertitles**. The audiences can then follow along with the *exact* sense of what is being sung, rather than just approximating the action from a plot synopsis. Most operagoers find this solution much easier than becoming fluent in Italian, French, and German.

Great Operatic Disasters

So much goes into an opera, from the creation of the work between composer and librettist to the execution of it among director, conductor, and singers/actors, that it is difficult to achieve the pinnacle of success with every aspect working together. Because the endeavor is so vast, the possibility for disaster can be distressingly great.

Opera lovers often take a perverse delight in some of history's more spectacular operatic failures. One such evening, recounted in Hugh Vickers' delightful little book *Great Operatic Disasters* (New York: St. Martin's Press, 1979) concerns a performance of Puccini's opera *Tosca* in New York's City Center in 1960. At the close of this highly dramatic work, the soprano in the title role is being pursued to the top of a castle. At the climactic moment, she turns, curses her pursuers, and leaps to her death from the top of the castle wall.

In such a performance, of course, the audience only sees one side of the castle wall and imagines the long plummet the soprano will make on her suicidal plunge. Behind the staged wall is normally a set of mattresses to cushion the fall of the singer. In this production, however, the soprano had been extremely temperamental, and the stage hands were thoroughly fed up with her by the end of the run. So, for the final performance, they removed the mattresses and replaced them with a trampoline. The star, thus, after a dramatic imprecation against her tormentors, leaped to her death, went down, and came right back up. The process was repeated about 15 times.

Problems of Baroque Opera

With the exception of the works of Monteverdi and Handel, it is rare to hear any Baroque operas given by a modern opera company. There are a few reasons for this. Perhaps the most important is that fairly quickly after opera originated, the grand conception of a synthesis of all aspects of artistic expression began to deteriorate. Baroque operas became extravagant spectacles whose primary purpose was to delight audiences with their special effects and to spotlight the star singers. To a great extent, any sense of dramatic continuity was lost. Contemporary audiences loved these works—opera became *the* major type of popular music for the next several centuries, and quickly spread throughout all of Europe.

Like most popular music, however, once the audience for whom the works were composed ceased to exist, so did any interest in the works themselves. Only a tiny handful of works managed to transcend their respective eras, and Baroque opera composers were more interested in their own audience's demands than in those of the future.

At least one authority dates the deterioration of the quality of opera from 1637, with the opening of the first public opera house in Venice. By public, we refer to a place in which anyone who had the price of a ticket could attend a performance. Opera was thus opened up to the middle and even the lower classes. The implication is that once the "commoners" are allowed into the opera, the level of quality will necessarily be lowered. This author finds such a view rather elitist. It has been his experience that the wealthy are just as capable of bad taste as the middle classes.

Regardless of the reasons why, it is true that most operas from the Baroque era seem foreign to a modern audience. Much of this stems from the problems already discussed, but another aspect is especially difficult to overcome. This is the use of **castrato** (pl. **castrati**) singers in the leading roles in Baroque Italian opera.

A castrato is an adult male soprano singer, of a vocal type which does not actually occur in nature. A castrato had to be created by surgically castrating a talented boy soprano prior to his reaching puberty. The singer would, then, grow to maturity without his voice changing. The resulting adult singer would have the purity of tone of a boy soprano, the flexibility and range of a female soprano, and the power of an adult male singer. The finest of the castrati, as we understand from contemporary accounts, were incredible singers and artists.

The modern mind has some difficulty with such a concept—one tends now to associate a deep voice with masculinity, and a male soprano now would be cast in somewhat effeminate roles. A Baroque audience, however, was quite accustomed to gender switching on the stage (especially in the theater—Shakespeare's plays, for instance, were done by all-male casts because English law forbade the use of women on stage). The sound must have been quite astonishingly beautiful and powerful because the castrati took roles representing great power: generals, emperors, and heroes.

This, of course, answers another question: why presumably loving parents would consent to such an operation on their child. The castrati were the "superstars" of their day; they were immensely famous and, for musicians, quite wealthy. If your son grew up to be a famous castrato, your declining years could be taken care of quite well by a wealthy son.

We really have little idea how a true castrato singer sounded. The taste for the castrato in Italian opera faded out by the end of the 18th century (it never caught on at all in France, which stubbornly maintained an independent style; Italian opera was dominant throughout the rest of Europe), and therefore castrati were no longer created. The one surviving recording of a castrato was done around 1903, of one Alessandro Moreschi. It was preserved on primitive recording technology, and Moreschi was only a mediocre singer. The recording gives only the slightest hint as to the real glories of such a voice. It is unlikely that the sound was like that of a countertenor, which is by nature a smaller-sounding quality. The great castrati were supposed to be tremendously powerful.

The problem, here, is how to deal with music written for a type of singer which, mercifully, no longer exists. In some operas, particularly those of Monteverdi, one can rewrite the castrato's part by dropping it an octave and assigning it to a tenor or even a baritone. Such a solution gains substantially in dramatic verisimilitude, while unfortunately losing some qualities in ensembles. The love duets in *Poppea*, in particular, lose some of the sensual beauty of two voices intertwining in much the same register.

Many later operas have such virtuosic parts for the leading castrati that they cannot be sung by a male singer, but need a singer with the flexibility of a female voice. In such an instance, one can only take a female singer and dress her as a male. The results of either of these approaches leave much to be desired. There is, frankly, no truly satisfying solution to the problem of the castrato in modern performance.

Monteverdi's *L'Incoronazione di Poppea*

Orfeo is the earliest surviving opera that is still performed with any frequency. It represents the earliest work in which all the modern elements of opera are substantially present. It is, however, a bit static for most modern tastes. Perhaps that is more a problem with our own age than with Monteverdi—we seem to be at a point in which we have little patience with anything that takes too much time to contemplate; we are poorer because of that. Nevertheless, for most modern listeners, Monteverdi's real masterpiece was composed during the last year of his life: *L'Incoronazione di Poppea (The Coronation of Poppea)*.

In 1613, Monteverdi resigned his position in Mantua and took the post of music director for St. Mark's Cathedral in Venice, a position vacated with the death of Giovanni Gabrieli. For the next three decades, Monteverdi was active mainly in church music. We have records of several operas that he composed during this time, but the complete scores for only two of these survive: *Il ritorno d'Ulisse in patria* (The return of Ulysses to his homeland, 1641) and *Poppea*. During the generation that separates *Orfeo* and *Ulisse*, a tremendous amount of activity took place in opera. A new generation of opera composers came onto the scene, all contributing to the development of the medium—many of these figures were pupils of Monteverdi.

Unlike *Orfeo*, *Ulisse* and *Poppea* use smaller orchestras, fewer instrumental interludes, and make little use of the chorus. Both works, however, represent a tremendous leap forward in the composer's ability to convey character, emotion, and action through music.

Poppea is indeed one of history's few truly great music dramas, worthy to stand with the masterworks of Mozart, Verdi, and Wagner. It is an unusual work in many aspects. First of all, it is a historical work; most of the earliest operas were based on mythology. Apart from an allegorical opening, in which Fate, Virtue, and Love are personified as deities and argue over which is more important in the lives of humanity, *Poppea* is a reasonably accurate history of the Roman Emperor Nero's relationship with his mistress Poppea. The libretto, by Gian Francesco Busanello, is based largely on the annals of Roman historian Tacitus, and while the chronology is altered to fit into the limited time span of the drama, the events described in the opera actually took place.

Nero was one of the most corrupt of a long line of corrupt Roman emperors. He fancied himself as much an artist as a politician—it likely was Nero who set fire to much of Rome so that he could redesign the city according to his own architectural plan. He blamed the fire on the newly emerging Christian sect and had hundreds crucified along the Appian Way. Nero also thought of himself as a poet and singer. He went to Athens to compete in the Olympic Games (which at the time included artistic competition along with athletic). He won all the events he entered because he brought along with him a large army and the Greeks were wise.

Monteverdi's opera recounts the story of Nero's love for the beautiful courtesan Poppea. Historically, Poppea was the wife of Ottone. Nero was enamored by her and sent her husband away on military duty to Lusitania (now Portugal). When Ottone returned, he found his wife was now the mistress of the Emperor, and he was barred from his home. Nero was madly in lust with Poppea and wanted to marry her so she could become the Empress of the Roman Empire. There was some opposition to his plan. His wife, Ottavia, was not amused. Nor was his old teacher, the Roman senator and Stoic philosopher Seneca. Nero managed to accuse Seneca of treason and forced him to commit suicide; his wife was found guilty of attempting to assassinate her rival, and was repudiated and banished. The way was then clear for Nero to marry Poppea, and the opera closes after her coronation as Empress.

The work does not include other events related to the liaison between Nero and Poppea. Nero's mother, Agrippina, was killed by him when she opposed the marriage. After the marriage, when Poppea was pregnant, Nero got into a drunken argument with her and proceeded to beat her to death. He later was so remorseful that when he saw a young boy who bore an uncanny resemblance to his dead wife, he had the boy surgically castrated and married him in a public ceremony. The ancient Roman equivalent of blogs commented that it was a shame Nero's father didn't marry such a wife.

Poppea is also an unusual opera in that it is particularly amoral. There are no real heroes: all of the four major characters are flawed, and none emerges as a force to champion good over evil. Such a cynical view will not be found in opera (or in any of the other arts) until the 20th century. Nero is seen as a weak, indulgent ruler, half-crazed with lust. Poppea is manipulative and grasping, willing to do anything to achieve a position of power. Seneca is portrayed as a blowhard, given to great moral pronouncements that have little relationship to the real pains with which humans struggle on a daily basis. Ottavia, seen at first as a noble figure struggling to bear her husband's public infidelity and his rejection of her with some grace and dignity, eventually shows her dark side when she threatens Ottone with torture and even death if he will not assassinate Poppea, his former lover.

Most importantly, *Poppea* is unusual in the extraordinarily high quality of its music, or perhaps more appropriately, in its magnificent marriage of word and music. Dramatically, the work is powerful; it combines passion, intrigue, humor, ethical argument, attempted assassination, suicide, and sex into a fascinating tale, filled with the intensity and extravagance that is characteristic of the greatest operas. Monteverdi has captured the essence of these emotions and actions with just the right musical setting. He has an uncanny ability to portray scenes with melodies and harmonic settings of unequaled poignance and intensity.

The Coronation of Poppea: **Characters and Story**
Characters:

> **Nerone** (castrato)—Nero, Emperor of Rome, son of Agrippina and Claudius
> **Poppea** (soprano)—Roman courtesan, formerly lover of Ottone, now mistress to Nero
> **Ottavia** (alto)—Wife of Nero
> **Seneca** (bass)—Stoic philosopher, Roman Senator, former teacher of Nero
> **Arnalta** (tenor)—Nurse/attendant to Poppea
> **Nutrice** (mezzo-soprano)—Nurse/attendant to Ottavia
> **Ottone** (countertenor)—Gentleman of Rome, husband of Poppea
> **Drusilla** (soprano)—Lady of Rome, in love with Ottone
> **Valetto** (mezzo-soprano)—Page boy for the castle

Other minor characters include servants, students of Seneca, a freed slave, and a few supernatural entities including Pallas Athena, Mercury, and the personifications of Fate, Virtue, and Love.

Story:

> **Prologue:** Fortune, Virtue, and Love argue over which is more important in the activities of humanity. Love wins the argument and proclaims that the events of the coming day will demonstrate the superiority of Love.

Act I: Ottone returns to the home of Poppea only to find that she is now mistress to the Emperor and that her house is surrounded by imperial guards. The guards exchange cynical comments deriding Rome, Nero, Poppea, and the military in general. Nero and Poppea emerge after a night of passion and reluctantly part, anxious for their next tryst.

The next few scenes feature an interaction of characters, first among Ottavia, Seneca, and the Valetto; then between Nero and Seneca; and finally between Nero and Poppea. They are discussed in greater detail below.

The act closes as Poppea rejects Ottone, having taken up with a higher class of lover. He then turns to Drusilla, who has been in love with him all along.

Act II: The act begins with the death of Seneca, discussed more fully below. It is followed by a bit of comic relief: a scene between Valetto and Damigella, one of the maidservants of the castle. The two are in lust for the first time and are determined to enjoy the experience.

Nero hears the news of Seneca's death and rejoices, singing praises to the beauty of Poppea with the poet Lucano. Ottavia, meanwhile, is determined to have revenge and commands Ottone to assassinate Poppea. Ottone is horrified, because he is still in love with Poppea, but agrees to comply when Ottavia threatens him with torture and death. She suggests that he disguise himself as a woman to accomplish the deed in secret, so Ottone borrows some clothing from Drusilla as he already has her voice.

Poppea falls asleep in her garden, soothed by a beautiful lullaby from her nurse Arnalta and guarded by Love. Ottone, disguised as Drusilla, comes upon the sleeping figure of Poppea. Though tortured by guilt, he attempts to strike Poppea with his sword, but Love knocks the sword from his hand. The assassination is foiled, and Ottone flees in the ensuing confusion.

Act III: Drusilla rejoices that her love for Ottone is finally requited, but her joy is cut short when Arnalta arrives and accuses her of attempting to kill Poppea. She is dragged before Nero, who threatens her with torture to find the truth. Drusilla refuses to betray Ottone, but he steps forward and confesses, revealing that he was working under Ottavia's orders.

Nero commutes the death sentence for Ottone to banishment, and allows Drusilla to accompany him into exile. Ottavia, however, is to be sent into exile, put aboard a boat and left to the mercy of the winds. Ottavia bids an anguished goodbye to her homeland in her moving *Addio, Roma*. Arnalta reflects on her good fortune in a cynical passage, and Nero and Poppea rejoice that the last obstacle to their love has been overcome.

The Consuls and Tribunes assemble for the coronation ceremony, as Poppea weds Nero and is made the Empress of all Rome and its empire. The opera closes with the exquisite duet *Pur ti miro*, as Nero and Poppea delight in their love.

Performance of *Poppea*

Modern performances of *The Coronation of Poppea* encounter several difficulties. Casting the opera is particularly complicated. The part of Nero was written for a castrato, as were several other characters. The nurse/attendant for Poppea is written for a male singer dressed as a woman, singing sometimes as a tenor and sometimes as a countertenor. Ottone was written for a countertenor rather than a castrato, to reflect his weakness of character. The part of the Valetto is to be sung by a mezzo-soprano, in what is often called a "trouser role"; this refers to the casting of a female singer to portray a young adolescent boy.

The trouser role is the only bit of cross-gender casting which outlived the Baroque—Mozart, Verdi, Strauss, and others have all cast such roles. The part of a young teenager could not be sung by an actual boy; the voice at that age is not sufficiently dependable. A mature tenor singer will have too strong a voice for the character, so opera composers will frequently use a mezzo-soprano or an alto in such a role.

More complicated than this, however, is the problem of the orchestral accompaniment. There is no surviving score for *Poppea* from the original performance; we only have two scores from revivals done, respectively, in Venice and in Naples, several years after Monteverdi's death. The scores differ in several details and are also substantially incomplete from the standpoint of the modern performer. They consist for the most part of only the vocal lines and the figured bass line for the continuo, with a small number of instrumental interludes.

This does *not* mean that was all that was played at those performances. Improvisation and embellishment were assumed parts of performance during the Baroque, and it is not uncommon to find scores with only the vocal line and continuo. In practice, however, the vocal line would be ornamented according to the practice of the time, and the accompaniment would be expanded with parts for wind and string instruments, created by the players at the time of the performance. The extra instrumental embellishment might take the form of extra instrumental interludes, or it might be an accompaniment for the voice, or even a counter-melody added to the written material. Such practice was sufficiently widespread that it was not thought necessary to notate—in much the same way that a modern jazz group can take a simple melody and chord progression found in a "fake book" and turn it into a vivid, varied, and colorful performance.

The central principle in *Poppea* is the dominance of the voice. The added instrumental material was always designed to support and enhance the singing, never to overwhelm it. With that in mind, players would create an accompaniment appropriate to the drama.

The modern performance, then, must rely on scholars and performers specializing in this period to realize an accompaniment appropriate for the work, as the skills of that particular era are no longer common. In recent years, several different performing versions have been published, some using modern instruments, most using period instruments. Each version has its own particular qualities that distinguish it from the others.

One thing most modern versions have in common is a variety of combinations of continuo instruments. Many go to great pains to match a particular combination to a specific character. For instance, Nero might be accompanied by a harpsichord, Poppea by a harp, Ottavia by an organ, and some of the less important characters by lute. In this fashion, the accompaniment contributes to the dramatic characterization of the opera.

A Closer Look
ACT I, Scenes 6, 9, and 10; ACT II, Scenes 3 and 4; ACT III, Scene 8, Final Duet

The intensity, extravagance and theatricality of the early Baroque can best be experienced through the medium of opera. Monteverdi's *The Coronation of Poppea* is unquestionably the greatest masterwork of its era, and we can experience something of the mystery and fascination of opera, and of the age of the Baroque, by taking a closer look at some specific scenes from *Poppea*. At a distance of more than three centuries, we can enjoy Monteverdi's wonderful ability to portray these situations and characters through a marriage of word and music. In **Act I, Scenes 6, 9, and 10**, we see a remarkable interaction of characters as the composer begins to define, so vividly, the personalities of the opera.

Scene 6 features Seneca and his students, Ottavia, and the Valetto. Seneca is written for a deep bass voice, a character filled with richness, wisdom, and moral authority (or so he presents himself). He seems to view Ottavia as a symbol of virtue, an example for his philosophy and teaching, but hardly as a real, suffering woman. Monteverdi seems to underscore the "windy" part of Seneca's character by giving him an impressively long **melisma**—several notes on a single syllable of text, designed normally to set off a particularly important word. Here, however, the word emphasized is "la," the Italian for the article "the."

Ottavia sees through Seneca's rhetoric, and with dignity and courtesy, labels it "specious vanity . . . a useless cure for suffering." The Valetto, however, is driven to distraction by Seneca's empty preaching and in a delightfully comic rage mocks the old philosopher, saying that his teaching amounts to little more than little ditties; whenever he sneezes or yawns, he tries to make it mean some great moral precept. Ottavia takes her leave, asking Seneca to plead her case with the people and the Senate, while she makes sacrifices in the temple, taking her case to the gods. The Valetto, in a final burst of rage, threatens to set fire to Seneca's beard, toga, and books if he does not help the Queen.

Scene 9 is an interaction between Seneca and his former student and current Emperor, Nero. Nero announces to his teacher that he has decided to repudiate Ottavia and to take Poppea as his wife. Seneca tries in vain to warn Nero that reason must take charge of passion or disaster will follow. The two impressive figures trade aphorisms, Seneca warning against moral collapse, and Nero asserting his power as that which gives him the right to do anything he desires. The two build to a point of utter fury toward each other in this remarkable exchange. Seneca particularly demonstrates courage—surely no one would speak so boldly criticizing the Emperor, except perhaps his former teacher. Nero finally cuts off debate—whether right or wrong, whether the people or the senate or Heaven or Hell approve, he intends this very day to have Poppea as his wife.

Seneca, frustrated at his pupil's stubbornness, asks Nero bitterly how a "mere woman" has caused such a failing in him, so unworthy of true royalty. In **Scene 10**, we see precisely the answer to that question. Poppea enters after Seneca leaves and languidly recalls their recent night of love. She asks her lord how he enjoyed her kisses, her breasts, the embrace of her arms. The setting here is as intensely sensual as the former scene was angry.

Poppea manipulates her lover with her charms like a master puppeteer controls a puppet with strings, and finally we see what she is hoping for. She drops a hint to Nero that Seneca might stand in the way of their happiness, and says she has heard him claim to be the real power behind the throne of Nero. Nero, conveniently, becomes furious, and sends orders that the "decrepit madman" must die this very day.

Part of Monteverdi's characterization of Seneca portrays him as a purveyor of empty concepts, but another side exists: the old philosopher truly believes his own teaching, and when he receives the orders to end his life, he goes to his death with dignity and serenity. In **Act II, Scene 3**, Seneca tells his disciples, whom he addresses as "friends," that his end is at hand, and it is now time to practice the virtues he has always advocated. Death is but a brief agony, after which the soul travels to true happiness on Olympus.

Seneca's students beg him not to die: they themselves have not yet accepted the serenity of his Stoic philosophy and argue that he has too much to live for. The old philosopher gently ignores their pleas and commands that they should draw his bath, so his "innocent blood" can mingle with its waters and he can die in peace.

Listen to the contrast of the moods Monteverdi has created here. The writing for Seneca is rich, noble, and serene; he is indeed ready to meet his inevitable death with dignity. The horror of his students at the thought of Seneca's unjust death is expressed in a tortuous overlapping series of rising chromatic scales—the anxiety of the scene is terrifically powerful, as harmonic tension reflects dramatic tension in a way that mere spoken word never could. As the students affirm their love of life, their unwillingness to leave its sweetness, the music becomes dancing, joyous, even a bit mischievous. The students repeat their plea to Seneca, after which the mood of dignity and serenity returns, as the old Stoic goes to his final rest.

The passage from mood to mood, emotion to emotion is flawless, no matter how broad the contrast. The structure of the scene is like an arching gateway. Seneca's noble outer sections frame the arch at its foundations, while his students' anxiety, first for Seneca, then for themselves, leads up to and away from the central passage, an affirmation of the sweetness and joy of life.

Scene 4 is a touch of comic relief—and perhaps more than just that. The scene between the page and the maid has nothing whatsoever to do with the drama, but it does bring a refreshing touch to the work. In contrast to the twisted passions of Nero and Poppea and to the manipulations and machinations of the various main characters, the innocent love and adolescent excitement of these two young characters is both amusing and touching. The characters are not even named—"Valetto" and "Damigella" indicate only the jobs of page and maid, respectively. The maid seems a bit more experienced than the page, and just slightly cynical. She calls the flirtatious boy "love's little rascal," but seems just as eager as he is. The sweet interplay of voices as they begin to enjoy their love and happiness lets the audience share in their delights.

The opera closes with the coronation scene itself, **Act III, Scene 8**. Nero and Poppea have by this point cleared away all active opposition to their marriage, and both are filled with joyous anticipation. After all the ceremony, the lovers are left alone on the stage, singing tenderly to each other of their love. The duet ***Pur ti miro***, which closes the opera, is certainly one of the most intimately beautiful in all of opera. It also demonstrates one of the advantages of using a soprano in the castrato role of Nero. While recasting the part as a tenor may be dramatically desirable for the modern audience, the parts of this duet were written to be in the same range, with the parts in close proximity of pitch—the melody lines embrace, rather like the lovers themselves, and the effect is quite beautiful.

example

Monteverdi, *The Coronation of Poppea*, Act III, Scene 8, duet, *Pur ti miro*, Nero and Poppea, excerpt.

In one fascinating modern production of this opera, the final duet features Nero gently embracing Poppea, while she gently embraces her new crown. The scene, in which each player has finally achieved his or her greatest desire, is perhaps a bit cynical, but remains true to the amoral quality of this opera.

Other Important Figures of the Early and Middle Baroque

Some scholars divide the Baroque into three periods: Early, Middle, and High. We are neglecting most of the middle period in favor of the massive explosion of genius that occurs in the High Baroque, but if you find this music interesting and attractive, you should explore some of these other figures.

Heinrich Schütz (1585–1672) was a German, but is a member of the Venetian School. He was influenced by Monteverdi and studied with Gabrieli, for whom he had special regard (he remarked of his teacher "Quantus vir!" which is Latin for "What a man!"). He succeeded Monteverdi (who had succeeded Gabrieli) as director of music for St. Mark's cathedral in Venice, and his music is mostly sacred. He continued the use of polychoral motets and expanded the use of instruments. Many of his works were designated "sacred concertos." These were not concertos like the instrumental works that evolved later, starting with Corelli, but vocal works that made use of the concertato principle by alternating choruses, soloists, orchestra, and continuo to explore a wide range of contrasts.

Girolamo Frescobaldi (1583–1643) was born in Ferrara and worked for most of his career in Rome. He was a keyboard virtuoso, and his music for organ and harpsichord is the finest of the Early Baroque. *Fiori musicali* is a collection of his organ music, generally thought to be his masterpiece, and his toccatas and partitas for harpsichord are also of interest.

Barbara Strozzi (1619–1663) was a poet, singer, and composer. She was the illegitimate daughter of Giulio Strozzi (who later adopted her). Her father, a poet and dramatist, founded the *Accademia degli Unisoni*, a musical branch of the local *Accademia degli Incogniti*, a literary organization. According to the minutes of the organization, Barbara sang for the members and suggested topics for debate among them. She studied with Cavalli, a protégé of Monteverdi, and her lovely, expressive melodies show much of Monteverdi's influence. Her output is entirely vocal, mostly written for the *Unisoni*. She remained an active member after her father's death and seems to have felt no particular difficulty as a woman composer. A note attached to one of her sets of songs says, "Since I am no more held back by feminine weakness than by any allowance made for my sex, I fly on lightest leaves in devotion to make my bow."

Alessandro Scarlatti (1660–1725) was the greatest composer of secular vocal music of the Middle Baroque and one of the most prolific—his output includes over 100 operas and 600 cantatas. The Italian secular cantata was developed when the Church banned opera performances during certain seasons and the opera-loving Italians needed something to take its place. The cantata was not staged and generally featured only a single singer, but otherwise the musical style and structure was similar to opera. Scarlatti's son Domenico will be discussed later; he was one of the great composers of the next generation, though he specialized in keyboard music.

Henry Purcell (1659–1695) spent most of his brief career as organist for his hometown congregation of Westminster Abbey, the center of the Anglican Church. His output includes all kinds of music, instrumental and vocal, sacred and secular. His **incidental music**, songs and instrumental interludes to accompany plays, were often so extensive that they are often called "semi-operas" (a term the author greatly dislikes, though no more so than "postmodern"). His acknowledged masterpiece is his only true opera: *Dido and Aeneas*. The work is one of the first great English operas, and the last until the works of Benjamin Britten in the 20th century.

Jean-Baptiste Lully (1632–1687) was the favorite musician of Louis XIV, that most absolute of all absolute monarchs, known as "The Sun King." He was born in Florence, Italy, and originally spelled his name Giovanni Battista Lulli, adapting to the French spelling when he joined Louis' court. He was the greatest composer of French music and developed a particularly French version of opera, which he called *Tragedie lyrique*. The form always combined dance and drama and altered the style of recitative to fit the French language. He also developed the *French Overture* to introduce the works. This was a two-part structure: a slow, grand opening with dramatic dotted rhythms and a faster, smoother, and more contrapuntal second section.

Arcangelo Corelli (1653–1713) was a rarity: an Italian composer who never wrote vocal music. Corelli was a violin virtuoso and teacher and left only six collections of music. Five were sonatas, trio and solo, and the sixth was a set of twelve *concerto grossos*. The form originated with Corelli (a set by Giuseppe Torelli [1658–1709] was published first, though there is evidence that Corelli's were being performed earlier than those). We will discuss the concerto more fully when we come to Bach and Vivaldi in the next chapter.

Elizabeth-Claude Jaquet de la Guerre (1665–1729) was a child prodigy. At the age of 10, it was reported that she could sing at sight complex and difficult music, could play the harpsichord with considerable skill, and was already composing. She caught the eye of the Sun King, who asked his mistress (who would later be queen) to take charge of the girl's education. She left a prolific body of music, including two sets of works for harpsichord, several sonatas, cantatas, songs, choral works, a ballet, and an opera. Her harpsichord music is a particular favorite, considered by the author to be equal to any of her era in France.

Dietrich Buxtehude (1637–1707) was the most famous organist of the Middle Baroque. He worked in Lübeck, at the Lutheran *Marienkirkei*, and was a powerful influence on Johann Sebastian Bach. Bach, the younger composer, once walked from his home in Arnstadt, some 250 miles away, to meet Buxtehude and hear him play. He remained there three months, and Buxtehude was an indelible influence on the man destined to become the greatest organist of his day. Buxtehude's works include not only organ music but a number of sacred choral works.

Glossary

Aria: passage in an opera, oratorio, or cantata for solo singer, with more melodic and rhythmic interest than in recitative

Basso continuo: the harmonic foundation of all Baroque ensembles, consisting of at least two instruments—a bass instrument such as bass viola da gamba or 'cello playing the bass line, and a chordal instrument such as a harpsichord playing the harmonies implied by the figurations on that bass line (see *figured bass*)

Castrato: a male soprano or alto, popular during the Baroque, created by surgically castrating a promising boy soprano so he grows to maturity with the range of a female voice, the purity of a boy soprano, and the power of a male chest cavity

Chorus: a passage in an opera, oratorio, or cantata for an ensemble of singers with more than one singer to a part

Concertato principle: the use of contrasting elements as a basic compositional goal

Doctrine of affections: the belief of Baroque musicians that the primary duty of art is to express the emotions, as vividly and powerfully as possible

Ensemble: a passage in an opera, oratorio, or cantata for more than one singer interacting

Figured bass: in Baroque compositions, a bass line with numbers indicating the harmony that is implied by the bass notes

Melisma: in vocal music, several notes on a single syllable of text

Movement: a section of a piece, complete in itself, but functioning as a part of a larger work

Opera: a play set to music, entirely sung or almost so; the form is a synthesis of all kinds of art: vocal and instrumental music, theatre, dance, literature, visual arts, and even architecture

Ornamentation: the addition of extra notes—trills, turns, scalar passages—to decorate the music, especially on repeated passages

Overture: the instrumental introduction to an opera or oratorio

Recitative: passages in an opera, oratorio, or cantata, which are declamatory and rhythmically free; an attempt to imitate and intensify the natural inflections of human speech

Terraced dynamics: in Baroque music, the tendency to change dynamics immediately, going from soft to loud, or loud to soft, rather than gradually increasing or decreasing dynamics

THE HIGH BAROQUE (1700–1750)

An Explosion of Genius

If this book gives short attention to the Middle Baroque, that can best be explained by the fact that most of the music pales in comparison to the towering geniuses of the late period. Georg Friedrich Händel and Johann Sebastian Bach created works that are recognized as the greatest of their age, indeed of any age. Antonio Vivaldi and Domenico Scarlatti specialized in particular types of music that had an indelible effect on later music.

1685 was a good year for composers. Three of these masters were born in that year, only Vivaldi was slightly older. We will begin with . . .

Händel on a commemorative stamp.
© Blue Moon/Fotolia.

Georg Friedrich Händel (1685–1759)

Händel was born in Halle, in what is now Germany, the son of a barber-surgeon (that seems an odd combination, but was quite common for the era—barbers often doubled as paramedics, a far cry in expertise from what we would now call a surgeon). His father discouraged his musical ambitions, desiring that he study law. He went so far as to forbid him to practice; young Händel responded by sneaking to a friend's home to practice.

He was orphaned early, and immediately went into the study of music full time. He was proficient on violin, oboe, harpsichord, and organ, and immediately started to compose. His goal was to become the best at the era's most popular music: opera. His first opera, *Almira*, premiered in Hamburg in 1705 when Händel was only 19. It was quite successful, despite the fact that the libretto was half in Italian, half in German, and wholly unintelligible.

Händel, however, was not satisfied, and decided in 1706 to travel to Italy to study techniques for writing Italian vocal music. He worked with, among others, Alessandro Scarlatti and produced some very fine works on the trip. In 1710 he returned to Germany and became music director for the court at Hannover. He endeared himself to the Elector of Hannover by requesting leave to travel to London and angered his employer by overstaying his leave.

In 1712, he further endeared himself to his employer by requesting another leave to go to London. That, surprisingly, was granted and Händel never returned. Then, in 1714, England got a new King: George I, the former Elector of Hannover, Händel's old employer.

Händel quickly and wisely made his peace with the King and established himself as one of the leading musicians in London, active as composer, conductor, organist, and producer. He changed the spelling of his name to George Frideric Handel (he dropped the umlaut from his last name, though he never lost his thick German accent). He was even made court composer for King George I. His main specialty was Italian opera, produced through his Royal Academy of Music, an entity that sounds something like a school, but was actually an opera company.

Handel was wildly successful until 1728, when a change in the public taste started to occur. Though Italian opera had been staggeringly popular, a growing segment of the population began to feel doubts. Watching emasculated singers singing in a language other than their own about tales of Greco-Roman history and mythology started to be seen as not only ridiculous but unpatriotic. Joseph Addison and Sir Richard Steele directly attacked Handel in *The Spectator*. Finally, public discontent coalesced around a satirical work, *The Beggars Opera*, by Gay and Pepuch, a play (later the source for Kurt Weill's *The Three-Penny Opera*) that made fun of the excesses and eccentricities of Italian opera. It became so popular that the public fascination with Italian opera was destroyed.

Handel attempted to revive his fortunes, without success, and in 1737 he suffered a debilitating stroke that left him partially paralyzed. He didn't emerge until 1741, when he turned to a new form of music: the oratorio. He had worked with this form before, and now he composed what was to become the most popular such work of all time: *Messiah*.

An oratorio is similar to an opera; in fact, it grew from failed efforts to set a sacred subject as an opera. It was difficult to reconcile the personal nature of faith with the theatrical nature of opera, but composers discovered that if the works were not staged, but given as concert works, they were quite successful.

Handel's oratorios are written in the same musical style as his operas. They differ in three important ways:

1. They are sung in English (which pleased the bourgeoisie), and based not on Greco-Roman mythology or ancient history, but based on the mythology of the English: Bible stories (which pleased the bourgeoisie even more).
2. They are not staged, though they were often done in costume at the time.
3. Greater prominence is given to the chorus.

Handel: *Messiah: All We Like Sheep*

All we like sheep have gone astray;
We have turned every one to his own way;
And the Lord hath laid on Him the iniquity of us all.

From *The King James Bible*

Handel: *Messiah: Hallelujah*

Hallelujah! for the Lord God omnipotent reigneth.
The kingdoms of this world are become the kingdoms of our Lord,
*   and of His Christ:*
And He shall reign for ever and ever.
King of Kings, and Lord of Lords. (Johnson)

From *The King James Bible*

Handel composed *Messiah* during a period of 24 days. His servants were worried about his health because he was going without sleep and food. When they heard him weeping uncontrollably, they broke into the room. He had completed the Hallelujah Chorus, and told them, "I did think I did **see** all Heaven before me, and the **great God Himself**."

Modern psychologists suspect, on this and much other evidence, that Handel suffered from what would now be called bipolar syndrome, and he composed *Messiah* during a manic swing. Were he alive today, he might be treated with some psychotropic drug, and we would have no *Messiah*.

With the premiere of *Messiah* in Dublin in 1741, Handel regained his popularity, which was uninterrupted until his death. He remained an active composer and conductor despite going blind in 1753. At his death in 1759, he requested a small funeral, restricted to a few friends. Instead, most of London showed up. He was buried in Westminster Abbey alongside England's most famous playwrights and poets.

Handel's most important musical quality is melody. His operas survive despite their somewhat lethargic dramatic qualities because of the sheer beauty of their vocal writing. Handel has a wonderful quality of conveying the most poignant of emotions in melodic terms. His use of polyphony and chromaticism is skillful but conservative.

His concentration was always on vocal music—first operas, then oratorios—but he wrote considerable instrumental works, mostly for chamber ensembles, but also for orchestra. A collection of his pieces for a party thrown by the King is called *Water Music*, because the party was mostly held on barges on the Thames River. The musicians were on their own barge, and were expected to play during the long trip to Chelsea, for the party ashore, and for the return journey. They must have been exhausted. Another famous set of his instrumental works is the *Music for the Royal Fireworks*. This was to celebrate a peace treaty that had been signed recently with France and was to include a massive fireworks display. Unfortunately, the fireworks exploded prematurely, demolishing the imitation Temple that stored them; the peace treaty didn't last very long, either, before it was violated. But the music survives to the present.

The original score was almost all winds, including 24 oboes, a dozen bassoons and French horns, loads of drums, and a pair of now obsolete brass instruments called *serpents*. This special instrumentation was needed for an outdoor performance. Winds carry great distances, but strings die out quickly. Other orchestrations are available for a standard orchestra, but the wind version is thrilling.

example

Handel: *Music for the Royal Fireworks: Overture*

Johann Sebastian Bach (1685–1750)

Johann Sebastian Bach led a career as restricted as Handel's was international. He never traveled more than 200 miles from his birthplace in Eisenach in the Thuringia district of what is now Germany. He was born into a family of musicians, and throughout his career thought of himself as primarily a craftsman rather than as an artist (though he was notoriously impatient with incompetence—as a student he was reprimanded for a knife fight with another student whom he had called a *Zipfelfaggotist*—a "nannygoat bassoonist").

Johann Sebastian Bach. © WO, 2010. Used under license from Shutterstock, Inc.

Bach was deeply religious and viewed all of his music, sacred or secular, as an expression of his faith. He often began a piece by inscribing the initials JJ, for *Jesu Juva* (Jesus help me), and ended with the initials SDG, for *Soli Deo Gloria* (to the glory of God alone). He was devoted to his large family, and had 20 children through two wives, of which 13 survived childhood. Just as he was expected to go into the family profession of music, he trained his sons to become musicians, and four became prominent musicians in the next generation.

Bach was known more as an organ virtuoso in his day than as a composer. When he took his post at Leipzig, the town council went on record as regretting that they had to settle for their third choice—the other two were G.P. Telemann and Graupner. The town council, and likely Bach himself, would probably be astonished to find that now, some 325 years after his birth, he is revered as one of the two or three greatest creative minds in the history of western civilization.

No, Bach was part of the bourgeoisie, a skilled craftsman who took pride in his work, but expected no glory. His life revolved around his work, his family, and his faith, all of which he considered part of the same essence. His major career centered in three cities, and the posts are important because what he composed was what was required at those positions. After his early training and some short-lived positions, in 1708 he took a post at Weimar where he was organist and music director for that city's main church. Many of his organ works date from this period.

In 1717, Bach took a post as music director for the court of the Prince of Cöthen. He had to delay the start of that position to spend a month in the Weimar jail, where he was sentenced for accepting a position without first getting the permission of the Duke of Weimar (labor protection laws were virtually nonexistent at the time). The Prince was a Calvinist, so music was not so important to his church, but at court he was a strong music lover. When he married, his new wife considered music an unnecessary extravagance, so Bach began looking for employment elsewhere. Also during this time, Bach's first wife Maria Barbara died. He married his cousin Anna Magdalena in 1721.

In 1723, Bach took what was to be his most important and long-lasting post: as Kantor for the St. Thomas and St. Nicholas churches in Leipzig. His great sacred choral works date from this period.

While at Leipzig, he taught music and Latin, prepared and performed music for the church services, and was obliged by contract to lead an exemplary Christian life. He could not leave town without permission. His duties alternated between two congregations, of which St. Thomas was by far the larger and more important. The principal service was from 7:00 AM until noon on Sundays, with three other shorter works during the day. The music for each Sunday included a motet, a setting of the Lutheran Mass (*Kyrie/Gloria*), hymns, chorales, and cantatas. There were required annually some 58 cantatas, Passions for Good Friday, and Magnificats for Vespers.

St. Thomas Church, Leipzig. © Andrea Seemann, 2010. Used under license from Shutterstock, Inc.

Bach completed four mostly surviving cycles of cantatas for the church year. Much of his music has been lost. Very little of his music was published, and what little survives is in copies by other writers—often even copies of copies. He wrote in all Baroque genres *except* for opera—probably because no one ever asked him to write one.

The neglect of Bach's music during his lifetime is puzzling to the modern mind. Several possibilities have been suggested for this, the most convincing of which is that Bach was in the wrong place at the wrong time. He lived when the Baroque style was beginning to lose popularity, to be replaced by the newly emerging Classical style, which came about in a direct rejection of the Baroque.

All of the figures of the late Baroque made concessions (or more accurately, innovations) to this new style, *except* for Bach. His sons certainly mastered the new ideas, surely encouraged by their teacher, but Bach reflected the essence of the Baroque so perfectly that he was found to be hopelessly out of fashion. Yet it is that very perfection that both sums up and transcends his era, so that while the Kuhlaus, Graupners, and the Telemanns of the era are the property of specialist academicians, Bach belongs to all humanity.

His music remained largely unknown and unperformed for almost a century after his death. The Bach revival was begun by Mendelssohn and his teacher Karl Philip Zelter when they revived the St. Matthew Passion in 1829, a century after it had first been written. The first biography, by Forkel, was published in 1802, followed by later ones by Philipp Spitta and Albert Schweitzer. The Bach Society was founded in 1850, and the first publication of his collected works came in 1900. His works were officially catalogued in 1950 by Wolfgang Schmieder, presented as *Bach Werke Verzeichnis* (*Bach Works Index*), and the BWV number is used to identify the works. They are catalogued by genre, with vocal works coming first, instrumental later.

His music is still recognized as among the greatest ever composed. That sense of humanity, of universality, received an interesting recognition some time ago. NASA sent out the Voyager 1 and 2 spacecraft in 1977, designed to travel past the farthest planets and beyond the solar system. They left Pluto in 1990, and currently Voyager 1 is the farthest manmade object from earth. A record, made of gold that will not corrode, was attached to both spacecraft. On it was inscribed several images, including the position of Earth in the Solar System and a drawing of a man and a woman, both stark naked. The record also included greetings in 52 languages, along with music to represent humanity. First among the selections was the music of J. S. Bach, his *Brandenburg Concerto no. 2*.

It is a quixotic quest; if one accepts that we are not the only inhabited planed in the universe, which seems likely, so many other conditions would have to be met. Assuming, however, that the Voyager is not destroyed in some collision, and it does pass an inhabited planet, and that planet is occupied not only by sentient creatures but those technologically advanced enough to retrieve the spacecraft safely, to understand the instructions on how to play the recording, to determine why the thing is in analog rather than digital recording, and to speculate where those people left their clothes—assuming all that, the first thing those beings will hear, representing Earth and its human inhabitants, is the music of Bach.

Bach's stylistic characteristics include:

- Absolute perfection of counterpoint (as Palestrina is the model for modal harmony, Bach is the model for tonal harmony);
- Free use of chromaticism;
- Powerful rhythmic flow;
- Carefully organized structure;
- Essentially abstract conception (Bach seemed to conceive of music as pure music; his music can be, and has been, played on nearly anything, from steel drums to harmonica, and still retains its beauty); and
- Extremely high consistency of quality.

The High Baroque used several standard forms of instrumental music, and Bach created the finest of each. We'll begin with a form that can be either instrumental or vocal: the Fugue.

The Fugue

We encountered this form before, in Britten's *Variations and Fugue on a Theme by Henry Purcell*. That was a somewhat untraditional fugue, but it still had the primary characteristics. Fugues in the Baroque were especially popular on organ, and as the world's leading organ virtuoso, Bach composed them throughout his life.

Any fugue is based on a single melody, called the **subject**, and any fugue is in a set number of **voices**—not actually human voices, though there are fugues for chorus, but in a range that would correspond to the soprano, alto, tenor, or bass voices on the instrument. Three- or four-voice fugues are the most common.

The subject enters alone, initially, in one of the voices. After that, it is heard again . . . but this time in another voice, at a lower or higher pitch level; and again, at another, until all the voices have stated the subject. When another subject enters, the first continues to play (sometimes called a **counter-subject**, sometimes in free counterpoint). This opening section, in which the subject is stated in each voice in turn, is called the **exposition**. For the rest of the fugue, the subject enters in various voices, and the entries are connected by transitional passages, called **episodes**, that link the entries of the subject.

All this sounds rather complicated, but if you listen to a fugue with someone pointing out the sections, it is actually easy to follow.

example

Bach's *"Little" Fugue in g minor,* BWV 578

This organ fugue (called *"Little"* to distinguish it from another longer and more complex fugue in the same key) is a classic example. It is in four voices, which enter from top to bottom in sequence, thus:

```
[=================Exposition=================] [===Episode===]
Subject 1, g minor  ======================================================
      Subject 2, d minor  ================================================
            Subject 3, g minor  ==========================================
                  Subject 4, d minor  ====================================
```

The subject is in a minor key, but some later entries are in major. The conclusion returns to the minor key, but ends on a major chord. This practice is called ending with a **Picardy Third**. Baroque musicians considered major more stable than minor (which, acoustically speaking, it is) and thus had greater sense of finality. You'll recall that the interval of the third is the difference between major and minor.

The fugue can have, and too often does, something of a dry quality, as if music has been replaced by mathematics—but never in Bach's music. Perhaps he recognized this danger and went to special lengths to assure a lyrical beauty to his fugues. The form concerned him for his entire life. His final work is *The Art of Fugue*, an exploration in 15 examples of the various techniques involved in composing fugues. The work is incomplete; Bach died while composing no. 15, dictating the work to his son who was notating the work because his father had lost his sight some years earlier. Some performances end at that very point, without completing the phrase, with a very eerie effect.

The *Concerto Grosso*

The *concerto grosso* is the most important form of orchestral music in the Baroque. You'll recognize a connection to the *concertato principle*, that Baroque characteristic that prized contrast as a structural foundation for music. In the *concerto grosso*, this is taken to its limit.

The form is based on an alternation between two instrumental groups, a small set of soloists called the **concertino** (the "little concert") and a larger group called the **ripieno** (Italian for "full"). The ripieno is typically a strong orchestra and *basso continuo*.

So we already have contrast of dynamics, since the larger group will be louder than the smaller. We also have contrast of timbre, since even if the soloists are violins, one alone sounds different from a section of violins.

The works were usually multi-movement works, typically three, alternating fast-slow-fast (with contrasts of tempo and, usually, meter). In these cases, the second movement is usually in another key, providing further contrast.

Bach wrote several concertos for various instruments, but his finest set is the six *Brandenburg Concertos*, so called because they were written for the Margrave of Brandenburg. Bach, like any professional musician, was always searching for a better position with a higher salary and better working conditions. He sent these *Six Concertos for Diverse Instruments* and attached a flowery dedication to the Margrave. The package was never even opened. Most, but probably not all, were performed at Cöthen—a terrible shame as most authorities consider the works the finest of the genre by any composer.

Bach *Brandenburg Concerto no. 5 in D,* BWV 1050

I. *Allegro*
II. *Affetuoso*
III. *Allegro*

The fifth *Brandenburg Concerto* has an unusual *concertino* of flute, violin, and harpsichord—unusual because the harpsichord was rarely used as a soloist, but rather as part of the *basso continuo*. This is the first concerto to use a keyboard soloist; in it, the harpsichord serves both functions.

Listen to the first movement and notice the amount of imitation, especially between the flute and violin. Listen also to the virtuosic part for the harpsichord, which not only has incredibly complex figurations at certain points, but also has a long solo just before the end. In the next period, this will be a regular part of the form, called a *cadenza*. Imagine Bach himself playing it, as he did at the first performance in Cöthen.

The second movement, in a minor key, dispenses with the *ripieno* entirely, with only the soloists of the *concertino* and the 'cello of the *basso continuo*. The violin and flute continue their dialogue.

The third movement returns to a major key, a quick tempo, and switches to a fast triple meter. It is some of history's greatest frolicking music, a delight from beginning to end.

The Suite

Suite implies a collection of complementary items. A bedroom suite consists of furniture appropriate for one's bedroom: a bed, chest of drawers, night stands, etc. In music a suite refers to a set of pieces that complement each other, with contrasting elements of tempo, meter, and key to make a satisfying whole. During the Baroque, the suite usually consisted of a set of dances.

The form was first standardized by Johan Jakob Froberger (1616–1667), a German keyboard virtuoso who wrote several dozen suites, and is credited with establishing the standard form of the Baroque suite: four dances of contrasting tempo and meter, with international origins:

- *Allemande* (a slow dance in duple meter, from Germany)
- *Courante* (a quick dance in triple meter, with different versions from France and Italy)
- *Sarabande* (a very slow dance in triple meter, from Spain)
- *Gigue* (a very fast dance in triple meter, from England)

This order was not always followed precisely. French composers, in particular, would often add fanciful titles that may or may not correspond to specific dances. Also, suites often began with an introductory piece, such as a *prelude, fantasie,* or *toccata,* and other dances were added, often between the sarabande and the gigue. Even the name of the suite varied—sometimes they were called partitas, or overtures.

Bach wrote suites for all instrumental combinations: keyboard, orchestra, and even sets for unaccompanied violin and 'cello. There are three sets of six each suites for harpsichord: the French Suites, all without a prelude; the English suites, all with a prelude (and more French in style than the French Suites); and the Partitas, the most complex and French of all. Notice that Bach here calls the prelude a *praeambulum,* and that he inserts two movements between the sarabande and gigue: a *minuet* and a *passepied.*

example

Partita no. 5 in G, BWV 829

Praeambulum; Allemande; Courante; Sarabande; Minuet; Passerpied, Gigue

---

Notice also that the performance we'll hear is not on a harpsichord but on a modern piano. There is considerable debate among musicians as to whether this is appropriate, but one suspects Bach wouldn't care. He frequently transcribed his music for more than one medium, and as long as it's played with love and conviction, it suffers nothing by the change. Bach's music, more so than any other, flourishes in any medium. One hears his music played on synthesizer, harmonica, steel drums, along with the modern piano or guitar, and it's still glorious!

The Sonata

The term *sonata,* at its root, simply means a piece played on instruments rather than sung (which would be a cantata). Early examples by Gabrieli were for a bass ensemble, and others used it for any instrumental work. From the Classical period on, the term has a specific formal meaning—in fact, it has several, all related, all of which we'll deal with in the next chapter.

Even in the Baroque, there are references to single-movement, binary form harpsichord solos called *sonatas* (which we'll cover under Domenico Scarlatti at the end of this chapter). But the primary meaning in the Baroque refers to a multi-movement work for chamber ensemble.

There were three types of sonatas: the **trio sonata**, the **solo sonata**, and the **unaccompanied sonata**. The names add to the confusion. A trio sonata was played by four players, a solo sonata by three, and only the unaccompanied sonata was done, as the title might imply, by a single player. Why these odd designations? Remember the *basso continuo*—that harmonic support unit in all Baroque ensemble music that used two players, a bass line and a harmonic instrument, like a 'cello and a harpsichord. Thus, the trio sonata used three musical units: two soloists and the *basso continuo.* The solo sonata still had the *basso continuo* of two players accompanying a solo player. Only the unaccompanied sonata was, well, unaccompanied. To be linguistically consistent, one or the other of the trio/solo sonatas should have been called a duo sonata; but, for whatever reason, that was not the practice.

Each of those could be one of two types: a *sonata da chiesa* (church sonata), or a *sonata da camera* (chamber sonata). The chamber sonata identified its movements mostly as dance pieces; thus, it was a type of suite for chamber ensemble. The church sonata only used tempo designations, since dance music in church would have been inappropriate.

Even if you don't get it all straight, the music is charming, intimate, and delightful, especially in examples from J.S. Bach. We'll hear one of his trio sonatas, a *sonata da chiesa*, since each movement is given only a tempo indication.

example

J.S. Bach, *Trio Sonata in G*, BWV 1039

Adagio; Allegro ma non presto; Adagio e piano; Presto

Bach and the Cantata

The term *cantata* at its root simply means a piece that is sung. There have been various definitions of the cantata; the Italian cantata of this period was secular, for a soloist, and something of an opera scene without staging or costumes.

Bach wrote the Lutheran cantata, which was similar to an oratorio. It used one or more soloists, always a chorus and orchestra, was set in multiple movements, and was based on a *chorale*. Strictly speaking, the *chorale* is only a melody and text, and is the heart of Lutheran liturgy (Martin Luther himself wrote several). In practice, the melody was harmonized in four parts for the liturgy.

Over 200 of Bach's cantatas have survived, enough for four annual cycles; likely many have been lost. His settings of the 140th cantata, *Wachet auf, ruft uns der Stimme* (Awake, the voice calls us) follows an ingenious pattern, typical of many of his cantatas, moving from complex to simple. An opening chorus would use the chorale melody (and the first verse) in an elaborate setting of vocal and orchestral counterpoint surrounding the melody sung in long notes. After that, there may be solos or duets for singers; these elaborated on the meaning of the text, rather than being based on the *chorale*. Another choral setting of the second verse will approach the music in some differing, somewhat less grand fashion. Then there may be another solo or duet, again elaborating on the text. Finally the *chorale* would be presented in its simple form, harmonized in four parts. The congregation often would join in at this point.

example

Cantata no. 140, Wachet auf, ruft uns die Stimme, BWV 140

The text is based on the parable of the five wise and five foolish virgins sent out to meet the Bridegroom, though it concentrates on the joys of the faithful rather than on the frustration of the unprepared. The overall structure is as follows (only the texts for the choral move):

I. Chorale (verse 1). This is the most complex and impressive setting of all. The chorale melody is sung in long notes in the soprano voice, while the other voices move contrapuntally around it. Each phrase is set off by an orchestral *ritornello* (returning passage) that solidifies the structure.

> *"Wake arise," loud call the voices*
> *of Watchmen so high in the tower,*
> *"Wake up, you town of Jerusalem!"*

Midnigh'st hour is now approaching
They call to us with lucid voices:
Where are the clever virgins now?

Behold, the Bridegroom comes
Rise up, take your lanterns
Alleluia!

Prepare yourself
For the wedding,
You must arise and go to him

II. Tenor Recitative (evangelist).

III. Soprano and bass duet with solo violin.

IV. Chorale (verse 2). Tenors alone sing chorale melody, accompanied by a counterline in the violins alone with the *basso continuo* ritornello. This was the subject of a popular chorale prelude for organ, structured in much the same way.

Zion hears the watchmen singing
The maidens' hearts leap with joy
They wake and quickly go to Him

Their Friend comes in Heavenly splendor
With graceful strength, and tender mercy
Their light is bright, their star doth glow

Now come, Worthy One;
Lord Jesus, God's own Son
Hosanna

We all follow
To that glad hall
To our Lord's table we are called

V. Bass recitative (Jesus).

VI. Soprano and bass with oboe. Here the text portrays Jesus and the believing soul in a warm, lyrical duet.

VII. Chorale (verse 3) in a 4-part, homophonic setting.

"Gloria" we all are singing
With earth and heaven our voices are ringing
With harp's and cymbal's clearest tone

Twelve great pearls adorn the portals.
At your fair city we are consorts
With angels high around Your throne

No eye has ever seen
No ear has ever heard
Such a rapture

Our song doth go
Io, Io!
Ever in dulci jubilo

From Cantata BWV 140, *Wachet auf, ruft uns die Stimme*, English Translation—Chorale MVTS Only, "Wake Arise," Loud Call the Voices. Translation by Marlon G. Hurst. Reprinted by permission of Marlon G. Hurst.

It may be useful to compare Bach's cantatas and Handel's oratorios. Remember that Bach's cantatas are liturgical, whereas Handel's oratorios are not. They are sacred theater music, but theater music, and consequently are distinctly different in their nature. Effectively, the oratorio is narrative while the cantata is contemplative.

The *Mass in b minor,* BWV 232

Among Bach's greatest works is the *Mass in b minor* (1733–1749)—and it brings up the question, what's a nice Lutheran boy doing writing a Catholic Mass?

As with the *Brandenburg Concertos,* this setting of Catholic liturgy was another attempt to get a better position. Bach sent a completed *Kyrie* and *Gloria* to King Frederick Augustus of Poland, then as now a predominantly Catholic country, to demonstrate his capacity to write for "the Church." He did not get the appointment, but his nature led him to complete the work, if slowly, from newly composed and recycled material. It seems Bach wanted to leave a complete example of Catholic liturgical composition.

It is far too long for liturgical usage, and some have doubts as to the sense of unity in the work. Others disagree, and consider the work the finest setting of the mass from any composer of the Baroque. The work is unified by cyclic use of themes, by a consistency of performance forces, and more or less by key. The combination of new and ancient styles is consistent with its concept as a compendium of Catholic sacred choral styles.

Bach: *Mass in b minor, Credo*

Crucifixus
He was crucified also for us, suffered under Pontius Pilate, and was buried.

Bach: *Mass in b minor, Credo*

Et resurrexit
And on the third day He rose again according to the Scriptures:
and ascended into heaven.

These two excerpts from the middle of the *Credo* give some idea of Bach's expressive power. The *Crucifixus* is appropriately somber, a funeral dirge set as a *passascaglia,* variations over a repeating bass line. The bass descends chromatically, a metaphor for Christ's descent from the cross into the grave. Yet the sections ends on a major key (not a *Picardy third,* but a change to the major key with the same minor key signature), as though hope is not utterly lost.

And it is not; according to the Christian scriptures, after three days, Christ rose from the dead. The music has banished any sense of mourning or loss, and rising trumpets, tympani, and voices seem almost to burst from the grave and ascend into heaven. Tone painting, as was heard in the Renaissance, was not as common in the Baroque, but here we witness it at its finest.

Two other composers are important to consider; both are specialists in a particular form, though they were more widely recognized in their day.

Antonio Vivaldi (1678–1741)

Vivaldi was born in Venice, though he had the bad taste not to be born in 1685 like the rest of the gang. He was ordained as a priest (nicknamed the "Red Priest" because of the color of his hair, not his Marxist sympathies) but was excused from his duties due to health. Most of his professional life (1703–1740) was spent as music director for the *Ospidale della Pieta*, a girls' orphanage, supposedly for "foundlings," but in practice for the illegitimate daughters of the aristocracy. The aristocracy of Venice appears to have been active because there were some 6,000 girls enrolled in 1730.

© Adam Fraise, 2010. Used under license from Shutterstock, Inc.

Vivaldi was reported to be extremely difficult to work with, and he died virtually penniless and friendless at the end of what should have been a thoroughly celebrated life. His output includes 48 operas, 59 cantatas, 60 sacred compositions, and 100 chamber works. But he is known today primarily as the composer of over 450 concertos.

Of these, 300 are **solo concertos**—structurally the same as the *concerto grosso*, but with only a single player in the concertino (which would become the standard for all future generations). His most famous work, *The Four Seasons*, is an unusual, but not unique, example of **program music**.

Program music refers to instrumental music that has some extra musical source of inspiration. In the case of *The Four Seasons*, we have four solo concertos for violin, each inspired by a sonnet that describes typical images of the season.

The opposite of program music is **absolute music**, music that exists only as music, with no extra-musical associations. The terms refer only to instrumental music. In vocal music, the text itself is the extra-musical element. Program music is uncommon, though not unknown, during the Baroque, but it becomes of great importance for the Romantic period.

example

The Four Seasons: *Le Primavera*

I. *Allegro*
Springtime is upon us.
The birds celebrate her return with festive song,
And murmuring streams are softly caressed by the breezes.
Thunderstorms, those heralds of Spring, roar,
Casting their dark mantle over heaven,
Then they die away to silence,
And the birds take up their charming songs once more.

II. *Largo*
On the flower-strewn meadow,
With leafy branches rustling overhead,
The goat-herd sleeps, his faithful dog beside him.

III. Allegro pastorale
Led by the festive sound of rustic bagpipes,
Nymphs and shepherds lightly dance
Beneath the brilliant canopy of spring.

Translation from http://www.baroquemusic.org/vivaldiseasons.html. Copyright by Baroque Music. Reprinted with permission.

Domenico Scarlatti (1685–1757)

Domenico was the son of Alessandro Scarlatti, one of the most famous composers of the middle Baroque. His father was so highly regarded that he had to leave Italy to escape his shadow and be recognized for his own talents.

A two-manual harpsichord like Scarletti played. © Nancy Brammer, 2010. Used under license from Shutterstock, Inc.

Scarlatti spent the bulk of his life on the Iberian Peninsula. In 1719, he went to Lisbon, where he was appointed the harpsichord teacher for Princess Maria Barbara. In 1733, after a few years in other posts, he rejoined Maria Barbara who was by now married into the royal family of Spain, living in Madrid.

Like Vivaldi, Scarlatti composed in a large number of genres, but is today known almost exclusively for a series of single-movement, binary form sonatas for the harpsichord. There are 555 of them, catalogued by Alessandro Longo during the 19th century and more recently—and more accurately—by Ralph Kirkpatrick, who is also Scarlatti's biographer. That catalog appeared in 1953. Sonatas are usually given a letter and a number, like K423 or L57, in addition to the key, to differentiate the works. The letters refer to either the Longo or the Kirkpatrick catalog.

The first collection of these was only published in 1738 when Scarlatti was in his early 50s, so his 555 published sonatas, which he labeled *esercizzi* (exercises), only represents a portion of his total output. Much of his other music was lost in a fire in Lisbon. His writing is as idiomatic for the harpsichord as that of Chopin or Debussy is for the piano—both of whom we will discover later.

example

Scarlatti: *Sonata in E*, K. 162/L.21

This work is unusual in that it uses two contrasting themes in the same piece: this was one way that Scarlatti anticipated the music of the next age. This was the only aspect of Baroque music that did *not* usually exploit contrast. Remember, Baroque thinkers believed that emotions were caused by the humors in the body (the sanguine, the melancholic, etc.) and thought it was unhealthy to affect different ones at the same time. Contrast of mood was achieved by writing another movement. The next generation did not share this conviction; indeed, contrasting themes became one of the most important aspects of music in the next age, the Classical period.

Glossary

BWV: for *Bach Werke Verzeichnis*, Bach Works Index, a cataloguing system for Bach's music, starting with the cantatas and other vocal works and then the instrumental compositions

Cantata: specifically the Lutheran liturgical cantata—similar to an oratorio but usually contemplative rather than narrative, and based on a Lutheran *chorale*; Bach's 200+ cantatas are the most important example

Concertino: in the Baroque *concerto grosso*, the small group of solo instruments

Concerto grosso: the most important instrumental form of the Baroque, consisting of two contrasting bodies of instruments: the *concertino*, a small group of soloists, and the *ripieno*, a larger body (usually a string orchestra with *basso continuo*; a third sound can be achieved by combining the two in passages marked *tutti*).

Fugue: a polyphonic musical form, instrumental or vocal, based on a single melody (the *subject*) that enters alone; it is then followed by subsequent entries of the subject until the structure of the fugue is defined (as three-voice, four-voice, etc.)—that passage is called the *exposition*; the rest of the fugue consists of various entries of the subject in each of the voices separated by linking passages called *episodes*

Oratorio: similar to an opera, but without staging or costumes; usually, though not exclusively, on a sacred text (grew from failed attempts at creating a sacred opera)

Program music: music based on an extra-musical source; very important during the Romantic period, but used occasionally in the Baroque (Vivaldi's *The Four Seasons* is a famous example)

Ripieno: in the Baroque *concerto grosso*, the larger body of instruments, usually a string orchestra with *basso continuo*

Solo concerto: in the Baroque, similar to the *concerto grosso* in structure, but with only a single soloist in the *concertino*; Vivaldi's nearly 300 such works are the most important examples

Sonata: in the Baroque, a type of chamber music; may be a *solo sonata*, played by three players (a soloist and two on the *basso continuo*) or a trio sonata, played by four players (two soloists and two on the *basso continuo*); not to be confused with the solo harpsichord sonata, of which Domenico Scarlatti's 555 works are the most important examples

Suite: in the Baroque, a collection of dances, usually *allemande, courante, sarabande,* and *gigue,* contrasting tempos and meters; often preceded by a prelude or other improvisatory work

References

Baroquemusic.org. n.d. *Antonio Vivaldi.* Available at: http://www.baroquemusic.org/vivaldiseasons.html.

Hurst, Marlon G. 2005. *Cantata BWV 140.* Available at: http://www.bach-cantatas.com/Texts/BWV140-Eng9.htm.

Johnson, Bruce L. 1998. *Handel's* Messiah. Available at: http://www.worshipmap.com/lyrics/messiahtext.html.

Tear-Out No. 2

Identify the following musical examples as music of the Renaissance or of the Baroque.

1. _____

2. _____

3. _____

4. _____

5. _____

The information in this table may help you:

	RENAISSANCE	BAROQUE
Rhythm	Gentle, often asymmetrical	Driving, powerful
Major solo instrument	Lute	Harpsichord in the court or organ in the church
Vocal music	Mostly *a capella*, or unaccompanied	Usually with contrasting instrumental accompaniment
Instrumental music	Mostly dance music, without *basso continuo*	Fugue, *concerto grosso*, *solo concerto*, always with *basso continuo*
Aesthetic ideal	A homogenous blend of equal sounds	A celebration of contrasting sound, intensity of emotion

Listening Exam

THE CLASSICAL PERIOD (1750–1809)
Papa Haydn and Mozart's Perfection

When most people refer to "classical music," they usually refer to the entire body of the cultivated, art music tradition that this course studies. But the term actually describes a rather narrow band of time, the second half of the 18th century through the early part of the 19th century. Historians generally agree to 1750 as its beginning (more precisely, the end of the Baroque with the death of J.S. Bach), but there is little agreement on its end. The transition from Baroque to Classical is fairly clear, because the new style was a deliberate rejection of the old. But the transition between Classical and Romantic was more direct, an evolution rather than a revolution. This book uses the date 1809 because on that date, something happened about which there is no dispute: Franz Joseph Haydn, one of the two greatest figures of the period, passed away.

The term *classic* is widely used, and really rather widely understood, whether referring to a classic car, classic rock, or Coke Classic—something is classic if it represents excellence, a model on which later creations can be patterned.

Even the term "classical antiquity" has specific meaning to the West: ancient Greco-Roman civilization. The art of the 18th century was actually called *neoclassic*, a conscious modeling of art and architecture after Greco-Roman models. Music was unable to do this as that time knew even less than we do now about Greek music, but it did use the term in another, related sense.

One aspect most things referred to as classic have in common is simplicity. That which is used as a model for later work must necessarily be direct, clear, and unambiguous. If the essential simplicity is not there, any attempt at later development will be compromised by aspects already developed from the simplest version.

And that, after all, was the essence of this classical revolution. The music of the Baroque had gotten too complex: so emotionally intense as to seem ridiculous; so heavily ornamented as to seem fussy. What was needed was a return to basics; to a reasonable, orderly, simple, and natural sort of expression.

The Enlightenment

In the history of philosophy, the period is known as **The Enlightenment**, or the **Age of Reason**. It was an age that valued clarity of thought and rationality above all qualities. This was the time that Diderot and the French Philosophers put together the first *Encyclopedia*, a compendium of all extant knowledge. It was when Emanuel Kant wrote his *Critique of Pure Reason*, setting the limits of human knowledge. It was the time Adam Smith wrote *The Wealth of Nations*, the first systematic study of political economy. Religious thought emphasized ethics over miracles; even operas started to use historical rather than mythological subjects.

It was, in short, an *Apollonian* age. You'll recall from the beginning of the course a short discussion of the Greek deities Apollo and

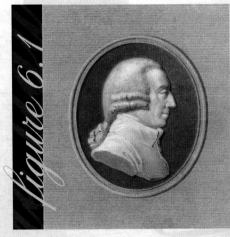

Adam Smith. © JupiterImages, Inc.

Dionysus; the former representing order, restraint, calmness, and reason against the latter's fascination with the free expression of emotion, with intoxication and revelry. In aesthetics, the study of the philosophical nature of art and beauty, *Apollonian* and *Classic* and *Dionysian* and *Romantic* are used to express these complementary opposites—as we observed before, any successful art will have both aspects in some sort of balance.

It may seem that this was an emotionless age, in which reason banishes passion. But in philosophy, music, and indeed, life itself, all things are some sort of a balance of the two. Consider the two most important events of the late 18th century, at least from a Western point of view: the American Revolution of 1776 and the French Revolution of 1789.

The American Revolution was bad enough for European civilization. Never before had a colony risen up and, by a violent revolution, severed the dominance of the mother country. But the French Revolution was on European soil, and the sight of the commoners rising up and throwing down the ruling aristocracy in a violent rebellion that left most of that aristocracy headless—*that* shook the continent to its core.

Imagine the emotions that went into those conflicts. Then go and reread the U.S. Declaration of Independence, the U.S. Constitution, or the French Declaration of the Rights of Man. These are all perfect expressions of the Enlightenment: calm, reasoned, not given to inflammatory rhetoric or extremes of emotion. Yet those documents are the reason behind these revolutions . . . the classical model, if you will. No, this was *not* an age without feeling; just an age that expressed its emotions within careful limits.

The Emerging Classical Style

The emerging classical style was a reaction against what was perceived as the excesses of the Baroque, a return to ideals of simplicity, grace, serenity, logic, and order, entertainment rather than profundity, naturalness (whatever that should be taken to mean), and a return to the ideals of ancient Greco-Roman civilization. Nearly all aspects can be summarized as a simplification of the earlier Baroque style.

- Melodies were simpler, with shorter phrases, and more prominent (it was considered a tuneful age).
- Texture was mostly homophonic.
- Rhythms were more relaxed and varied (part of the Baroque's rhythmic energy derived from repeated rhythmic patterns).
- Dynamics made greater use of crescendo/decrescendo (rather than the Baroque's terraced dynamics).
- Harmonies were simpler, with less chromaticism. (The *basso continuo* became not so much unfashionable as irrelevant. It was no longer necessary to define harmonies that were so simple already.)
- New instruments were developed: the pianoforte replaced the harpsichord; a new single-reed woodwind, the clarinet, was developed; the trumpet added sets of valves so the instrument could play any note in the chromatic scale.

With the exception of Bach, whose music was wholly Baroque, all the other great figures of the Baroque had aspects of their music that prefigured the new style. **Handel's** abilities as a melodist let him to favor homophonic texture over polyphony. **Vivaldi's** preference for the solo concerto also favored homophonic texture, and the solo concerto would be the model for nearly all such works in the Classical era. **Scarlatti** also preferred homophonic texture, and in some of his later works, used contrasting thematic material in the same movement.

To that latter assertion, you may simply say "big deal." But it was a big deal, and it led to a compositional system that would dominate instrumental music for a century and a half.

Sonata-Allegro Form

Sonata-allegro form is the most complex form we will deal with, yet it is not terribly complicated. Its foundation is a movement based on two themes: themes of contrasting character and key that we will call Theme 1 and Theme 2. The movement is in three parts: the **Exposition**, the **Development**, and the **Recapitulation**. An outline would look like this:

> **Exposition** (usually repeated): Theme 1 (key 1), transition, Theme 2 (key 2), closing
>
> **Development**: of Themes 1 and 2, possibly with new material, passing through various keys
>
> **Recapitulation**: restatement of Themes 1 and 2, now both in key 1, usually followed by a coda

The **exposition** exposes the materials that will be used for the movement, in their original form. The two themes differ not only in key but also in character. Typically Theme 1 was dramatic, 2 was lyric (less enlightened thinkers in earlier times described 1 as masculine and 2 as feminine).

The **development** takes those materials, and (for want of a better term), develops them . . . perhaps they might be extended, or shortened, or altered yet still recognizable; and they usually appear in various keys.

Recapitulation just means repeat. The materials are repeated just as before, with one exception: they are both now in the same key. Otherwise, the piece would end in a key other than that in which it began—a horror for the Age of Reason! And the **coda** (which we encountered earlier when we met the rondo) brings the piece to a satisfying conclusion.

Like the fugue, it all seems complicated until someone guides you through it with a musical example. For this, we'll use the first movement of the work *Eine kleine Nachtmusik*, by one of the two great figures of the period: Wolfgang Amadeus Mozart.

example

Mozart: *Eine kleine Nachtmusik*

I. Allegro

The Sonata Cycle

We claimed earlier that the sonata-allegro form was the most important development in instrumental writing to date, but this only deals with a single movement. If it is to be so significant, it has to be something that can be adapted to a broader scope. That's easy enough with the **sonata cycle**.

The sonata cycle is a four-movement sequence for instrumental composition, the first movement of which is in sonata-allegro form. The second movement may be in a variety of forms, but is usually slow, lyrical, and in another key.

The third movement was called a **minuet and trio** in the 18th century and a **scherzo and trio** in the 19th. The minuet is a graceful, courtly dance, without the capacity for drama that the Romantic period desired, so it was faster and more intense. But both were in the same form: binary (with each section repeated). The **trio** was another minuet (or scherzo)—usually lighter, slightly slower than the first minuet, and often in another key. The arrangement goes back to the Baroque, when the instrumentation of the trio would actually reduce to that of a trio sonata. That was lost by this point, but the trio continued to be a lyrical contrast to the minuet or scherzo. After the trio, the minuet was repeated, so one ended in the same key, and usually without repeats. The form would look like this:

Minuet (Scherzo): AABB

Trio: CCDD

Minuet: AB

The fourth movement might be in a variety of forms—sonata form, rondo, or variations were all popular—but it was nearly always fast, with a playful or heroic character.

Sonata Cycle (for symphony, concerto, chamber music, solo sonata):

I. Sonata form, fast, dramatic

II. Slow, lyrical, in another key

III. Minuet (18th century) or Scherzo (19th century) and trio

IV. Fast, in a playful or heroic mood. Sonata form, rondo, variations, or sonata-rondo

Eine kleine Nachtmusik is a four-movement work that follows this pattern, so let's hear the remaining movements.

example

Eine kleine Nachtmusik

II. *Romanza*

III. *Minuetto*

IV. *Rondo*

You'll notice that we are not specifying a specific type of ensemble for the sonata cycle. That's because the outline was used for any and all types. A work based on the sonata cycle for full orchestra is called a **symphony**. The form is so connected to the ensemble that it is often called a symphony, as in the New World Symphony or the Chicago Symphony Orchestra.

The identification with the ensemble is even more confusing when dealing with chamber music: A string quartet is a piece based on the sonata cycle written for a string quartet. A piano trio is a sonata cycle for piano trio.

We should note here that a chamber ensemble can be composed of pretty much anything, but there is some specific instrumentation: a string quartet consists of two violins, a viola, and a 'cello. Anything else that had four strings would have to specify the combination. And if you add another instrument to a string quartet, it becomes a [that instrument] quintet. A piano quintet is not five pianos, but a piano and a string quartet.

The other standardized form is the piano trio; again, not three pianos, but piano, violin and 'cello. Those two types of ensembles make up the bulk of professional chamber groups. If they want to do a different instrumentation, they usually add or delete instruments as appropriate.

There are also sonata cycles for solo instruments, assuming the instrument can play harmony. There are thousands of piano sonatas, and several also for harp, guitar, and organ.

And there is one other orchestral form that is based on the sonata cycle: the **concerto**. The Classical concerto differs from the Baroque in that in it, the featured soloist (usually only one) does not alternate with the orchestra, but is accompanied by it.

Otherwise, the form is rather like the symphony, with a few major differences. In the concerto first movement, in sonata-allegro form, the exposition is repeated, like it is with most sonata-allegro forms. But here, it's not repeated exactly. The first time through it is given to the orchestra alone; the soloist only enters on the repeat. So it's not an exact repeat—not only does addition of the soloist change the sound, but the soloist typically plays a much more elaborate version of the music, since he or she is the featured soloist.

One other difference occurs near the end of the movement. After the recapitulation, but before the coda, the orchestra reaches a cadence and stops. The soloist then plays a complex passage alone, often (though not always) an elaboration of earlier material. This is called the **cadenza**; during the 18th century, these were usually improvised, though as the music got more complex, composers began to furnish their own cadenzas.

The other difference in the concerto is that it is usually in three movements. Part of this is a throwback to the Baroque's fast-slow-fast sequence, but it is also because of the fact that the minuet and trio is highly stylized, restrained, graceful music. Most concertos are very dramatic and assertive; the elegance of the minuet would be out of place.

The sonata cycle formed the foundation for much of instrumental music for the next 150 years, and is still being used today, if less widely. What makes the sonata cycle so useful is its incredible flexibility. It is a set outline, but there is room for tremendous innovation. Composers may add extra movements, or delete expected ones, or compress the character of the four movements into one. The differences between themes in the sonata movements may be slight or great; there may be three or more themes in use.

One student once inquired whether, as the pattern was so frequent, could the movements from one work be exchanged with another. The answer is no, partially from the need for the keys of the movements and sections to be complementary. The main reason, however, is that there is an emotional, aesthetic balance in the creation of a satisfying sonata cycle. The whole is greater than the sum of the individual parts, at least in the best of such works. And you'll see the pattern again and again.

The Mature Classic Style: Franz Joseph Haydn (1732–1809)

Franz Joseph Haydn. Library of Congress, Prints and Photographs Division, Bain Collection, Reproduction Number: LC-USZ62-60866.

We have already met Mozart, one of the two figures who dominated the Classical Era. The other was Franz Joseph Haydn. He was the son of a wheelwright, born in the city of Rohrau, near Vienna. His early career was as a boy soprano in local choir. At this point, the taste for the castrato was fading, so Haydn reached adolescence intact. But when his voice changed, he was no longer a boy soprano, and he had to leave the choir. He was 18 at the time (boys matured more slowly then because of poor nutrition and medical care), and he made his living as a freelance teacher, performer, and composer, with precious little success.

His first break came in 1761, when he acquired a patron: Prince Paul Anton Esterhazy. Nearly all 18th-century musicians worked under what was called the **patronage system**. Keep in mind that this is not only the days before the mp3 file, but before any recording technology. All music was live performance. If a ridiculously wealthy aristocrat wished musical entertainment for him- or herself, his or her family, or his or her social events, a staff of musicians would be employed for those tasks. Just like aristocrats would have cooks and valets for meals, musicians for musical desires would be present. The musicians were servants and had uniforms to befit their status.

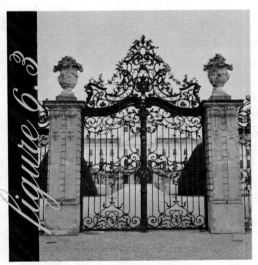

Entrance gate of the Esterhazy Palace. © Ungor, 2010. Used under license from Shutterstock, Inc.

The following year, Paul Anton passed away, to be succeeded by his younger brother, Prince Nicholas "The Magnificent," who turned the Esterhazy estate into a center for music/ art patronage second only to Vienna. Haydn was thus in a real plum of a position, as the patronage system went. He was appointed *Kappelmeister*, the music director for the court; he had a ready market for all his compositions, and a staff of fine musicians to perform them. The Esterhazy estate even had its own opera house.

The only drawback to this excellent situation was that Haydn's duties were so intense that he had no real opportunity to travel and keep up with current developments in the musical world. He responded philosophically, saying that his isolation kept him from distraction and forced him to become original.

In 1790, Prince Nicholas "The Magnificent" passed away, replaced by Prince Nicholas II. Nicholas II has less taste for music and promptly dismissed most of the musical staff. Haydn, having been with the family for nearly 30 years, was retained—at this point, he was practically a member of the family—but his duties were reduced. He was allowed to take an apartment in Vienna and was given freedom to travel.

Haydn promptly received an invitation from Peter Salomon, a London producer, who asked him to come to England to compose six symphonies for the next concert season. He in fact made two such trips, from January of 1791 to July of 1792 and from February of 1794 to August of 1795. His last 12 symphonies, along with other works, were from these trips. He was received with great acclaim in England, had an audience with the Royal Family, and was awarded an honorary Doctorate from Oxford.

He was impressed with the size and quality of English orchestras and was inspired by commemorative performances of Handel's oratorios to turn to sacred choral compositions during his last years when he composed six masses and the oratorios *The Seasons* and *The Creation*.

One such work is the *Mass in Time of War*. It was actually composed in time of war. The year was 1796, and Austrian troops were being defeated by Napoleon's army. Vienna was in danger of being taken by the French. The final phrase of the *Agnus Dei: Dona nobis pacem* (Grant us peace) was never delivered with such need . . . or such a confidence that the prayer would be granted!

example

Haydn: *Mass in Time of War: Agnus Dei*

Haydn's works are cataloged by Anthony van Hoboken, grouped not chronologically but by genre. You may occasionally see a work with an odd designation like Quartet in Eb, Hob. III 38.

This means the Hoboken catalog, volume III (string quartets), the 38th such work chronologically. Haydn himself often used Opus numbers for his works, or sets of works. The Opus number (abbreviated Op.) indicates the order of publication. This usually is related to order of composition, but occasionally a composer will publish a work well after it was composed, so a late opus number does not always mean a late work.

Haydn was called "Papa" by his musicians (and by Mozart) because of the fatherly concern he expressed for them. He was always conscious of, and accepting of, his lowly origins and his status as a servant. His personality is one of restraint, balance, order, and wit—the very qualities of the age itself. In his way, Haydn is as much a summation of the Classical era as Bach was of the Baroque.

Haydn is still sometimes called Papa, but now in recognition of his role as the father of the symphony and the string quartet. He took both forms from vestigial states to the mature forms we now recognize. He has 104 numbered symphonies and over 70 string quartets, all based on sonata cycle.

Early string quartets tend to be dominated by the first violin, essentially sonatas for the violin with string accompaniment, but Haydn's later compositions build the form to the point that all the instruments are of equal importance.

Haydn's sense of humor often found its way into his music. His Quartet, Op. 33, no. 2 has the nickname "Joke" because in the last movement, Haydn writes a series of false endings. He had a bet with a friend that he could get the audience to applaud before the work was over (he won the bet).

example

Haydn: *Qt. Op. 33 no. 2 in E-flat, "Joke"*

IV. Allegro

Haydn's last 12 symphonies are his greatest in the form, all written for those trips to London (and often collectively called the *London Symphonies*). The second work of the first journey, *Symphony no. 94 in G* has the nickname "*Surprise*," another example of Haydn's wit. The first movement begins with a slow introduction, thematically unrelated to the rest of the movement. Haydn used this devise frequently in his later works, and in most of his last 12. It establishes a sense of grandeur and allows the audience to focus before the rollicking *allegro* begins.

The surprise is in the second movement. Haydn was received with much acclaim on these London journeys, but he was a bit annoyed at the British audience's tendency to nod off during the slow movements. Here he begins the movement quietly and simply, outlining a C-major triad, then a G triad . . . then he repeats it, even more slowly . . . until the end of the phrase, hit by a grand, *fortissimo* chord! It worked well. The surprise over, the audience alert, they can then enjoy the rest of the movement: a theme and variations.

example

Haydn: *Symphony 94 in G, "Surprise"*

I. Adagio-Vivace assai
II. Andante

Wolfgang Amadeus Mozart (1756–1791)

Musicians make their mark in history in one of two ways—some, like Bach and Haydn epitomize their era, bringing the essential character of the age to a level of perfection. Others are innovators, who challenge the norm and take the art to the next level . . . if not to several levels higher. Mozart is the latter; he looks forward to a new age, the Romantic period, by taking music to a higher level of sublimity. By refusing to accept the role of the 18th-century artist, he changed society itself.

Johannes Chrysostomus Wolfgangus Amadeus Theophilus Gottlieb Mozart was born to **Leopold** and **Maria Anna Mozart** on January 27th, 1756. The normal practice was to name children after various family members, saints, etc.; it is worth noting that *Amadeus* in Latin, *Theophilus* in Greek, and *Gottlieb* in German all mean the same thing: the love of God, or one who is loved by God.

figure 6.4

Mozart and his sister at the piano, with Leopold looking on and Maria Anna's portrait. © JupiterImages, Inc.

The family lived in **Salzburg**, at the time an independent theocracy ruled by a Church-appointed Prince-Archbishop. **Leopold** was a prominent composer, violinist, and teacher of the preclassic period. He was also his son's only teacher; he taught Wolfgang everything—music and general education, including languages: French, Italian, and English, with some Greek and Latin.

Wolfgang was an amazing prodigy. He was playing violin by the age of 4, and his first compositions were done at 6. He composed his first symphony at the age of 8, his first oratorio at 11, and his first opera at 12. His early years were spent traveling with his family throughout Europe to show off his talents—and, incidentally, those of his older sister Nannerl, who seems to have been as talented as her brother. It is a pity that the age was so rigid in its gender roles. Nannerl was not allowed to develop her talents and is never heard from as a musician after childhood.

Between the ages of 6 and 15, Mozart embarked on a series of tours with his family, during which he would perform as pianist, violinist, and composer for courtly gatherings throughout Europe. He was "on the road" for almost half of his life during this time, so that Leopold could display "the miracle God let be born in Salzburg."

Salzburg, historical center, with much of the architecture preserved from Mozart's day.
© JupiterImages, Inc.

While there is certainly an element of calculation in Leopold's leadership at this time, it is incorrect to see him as a mediocre talent exploiting the abilities of his son and daughter. Leopold Mozart was a prominent figure of his age, but nevertheless was never appointed to the rank of Kapellmeister, despite his reputation and importance. Part of this had to do with prevailing prejudice. Italians were considered to be the ultimate musicians (with the French not far behind), and Germans were thought to be inferior. There was only one German Kapellmeister appointed during Leopold's 40 years of service in Salzburg. But the main reason for Leopold's professional neglect was doubtless his repeated absences from the court for tours with his children. He had enough artistic acumen, or common sense, to realize that his son had a far superior talent to his own and was willing to sacrifice his own career so that Wolfgang could have one.

The travels of those early years were profoundly influential for Mozart, in four ways.

- **Educational:** Mozart, unlike Haydn, was exposed to the entire musical traditions of Europe on these trips, and his abilities were so astonishing that he discarded what he didn't like, absorbed what he liked, and usually improved it. Important influences include Haydn and J. C. Bach, Johann Sebastian's youngest son, with whom Mozart worked for over a year in London.
- **Psychological:** By being forced into adult life and adult responsibilities at an early age, Mozart never had a real childhood. His lack of maturity in his later years can perhaps be traced to this.
- **Physiological:** His chronic ill health later on can perhaps be blamed on being forced to travel and work at such a young age, regardless of his state of health and the conditions of travel.

Mozart as a boy. © JupiterImages, Inc.

- **Social:** Mozart the child was celebrated by the greatest heads of state in all of Europe; he was fawned and fussed over by queens and princesses. He gained a strong sense of his value and importance, and when it came time for him to behave like a properly submissive servant, in the 18th-century tradition, he was unable to do so. He constantly fought with his employer in Salzburg.

figure 6.1

Mozart in the Vienna period.
© JupiterImages, Inc.

Mozart entered the employment of Archbishop Hieronymus, Count Colloredo as court musician in 1774. Colloredo was the opposite of his beloved predecessor—he was an authoritarian with specific ideas as to how the world should work, among which was the place of the serving class, including musicians. He and Mozart clashed from the beginning, and the next three years were terribly unhappy ones. He traveled to a variety of places seeking a position, but found that despite his talents, no one would offer a leading position to a man so young. On one trip, accompanied by his mother because Leopold could not arrange leave, his mother passed away.

In 1781, Colloredo and his entourage, including the musicians, went to Vienna for the funeral of Empress Maria Theresa. On this visit, Mozart got into an argument with Colloredo, and found himself literally thrown out of his service for repeated insubordination.

After two men tossed him into the street, Mozart brushed off the dust and considered his situation—he was now unemployed, but he was no longer in provincial Salzburg. He was in Vienna, the world's most important musical capital. He made the decision to live outside of the patronage system, by sales of his music, teaching, and by offering a series of subscription concerts for each season promoting his music and his performance and conducting.

At this, he became wildly successful. At the peak of his popularity, his income was 10,000 gulden annually. (In comparison, a maid would have made 12 gulden a year, a violinist 400, a surgeon 1200, and a hospital director 3000). He was married, in 1782, to the former Constanze Weber, and the two were passionately in love for the rest of Mozart's days in Vienna (if neither partner was completely faithful).

sidebar

Mozart and the Freemasons

In 1784, Mozart joined the Freemasons. That group is still active, a rather conservative service organization in our times. But during the 18th century, the Freemasons were considered quite subversive.

The Masons were at the forefront of many of the dramatic changes of the late 18th century. Their philosophy combined all of the humanitarian teachings of the day and systematized them, illustrated them with symbols, and set up an organization within which they could be actualized.

The secret nature of the society and its penchant for using mystic symbolism led to the circulation of all manner of fantastic stories. It has been cruelly repressed by totalitarian governments throughout its history. Members rarely bothered to defend themselves against such drivel, and consequently they continued to circulate. Actually, secrecy is not really key to Freemasonry—most, if not all, of their ritual and philosophy is available to the public in books and manuals. At the core of its mysticism is the belief in true love for all mankind, in a Divine being (possibly though not necessarily the Judeo-Christian God), and a rejection of both hereditary authority and the central rule of the Church.

The 18th century is considered the pinnacle of Masonic history. During the Age of Reason, the best and brightest figures of its age joined the lodges. Many of the founding fathers of the United States were Masons, including Washington, Franklin, and Jefferson, as were literary giants such as Chamisso, Klopstock, Beaumarchais, Sterne, Swift, Pope, and Goethe. Many musicians were Masons, including both Mozart and Haydn.

There was, in fact, a dual aspect of Masonry, the rational and the mystical, that must have attracted Mozart. The sense Masons had of being "brother to a King, companion to a Prince" surely had a terrific attraction to Mozart. He struggled throughout his life under rejection by the aristocracy and by the Italian musical establishment. The ideals of strength, wisdom, and beauty; the elevation of reason, generosity, and justice; its rejection of bigotry, narrow-mindedness, and intolerance; and the image of mankind struggling, indeed destined to attain, not the horror of final judgment and damnation, but the pure light of goodness—all these images were surely important to Mozart and to the leaders of his world. The periodic suppression by Emperors fearing the Masons' influence on society or by the Catholic Church sensing the Masons' rejection of its absolute authority and tolerance of dissent could not stop the changes in the world that were ready to occur.

Around 1786, Mozart began to have financial troubles. It has never been established exactly why. There is some truth in the popular image that Mozart was overly extravagant—his income was spent, not saved. His tailor bills were high, though it was a professional necessity for musicians to look appropriately fashionable in performance. Constanze was nearly constantly pregnant and often required expensive medical care.

Two other aspects are important: after 1787, Mozart's music began to take on a complexity that confused both audiences and musicians, and his popularity declined as his debts rose. Another reason rarely mentioned is that Mozart was not the only person in Vienna with money troubles. Emperor Joseph II, Maria Theresa's son and successor, was waging wars on two fronts and had to raise taxes to support the effort. That sent Vienna into a deep recession, and that as much as anything was behind Mozart's troubles.

During the summer of 1791, while on a walk with Constanze, Mozart said he believed he had been poisoned. There is no surviving record of by whom, or for what reason, but there is a record of by what: a substance called *acqua toffana*, a mix of chemicals that was both deadly and long-acting. It was virtually undetectable by the science of that day, and it would kill only after several months.

Later in that summer, Mozart was approached by a mysterious stranger who commissioned a *Requiem Mass*, or a mass for the dead. The person was an agent for one Count Walsegg, who intended to plagiarize the work and present it as his own. Walsegg had done this before; he would buy a work from a composer and replace the name on the title page with his own. He was married to a beautiful young woman who died at a young age, and he wanted to memorialize her with a work by the world's greatest composer. But Mozart did not know this, was haunted by the anonymous nature of the commission, and became obsessed with the idea that he had been approached by Death himself and was writing his own *Requiem*.

The work was incomplete 6 months later at his death—it had to be completed by his student (and tenant) Süssmayr. While this in itself is not unusual, for Mozart it was. He had an uncanny ability to compose music *in his head*. After it was done, he had total recall and actually preferred to write the score while distracted by lively conversation or a game of billiards.

There is, however, the powerful psychological element that if one is indeed composing one's own requiem, then there must be a sense of reluctance to finish, for to write "the end" really means it.

On December 5, Mozart was dictating portions of the *Requiem*. He was battling a long, undiagnosed illness. He went to sleep and died in his sleep just after midnight. Five doctors examined his body and came up with five different diagnoses. For some time, uremic poisoning was suspected but those suffering from this are normally in a coma for some time before death; Mozart was rehearsing singers for the *Requiem* earlier that evening.

The funeral was held the next day, rather than observing a customary mourning period. The funeral party did not follow his body to the cemetery, allegedly because of bad weather, though the records of the day indicate the weather was clear. His body was buried in an unmarked pauper's grave, with no witnesses except for the workmen who tossed the body into a pit and covered it, and those decaying around it, with lime.

Despite his debts, which were discovered to be far less than formerly expected, this should not have happened to a musician of Mozart's internationally recognized stature. He was anything but indigent; he had a home, tenants, and servants. The possibility is unavoidable that Mozart's body was deliberately lost to prevent traces of poison from being detected.

Theories abound concerning Mozart's death, including natural causes of a wide variety, both illnesses and inadvertent overmedication. Mercury poisoning has been suggested. The substance could have been added to his food over a period of months, causing gradual deterioration and ultimately death; or perhaps Mozart had taken mercury himself, as this was a popular cure for venereal diseases. Contemporary composer Antonio Salieri has been accused, along with the Freemasons, though neither stands up to investigation. A possible explanation is that one of the spouses of Mozart's lovers or a lover of Constanze may have been driven to such extreme lengths (though there is no conclusive evidence of this beyond rumors).

Whatever the truth, the tragedy of this is that perhaps the most gifted musician who ever lived was cut down in the prime of his life—what he could have produced in another 10 years, or 5, or just 1, is incomprehensible. For all his remarkable innovations of his last decade, he said on two occasions during his final months that he thought he was just then learning to compose.

Mozart was never completely able to cope with adult responsibilities, nor to treat aristocrats and fellow musicians with an expected level of respect. He was both devout Catholic and a Freemason, deeply believing while questioning aspects of the church as an institution. He freed his professional life from the 18th century patronage system and is largely responsible for changing society and its view of Art and Artist.

Mozart's musical style is essentially vocal and lyrical. His thematic material is chosen for its aesthetic beauty, rather than for its structural potential (unlike that of Haydn). Mozart's music goes straight for the heart, rather than the brain, though there is plenty of intellectual depth as well. By relating all to the voice—even his instrumental themes could often be set for voice—he gives his music a sense of humanity, a universality, that speaks to all ages.

Mozart's Music

Mozart's compositional output has been divided into three periods:

- Childhood and early youth (1762–1774)
- Salzburg (1774–1781)
- Vienna (1781–1791)

Much of the works of his childhood are astonishing simply because they were composed by a child. His compositions began to reach the level of maturity in the seven years he spent in the employ of Archbishop Colloredo. But only after his move to Vienna, in his final decade, did his works attain the heights from which he changed the world of music.

Instrumental Music: The Concerto

Mozart was easily Haydn's equal at first in symphony and string quartet—in the Vienna period, he quite surpassed his older friend. His greatest achievement in instrumental music is in his 27 piano concertos. He is the first composer to bring to that form the sort of depth of expression and structure that had previously been reserved for the symphony. Many of these works were composed for Mozart himself to play, usually at subscription concerts; others were designed for one of his pupils, with Mozart conducting.

He wrote a total of 27 concertos for piano, and they are all perfect, with the possible exception of a few early works composed on other people's thematic material. George Bolet, one of the greatest pianists of the 20th century, once was asked to comment on the most difficult pieces in the piano repertoire. He thought for a moment, listed a work by Franz Liszt that is famous for its treacherous difficulty . . . and then said "or a Mozart concerto."

Presumably he meant any of them. What he referred to is the absolute clarity and transparency of the works; for them to be successful, the player needs to have absolute perfection. Any flaws are impossible to cover. If you have ever tried to play an instrument, you'll discover that to get to 95% accuracy is not terribly difficult. But real perfection is extraordinarily difficult.

Mozart praised smoothness over all. His highest compliment was to say that his, or another's, playing "flowed like oil."

. . . {these concertos achieve} a happy medium between what is too easy and too difficult . . . very brilliant, pleasing to the ear, and natural, without being vapid. There are passages . . . from which connoisseurs alone can derive satisfaction, but those passages are written in such a way that the less learned cannot fail to be pleased, though without knowing why.

For the 1786 season, Mozart composed three piano concertos: no. 22, K. 482 in E-flat; no. 23, K. 488 in A; and no. 24, K. 491 in c. They make a fascinating set to consider as a group. The first of this set was first performed at a concert on December 12th to an audience of 120. The work was written for Barbara ("Babette") Ployer, to whom Mozart also had dedicated no. 14 and no. 17. The concert had to encore the second movement.

example

Mozart: *Concerto no. 22 in E-flat, K. 482*

I. *Allegro*
II. *Andante*
III. *Allegro*

This is the biggest and longest of the concertos. Its orchestra is the only one that includes both clarinets and oboes. In the late concertos, there is in general a greater sense of thematic development, formal integration, a greater emotional weight, and a greater use of wind instruments.

Movement I is more traditionally festive than innovative; listen for the tympani and trumpet in the orchestration. Note, however, the careful thematic integration, the variation of repeated motives, and the modulations in the development.

The second movement is in c minor, one of the most poignant and haunting movements in all of music, with a depth of feeling that completely transcends the "light, entertaining" ideal of the classical style. It is rondo form, ABABC—the B section is in major, with an emphasis on the winds.

The finale returns to Eb, a rollicking 6/8 rondo, with a hunting horn–like main theme. Note the contrasting slow section interpolated in the middle, like a similar section in Concerto no. 9 (which is also in Eb). The finish, however, is light and brilliant.

Vocal Music: Opera

Mozart is without question the preeminent genius of 18th century opera. In contrast to Gluck, who proclaimed that the text the most important aspect of the form, Mozart stated that "in opera, the poetry must always be the obedient servant of the music." Yet his music is hardly the sort which will fail to serve the needs of the text.

Why was he so adept at vivid characterization and drama? Perhaps, for Mozart, music and humanity, or "humanness," were inseparable. His letters show him to be an avid people watcher. In fact, in Mozart's operas, the music, character, and situation are united in a perfect balance that has only rarely been equaled and never surpassed.

Mozart composed all the major types of opera of his day: *opera seria*, *opera buffa*, and *Singspiel*.

Opera seria, serious opera, was something of a stylistic throwback to Baroque opera—they tended to be static, with series of recitatives and aria and the occasional ensemble or chorus. These continued to use castrato singers. As this was the Enlightenment, the mythological stories were less common than historical ones, and supernatural spectacle was replaced by more reasonable, if somewhat duller, plots.

Mainly, *opera seria* were intended to convey a broad, morally uplifting theme. Audiences of the day were as interested in being morally uplifted as they are currently, so to keep audiences amused, *opera buffa* was developed.

These were originally one-act intermezzi between acts of *opera seria*. Eventually, rather than presenting two separate works, two-act operas became the norm. Audiences didn't mind at all skipping between the two, and eventually the *opera buffa* began to take on a life of its own and was performed separately. In contrast to *seria*, *opera buffa* was in contemporary, mostly domestic settings. They had their own stock characters and tended toward slapstick comedy—and they never used castrati.

The *Singspiel* is a German-language opera that replaces recitative with spoken dialog. Italy never even thought to do this; the Italian language is so naturally musical that there was never any need to do so. But other nations all developed such versions of opera. In France, it was called *opera comique*; in Spain, the *zarzuela*; in England, the *operetta*; and in the United States, the *musical comedy*.

For someone who has never encountered opera, Mozart's four greatest works are the best introduction:

- *Le Nozze di Figaro*, K. 492, opera buffa, 1786
- *Don Giovanni*, K. 527, dramma giocosa, 1787
- *Cosi fan tutte*, K. 588, opera buffa, 1790
- *Die Zauberflote*, K. 620, singspiel, 1791

The first three all had librettos by the same person: **Lorenzo da Ponte** (1759–1838). He was born Emmanuele Conegliano in a Jewish ghetto in Venice. His father was Geremia, mother Rachel, and his brothers were Baruch and Annania. He was sent to the Church for his education and took the name of the priest who taught him at seminary.

He took holy orders in 1773 and promptly began breaking his vows of celibacy. In 1774, he became professor of rhetoric at Treviso, only to be dismissed two years later for insubordination. He worked in Venice until an affair involving the wrong aristocrat's wife resulted in his choice of sentence—banishment for 15 years or 7 years in the dungeon. He chose the former and moved to Austria.

He remained outside of Vienna until the death of Empress Maria Teresa, after which things got somewhat more relaxed. He collaborated with many of the most successful composers, including Mozart on *Figaro, Don Giovanni*, and *Cosi fan tutte*.

The Other Three Operas

Don Giovanni

Don Giovanni was called not *opera buffa*, but *dramma giocosa*. Some sources take this to mean "comic drama," indicating a mix of comedy and drama, though the 18th century used the terms interchangeably. *Giovanni* is the Italian version of the name *John*, or the Spanish *Juan*. The opera is about Don Juan, more specifically Don Juan Tenorio (for those of you who didn't know he had a last name). Even today, a man who habitually seduces and abandons women is called a "Don Juan," but many don't know this figure has a rich literary history.

The legend goes back into the Middle Ages, in Spain, when a nobleman was having his way with as many young ladies as he could seduce. The monks in the local monastery were disgusted with his behavior and kidnapped and killed him; after that, they spread the story that he had actually been dragged off to Hell by the Devil for his dissolute and unrepentant life.

The opera does have serious, dramatic elements, and productions from the 19th century tended to emphasize that aspect. For some, Don Giovanni represents something of a Nietzschean Superman: one who stands apart and bends life to his will. Don Juan will not be subject to the mores of society, the dictates of religion, or the laws of the nation; he takes what he desires, whether women, power, or wealth.

It is hard, however, to believe that Mozart intended the work to have such grand significance for the primary reason that, despite several attempts, the Don doesn't manage to successfully seduce any woman throughout the work. Final Score: Women = 12; Don Giovanni = 0.

And, in the end, the Don is visited by the stature, now chillingly come to life, of the town's former ruler, whom he killed in a duel in act I. He is given the choice of repenting or being dragged off to Hell and eternal punishment. He is Don Giovanni. He does not repent. Finally, with his servant cowering under a table singing, "Oh, boss, we're all gonna die!," he grasps the statue's hand and is engulfed in freezing cold. He is last seen being dragged to Hell, or at least to some place below the stage, and the remaining characters unite in a moralizing ensemble.

Cosi fan tutte

The title literally translates as "Thus Do They All"; more idiomatically, "All Women Are Like That" (*tutte* means everyone; with the feminine ending e, it means all women). It is the tale of two pairs of lovers, and as it opens, the two men are bragging about the beauty and fidelity of their partners. Their friend, the cynical Don Alfonso, claims that all women will cheat, given the opportunity, so the make a bet on it. The two pretend to have been called off to war, and after their departure, they return disguised as Albanians, and each tries to seduce the other's lover.

Really. I am not making this up.

Yes, that does sound supremely silly. *Cosi fan tutte* is a bit of fluff, horribly sexist by modern standards (though there are deeper and more enlightened sentiments at the core), but is not to be taken seriously. It contains some of the most ravishingly beautiful music Mozart ever composed and some of the most delightful ensembles. In the end, Don Alfonso wins the bet when both ladies succumb to the charms of their Albanian gentlemen pursuers, the plot is revealed, and the marriages occur. It is not, however, entirely clear which of the parings, the original or the latest, actually does wed.

Die Zauberflöte (The Magic Flute)

The Magic Flute is quite different from the other three great operas of Mozart. It is in German, by type a *Singspiel* . . . but it is radically different from the usual *Singspiel*. Austrians were used to these works as slapstick comedies, sort of like the Three Stooges, but less sophisticated. In *The Magic Flute*, there is actually only one comic part. The rest is something between a fantasy and a morality tale.

During Mozart's last year, his friend and Masonic Brother Emanuel Schikaneder proposed the work. Schikaneder furnished the libretto, and he managed a theatre in the outskirts of Vienna. He asked Mozart to write some easy baritone arias that he could sing for the comic part; Schikaneder would produce the opera. They would split the profits.

The work is more than a simple comedy. It was filled with Masonic symbolism and philosophy, and it is very likely that, after the death of Emperor Joseph II, Mozart and Schikaneder wanted to present a work to the world that showed the Masons in a positive light. The succeeding Emperor Leopold would prove less tolerant than Joseph had been.

The work is a fascinating combination of delightful comedy, intrigue, and idealism. The music, and its portrayal of the characters and events, is incomparable.

Le nozze di Figaro (The Marriage of Figaro)

Let's take a closer look at the first really great masterpiece—the finest opera ever composed by that point in history, and rarely equaled afterwards.

A complete synopsis and cast of characters is included below. It is rather complicated, but if you have the opportunity to see the work in its entirety, either live or on a video recording, the details will be helpful for your enjoyment of the experience. Bur for now, let's just examine a few sections of the first act and the beginning of the second as examples of Mozart's mastery in conveying emotions in music.

example

Mozart: *The Marriage of Figaro*

Overture; Opening Duet

After the overture sets the mood, the curtain opens to find Figaro and Susanna together in their new quarters. Figaro sings, "*Cinque . . . dieci . . . venti . . . trenti . . . trentasei . . . quaran-tatre,*" which translates to, "*Five . . . ten . . . twenty . . . thirty . . . thirty-six . . . forty-three.*" Not terribly engaging dialogue, until one realizes that he's measuring a space in the room in which they are to be housed after their marriage. Susanna, meanwhile, is trying on the cap she has made by herself for the wedding, asking Figaro to look at it and approve. He tells her it is lovely, not bothering actually to look at her until a well-placed knock on his head from his bride brings him around.

In the ensuing recitative, we learn that Figaro is tremendously pleased with the quarters because they are so convenient, being just a few steps away from the Count's quarters. Susanna is appalled at the quarters for much the same reason: unknown to Figaro until Susanna now reveals it, the Count has been trying to seduce Susanna prior to her wedding. Left alone, Figaro vows revenge, in his aria *Se vuol ballare*—not by a violent rebellion, but by outwitting his employer.

example

Mozart: *The Marriage of Figaro:*

Se vuol ballare

After a few other scenes, we meet Cherubino. He is a young man, just past puberty. He's discovered that there are two genders of people and that he's deeply interested in the opposite one. He has made a nuisance of himself flirting shamelessly with nearly every female in the castle, and his opening aria, *Non so piu*, is the expression of the breathless excitement of a young man in love for the first time.

Mozart: *The Marriage of Figaro:*

Non so piu

In the second act, the Countess is introduced for the first time, with her poignant aria *Porgi, amor*. Her character has really little comedy—she is a noble, suffering figure. When her husband was courting her, he went to amazing lengths to win her hand . . . and now he's chasing the castle servants.

example

Mozart: *The Marriage of Figaro:*

Porgi, amor

These short examples—the domestic warmth and humor of the opening duet; the seething defiance of Figaro's opening aria; the breathless excitement of Cherubino's aria, an adolescent in the throes of his first crush; and the Countess' aria, singing of a love which is betrayed but not forgotten—all serve to demonstrate only the merest sample of Mozart's vivid genius on the operatic stage.

The opera may seem strange to us, with all of its 18th-century frippery, manners, and customs. Yet, if we strip it of its setting, what do we find? We find love, of course, but also conflict—conflict between lovers and between those who want to take a lover away from her love. We also find class struggle and conflicts between employers and employees. Is any of this familiar to anyone in this class? At its root, *The Marriage of Figaro* is timeless, universal, and therein lies its ability to touch listeners, centuries after it was created.

sidebar

Mozart, *The Marriage of Figaro*: Characters and Plot

Characters

Count Almaviva (bass), cheating nobleman
Countess Rosina (soprano), long-suffering wife
Figaro (baritone), valet to Count Almaviva
Susanna (soprano), maid to Countess Rosina
Cherubino (mezzo-soprano), page-boy, in love with all the feminine members of the court
Dr. Bartolo (bass), former guardian to Rosina
Marcellina (mezzo-soprano), lady, well past what was never much of a prime, in love with Figaro
Don Basilio (tenor), music teacher and scoundrel
Barbarina (soprano), underage cupcake, daughter of
Antonio (bass), drunken gardener
Don Curzio (tenor), nondescript notary, often doubled by singer for Don Basilio

Synopsis

ACT I: Figaro and Susanna are together in their new quarters. Figaro is tremendously pleased with them because they are so convenient, being just a few steps away from the Count's quarters. Susanna is appalled at the quarters for much the same reason: unknown to Figaro until Susanna now reveals it, the Count has been trying to seduce Susanna prior to her wedding. Left alone, Figaro vows revenge, in his aria *Se vuol ballare*—not by a violent rebellion, but by outwitting his employer.

Bartolo and Marcellina enter: Marcellina has a contract with Figaro that if he does not pay off a debt owed her, he must marry her. Bartolo, who has his own grudge with Figaro, vows to help her with his mastery of the law, realizing that revenge is a dish best served cold. Susanna enters, and she and Marcellina sing the most catty duet in all opera.

Enter Cherubino, who has crushes on Susanna, the Countess, Barbarina, Madonna, and presumably Laura Bush. His opening aria, *Non so piu*, is a masterpiece of expression of the breathless excitement of a young man in love for the first time. Music teacher and scoundrel Basilio then enters, and Cherubino hides. Bartolo fronts for the Count and drops innuendo about Susanna and other men. The Count enters to seduce Susanna, and after some seducing, discovers Cherubino under a cloak in a chair. Furious with Cherubino for seducing (yes, you read that correctly), he is about to send for Figaro when he realizes that the page has overheard everything he said to Susanna. Cherubino, however, "tried not to listen."

Figaro then complicates matters by entering with a chorus of servants singing the praises of the Count for abolishing the *droit du signeur*, effectively the right of the lord of the castle to have sex with any of the servant girls who were to be wed. Figaro and Susanna present themselves to be formally joined, and the Cherubino has to do some fancy thinking to get out of his situation while omitting the possibility of Susanna's seduction. He says he wants time to prepare a major party to celebrate. No one is fooled, but the chorus reprises its hymn of praise and exits, leaving Bartolo, the Count, Cherubino, Figaro, and Susanna.

Cherubino is distraught over his dismissal, and the Count decides to pardon him and instead commission him in his army. There is a war going on, and he is needed at the front. As you can imagine, Cherubino is overjoyed; he hasn't been this happy since he broke his left leg in three places a few years ago. Figaro, in an aside, tells Cherubino to see him privately later, and closes the act with an incredibly sarcastic aria that everyone but Cherubino has been anxious to hear since he reached puberty and began making a nuisance of himself.

ACT II: Here the Countess is introduced for the first time, with her poignant aria *Porgi, amor*; her character has really little comedy about it—she is instead a noble figure, suffering with a love that has been betrayed but not forgotten.

In conference with Susanna and later Figaro, they decide on a plan: the Cherubino has already been sent a letter warning him of the Countess' intention to meet a lover in the garden that night. Susanna will make a date to meet him in the same place, but they will send Cherubino dressed as a girl instead. This, of course, is not difficult, as Cherubino is already being played by a girl.

Cherubino duly arrives, sings a touching love song, and is put in drag. Susanna is sent away, and then the Count arrives. Cherubino locks himself in the closet, and the Countess commands him to be silent when the Count commands him to come out (she has told the Count that it is Susanna in the closet). He threatens to have the door broken down, but rather than expose scandal to the servants (not that they don't know already), he leads her away to get the key. Meanwhile, Susanna has come back, and sends Cherubino away by leaping out of a second story window and running, jackalope-like, for the hills.

When the Count comes back, the Countess admits it is Cherubino in the closet and protests innocence (while the Count sings something like "death to Cherubino"). She is as surprised as he when Susanna comes out of the door, but, being quick-witted, turns the situation to her advantage claiming the situation to have been a great practical joke in response to his overbearing jealousy.

Figaro then arrives with musicians for the wedding. The Count asks him about the letter, which he will not admit to writing, but instead turns the question back to the Count: when will you perform our marriage? The Count is backed into a corner, but then Antonio the Drunken Gardener arrives, complaining of the man who leaped from that window into his garden, ruining the same. The Count smells vermin and questions Figaro about the matter. With help from Susanna and the Countess, Figaro explains that it was he who leapt into the garden, ruining the same, and otherwise confirms his part in the matter. Finally, Antonio leaves and is replaced by Bartolo, Marcellina, and Basilio. Utter chaos then reigns, and the situation is excellent.

ACT III: The Count and Susanna agree to meet after hours for canoodling. Figaro enters, and the Count overhears him and Susanna conferring. Figaro then sings a furious aria lamenting the unfaithfulness of women. Then Marcellina and Bartolo appear with Don Curzio, the notary, to finalize plans for Susanna and Figaro's wedding, at gunpoint, as it were. In the ensuing recitative, however, it is discovered that Figaro is the long-lost illegitimate son of Marcellina and Bartolo (something about a birthmark). There is a large and very funny ensemble of reconciliation, made even better when Susanna arrives with money to pay off Figaro's debt and finds him in the arms of Marcellina. Everyone is happy but the Count.

The next scene begins with the Countess' aria *Dove sono*, in which she laments the loss of love that has driven her to such drastic measures. She is then joined by Susanna in the "letter duet," inviting the Count to meet Susanna (who will actually be the Countess dressed as Susanna) later for the aforementioned canoodling.

The villagers return, led by Barbarina and Cherubino in drag, bringing flowers to the Countess. The Count discovers Cherubino and rejects his Max Klinger-style attempt to get out of military service, but Barbarina then reminds the Count how when kissing and cuddling her he promised her anything she might want. She asks for Cherubino for a husband (he, after all, is so pretty) and her wish is granted, for she gave good cuddle. The act closes with a bridal march and fandango (the only element of Spanish color in the whole opera, though set in Seville), preparation for the upcoming celebrations.

ACT IV: Barbarina opens, lamenting the loss of the pin on Susanna's letter. Figaro hears this and is appalled at his bride's faithlessness. Susanna and the Countess arrive, attired in each other's clothing. Susanna knows Figaro is there and sings of her anticipated meeting with her beloved—she means Figaro, but he overhears and thinks she means the Count. She hides. Cherubino comes in and flirts generally. The Count enters and begins seducing his own wife, dressed as Susanna. Figaro, behind the shrubbery, then flirts with Susanna as though she was the Countess (he knows by now, having recognized her voice). She is furious and begins beating the stuffing out of him, which he

enjoys. When they both eventually determine where each other stands and join their voices in a gorgeous duet, they are discovered by the Count, who temporarily interrupts his seduction of Susanna (actually the Countess) to call for lights and witnesses to the supposed infidelity of his wife with Figaro. He then succeeds in demonstrating to the entire castle what an ass he is—but, in one of the most moving moments in all of opera, his wife comes out from behind the scenery, dressed as Susanna; he has no choice but to fall on his knees and beg forgiveness. She gives it to him. The moment is too intense for the 18th century, and the opera ends with a chorus of general rejoicing.

Glossary

Cadenza: a passage in a *concerto* in which the soloist plays an extended solo passage without orchestra, typically after the recapitulation and before the coda; during the Classical period, these were often improvised

Concerto: a work for orchestra with a featured soloist based on the *sonata cycle*; usually only three movements, omitting the *minuet (scherzo) and trio*

Esterhazy: the family that was patron to Franz Josef Haydn; particularly Nicholaus "the Magnificent" who was a very strong music lover

Hoboken: Anthony van Hoboken, the cataloguer of Haydn's works; they are abbreviated *Hob.* and arranged by genre (indicated by a Roman numeral) and chronologically within the generic catalog

Köchel: Aloysius Ludwig Köchel, the cataloguer of Mozart's works; they are abbreviated *K.* and arranged in chronological order, rather than by genre

Minuet and trio: the third movement of a **sonata cycle** during the 18th century, each in binary form, with each section repeated, and the minuet played again afterward (usually without repeats)

Opera buffa: Italian-language comic opera from the Classical and early Romantic periods; usually in two acts, without use of *castrati*

Opera seria: Italian-language serious opera from the Classical period; usually in three acts, with a historical or mythological libretto, and frequently featuring *castrati* in leading roles

Opus: the designation used by most composers to keep track of their works, indicating the order of publication (usually abbreviated *Op.*); Op. 9 would be the ninth work or set of works published by a given composer

Patronage system: the system of employment for most 18th century musicians—a wealthy aristocrat would hire a set of musicians for the musical needs of the court, in exchange for a salary and living quarters for the musician and his family

Piano trio: an ensemble with piano, violin, and 'cello; also a composition for the ensemble based on the *sonata cycle*

Pre-classic period: the transition between the Baroque and Classical periods, roughly 1730–1770; the sons of Bach were the most important contributors

Scherzo and trio: the third movement of a *sonata cycle* during the 19th century; in the same formal arrangement, but faster and more dramatic

Singspiel: a German-language opera, usually a comedy, with spoken dialogue instead of recitative; Mozart's *The Magic Flute* is the most important example

Sonata: a composition based on the *sonata cycle* for a solo instrument (such as a piano, guitar, or harp); sometimes for piano and solo instrument, such as piano and violin, or piano and flute

Sonata cycle: a four-movement framework for instrumental composition, the first movement of which is in *sonata form*—followed by a slow, lyrical movement in another key; a *minuet and trio* (18th century) or *scherzo and trio* (19th century); and a fast, playful, or heroic finale

Sonata form: a musical form based on two contrasting themes, each in a different key and with a different character, presented in the *exposition,* worked out in the *development,* and restated in the same key in the *recapitulation*; the most important development in instrumental composition in the Classical period; also *sonata-allegro form*

String quartet: an ensemble with two violins, a viola, and a 'cello; also a composition for string quartet based on the *sonata cycle*

Symphony: a work for full orchestra based on the *sonata cycle*; also the ensemble that plays such a work

LUDWIG VAN BEETHOVEN

Struggle and Triumph

". . . Beethoven's work is built on the conventions, genres, and styles of the Classic period. Through external circumstances and the force of his own genius, he became the source of much that was characteristic of the Romantic period. But he himself is neither Classic nor Romantic; he is Beethoven, and his figure towers like a colossus astride the two centuries."
Donald Jay Grout

Historians often consider Ludwig van Beethoven (1770–1827) as part of the First Viennese School, along with Haydn, Mozart, and Franz Schubert (1797–1828). The group has much in common: all spent most of their mature careers in or near Vienna, all shared a common language and basic time frame, and most importantly all contributed to the development of forms and genres based on the sonata cycle, which had been developed during the Classical period.

Beethoven occupies a unique position in history. In many ways, his music is a bridge between the classic and the romantic; it is founded on the structural principles of classicism, yet it approaches those principles with a sense of freedom and individuality, and with a quality of emotional power that is far beyond the classic ideal of restraint and serenity. Indeed, while Mozart, in his exquisite perfection, seems to be sitting on the very clouds of heaven beckoning us to join him, Beethoven seems to be trying to storm the gates of that heaven and to break down those gates by the sheer power of his music.

Yet it would be incorrect to see Beethoven as the beginning of the Romantic period. While much of his music has clearly romantic qualities, he had little *direct* influence on the early romantic composers. None of the composers who followed Beethoven continued in his style—not because they thought that his music was old-fashioned, as the composers of the High Baroque felt about Bach's music, but because they knew they lacked the genius to continue his musical direction. Even those who truly comprehended Beethoven's late works lacked the capacity to continue their development; it wasn't until a generation later, in the person of Johannes Brahms, that a figure came on the musical scene capable of continuing what Beethoven had begun. Immediately after Beethoven, leading creative figures felt that he had brought to perfection the possibilities of the development of absolute music. As perfection is not improvable, the future of music must lay in another direction; this direction will be discussed at some length in the next chapter.

Symphonies, String Quartets, and Piano Sonatas

While Beethoven composed works in all the genres of his day, his development can be seen most clearly in three specific types of compositions, all based on the sonata cycle. Beethoven's

9 symphonies, 16 string quartets, and 32 piano sonatas are at the core of his output, and are spread chronologically throughout his life in all his compositional periods. At first glance, the totals of these works might seem rather slight. Haydn, after all, composed some 104 symphonies, almost 70 string quartets, and more than 50 piano sonatas. Mozart, in his brief 35 years, exceeded Beethoven in total number of works composed. What then accounts for the difference?

Surprisingly, Beethoven's deafness did not interfere with his compositional output. In fact, immediately after Beethoven's loss of hearing had been declared to be both incurable and irreversible, he entered one of the most prolific periods of his life. There are three other aspects of Beethoven's life that account for his comparatively lesser output.

It must be realized that Beethoven's works tend to be longer and more complex than those of his predecessors. A superficial understanding of the sonata cycle might leave the impression that a mediocre composer could simply plug thematic material into the right places and a symphony or string quartet could be produced with comparatively little effort. While neither Haydn nor Mozart ever resorted to such an automatic level of composing, neither of them ever tried to expand the elements of the sonata cycle far beyond their limits. Beethoven, however, was constantly expanding on those limits, from the standpoint of form, harmony, and other aspects of musical structure. Naturally, it takes longer to compose a work which is itself longer and more complicated.

It must also be observed that Beethoven was living during a time of tremendous social and political upheaval. The aftermath of the French Revolution set in motion a chain of events that would eventually change the governmental landscape of the whole of Europe. For the musician, the demise of the dominance of the aristocracy meant that dependence on the patronage system would soon be a thing of the past. Musicians would begin to trade the financial security of employment by a wealthy patron for an increased sense of personal and social worth, and for real freedom to create what was in their imagination. The cost of this freedom was the financial insecurity that made the image of the "starving artist" a frightening reality; yet this was a risk that artists would take in exchange for the possibilities of personal expression.

Beethoven was the first major musical figure to exist successfully outside of the patronage system. Mozart had tried earlier, and failed because, in large part, of forces outside of his control. Haydn lived contentedly as a servant throughout his long life; one of the main reasons his output is so prolific is that his position permitted this. Haydn had little else to do but compose and perform for his patron. Beethoven, on the other hand, had to spend considerable time in the development of his career, negotiating with promoters and publishers, creating his own market for his artistic output. This effort, quite naturally, took time and energy away from composing.

Finally, and in many ways most importantly, Beethoven did not possess a natural facility for composing. Actually few if any composers have had Mozart's natural gifts; Beethoven lacked the ease of Haydn, or any of a host of other composers. He did not compose in his head, but on paper; he left sketches for many of his compositions, sketches that were often many times longer than the finished work. These sketches testify to a figure struggling with the very act of composing. Beethoven's early ideas often are no more distinguished than material coming from a marginally advanced composition student. Yet his works did not remain at this point: he fought and struggled with his ideas, refining and developing them until they became the works of genius by which the world now knows Beethoven.

Childhood and Early Youth

The sense of struggle, of a titanic force fighting fierce opposition and ultimately triumphing, is the central characteristic of Beethoven's music. It is in this that he is most clearly romantic—one of the constantly recurring images in romantic art, music, and literature is that of the struggling and triumphant hero, a figure grappling with impossible obstacles and finally overcoming them. The reasons for this in Beethoven are manifold. Certainly, the political struggles of the French Revolution and the Napoleonic Wars were of considerable importance to Beethoven. In contrast to the stubbornly apolitical Mozart, Beethoven was conscious of the class struggle that was being waged in Europe and of its potential consequences in his own life and art as the common citizen eventually triumphed over the aristocracy. The seeds of Beethoven's sense of struggle, however, were sown earlier and on a more personal level: in his abusive childhood and his eventual triumph over the tyranny of his father.

Beethoven as a young man. © JupiterImages, Inc.

Beethoven was born in Bonn, the capital of the former West Germany, to Johann and Maria Magdalena Beethoven. Young Ludwig was more strongly and affectionately attached to his mother than to his father. Johann Beethoven was himself a musician; he had sufficient talent to recognize at least some of his son's gifts, but not enough to discover that Ludwig was no child prodigy on the level of Mozart. Johann apparently intended to use his son's talents to increase his own limited fortunes and determined to turn him into another Mozart. Ludwig's early education was limited almost exclusively to music—his letters throughout his life testify to the deficiencies of his studies in grammar, spelling, languages, and mathematics. From a very early age, Ludwig was set to many hours of work at the keyboard every day. Neighbors recalled him standing on a footstool so he could reach the keyboard of the family piano, weeping at the unremitting demands of work his severe and implacable father had assigned him, with the threat of punishment if he should fail. One of Ludwig's early teachers, Tobias Friedrich Pfeiffer, gave him lessons, but only erratically. Often, he and Johann would spend the evening drinking, coming home late and rousing nine-year-old Ludwig for his lessons, keeping him at the piano until morning.

Such a childhood caused Beethoven to develop a deep resentment against his father, but surprisingly not against music. Such unremitting toil did indeed cause him to develop into a prodigy of sorts. He performed as a piano virtuoso from an early age (his father publicly understated his age by two years to make his accomplishments seem more astonishing), and even composed during his Bonn childhood and adolescence, though nothing of any substance was produced until after he moved to Vienna.

That move came about with the help of Franz Joseph Haydn, who in January of 1792 was returning from his immensely successful first trip to London. Haydn passed through Bonn on his return, and Beethoven joined him on his journey to Vienna. Interestingly, Haydn and Beethoven did not get along very well. The young firebrand was far too adventurous for the conservative Haydn, and Beethoven found his older teacher too restrictive on his imagination.

There may have been another dynamic at work here: Haydn was called "Papa" by many of the younger musicians working under him as conductor or teacher. He was held in considerable affection by many, who saw in him a father figure—but for Beethoven, the father figure was not one of love but of harshness and coldness, learned from the model of his own father. At this point in his life, Beethoven would likely have had difficulty responding to any fatherly image, regardless of how unlike his own father that figure was. Such hostility may have explained why Beethoven always claimed to have learned very little from Haydn, despite the obvious roots in style. Beethoven's compositional methods were actually much closer to Haydn's than to Mozart's.

Haydn, Mozart, and Beethoven

Beethoven had long admired Mozart and intended to study with him when he moved to Vienna. He had played for Mozart when he was a boy, improvising so perfectly at the keyboard that the older composer accused him of having prepared the piece. Beethoven was upset by this accusation and asked Mozart to give him a theme on which he could improvise. He again played magnificently, and Mozart, much impressed, said to some friends, "Watch out for him; he will have something to tell you."

Beethoven's desire to study with Mozart was thwarted by Mozart's untimely death just a few weeks before Beethoven arrived in Vienna. He traveled there, however, with Haydn, and studied with Haydn for some time after he settled in that musical capital.

The connection of Beethoven with Mozart and Haydn was apparent to some from a very early time. When Beethoven began his life in Vienna, his friend, Count Waldstein, wrote to him:

> *. . . You are now going to Vienna in fulfillment of a wish that has for so long been thwarted. The genius of Mozart still mourns and weeps the death of its pupil. It has found a refuge in the inexhaustible Hayden (sic), but no occupation; through him it desires once more to find a union with someone. Through your unceasing diligence, receive* Mozart's spirit from the hands of Hayden. (Landon)

Deafness

Beethoven's early career in Vienna was quite successful. From the beginning, he affected a certainty of his own worth. That same certainty had seemed arrogant in Mozart and had gained him more enemies than friends; but at this point in time, society was changing, and Beethoven's confidence was seen as a positive aspect in society. As he himself put it, "It is good to mingle with aristocrats; but you must know how to impress them."

At the height of his popularity, however, about 1798, Beethoven began to experience a gradual loss of a musician's most valued sense: his hearing. This condition began in his left ear, and gradually progressed to include his right; the deafness was partial at first, often accompanied by tinnitus, a ringing or a roaring in the ear. When his deafness became total, after 1815, the tinnitus mercifully ceased. By 1802, his condition had become profound, and the physicians treating him had all concurred that his condition was both irreversible and incurable.

During the summer and fall of 1802, Beethoven sunk into a severe depression over his malady. He had moved to the town of Heiligenstadt for the summer, and while there he wrote a letter detailing his response to his suffering and how he came to terms with it. The letter, addressed to his brothers and intended to be read after his death, is a sort of last will and testament and has come to be known as the *Heiligenstadt Testament*. It divides his estate between his two brothers, but more importantly, and at much greater length, it describes his struggles and suffering, his sense of isolation, his contemplation of suicide, and his ultimate rejection of that solution.

Interestingly, it was not so much the lack of hearing, particularly hearing music, that disturbed Beethoven, but the feeling of separation from his fellow man which drove him to contemplate ending his own life. For any musician, the real world of music exists not so much in the ears as in the mind, in the imagination. Musicians are trained to be able to look at a score and have some idea what it sounds like; Beethoven, one of the most supremely gifted figures of all time, had perfected this ability. So his loss of hearing did not mean a loss of musical ability; in some ways, his isolation may have been the source of much of his originality. His pain came in being cut off from the rest of civilization.

Even in our supposedly enlightened times, those with disabilities can feel isolated from the mainstream of society; in Beethoven's day, deaf, blind, or otherwise impaired individuals were indeed cut off from real integration with the community. Beethoven was truly a child of the French Revolution, and the ideal of the universal brotherhood of mankind was of supreme importance to his world view. To be cut off from that brotherhood by this infirmity was almost more than he could bear. In the end, his compulsion to create was stronger than his urge to destroy. It was his *Art* that kept him from suicide—he felt unable to leave the world until he had said all that he felt was within his creative imagination.

sidebar

The Heiligenstadt Testament

Oh my fellow men, who consider me or describe me as unfriendly, peevish or even misanthropic, how greatly do you wrong me. For you do not know the secret reason why I appear to you to be so . . . For the last six years I have been afflicted with an incurable complaint which has been made worse by incompetent doctors. From year to year my hopes of being cured have gradually been shattered and finally I have been forced to accept the prospect of a permanent infirmity . . . Though endowed with a passionate and lively temperament and even fond of the distractions offered by society I was soon obliged to seclude myself and live in solitude . . . I could not bring myself to say to people: "Speak up, shout, for I am deaf." Alas! how could I possibly refer to the impairing of a sense which in me should be more perfectly developed than in other people, a sense which at one time I possessed in the greatest perfection, even to a degree of perfection such as assuredly few in my profession possess or have ever possessed . . . Moreover my misfortune pains me doubly, in as much as it leads to my being misjudged . . . I must live like an outcast. If I appear in company, I am overcome by a burning anxiety, a fear that I am running the risk of letting people notice my condition . . . how humiliated I have felt if somebody standing beside me heard the sound of a flute in the distance and I heard nothing, or if somebody heard a shepherd sing and again I heard nothing—such experiences drove me almost to despair, and I was on the point of putting an end to my life—the only thing that held me back was my art. For indeed it seemed impossible to leave this world before I had produced all the works that I felt the urge to compose . . . Joyfully I go to meet Death—should it come before I have had an opportunity of developing all my artistic gifts, then in spite of my hard fate it would still come too soon . . . Yet even so I should be content, for would it not free me from a condition of continual suffering? Come then, Death, whenever you like, and with courage I will go to meet you . . .

    Ludwig van Beethoven
    To be read and executed after my death
    Heiligenstadt, October 10, 1802

    Thus I take leave of you . . . Oh, Providence—do but grant me one day of pure joy—for so long now, the inner echo of real joy has been unknown to me . . . Oh, when, Almighty God—shall I be able to hear and feel this echo again in the temple of Nature and in contact with humanity—Never?—No!—Oh, that would be too hard.

From *Beethoven's Letters 1790–1826*, (ISBN 0-486-22769-3). Translated by J.S. Shedlock. Copyright © 1972 by Dover Publications, Inc. Reprinted by permission.

Portrait of Beethoven. © JupiterImages, Inc.

Last Years

Beethoven's final years were a time of increasing isolation. He wrote in one of his conversation books (notebooks he kept with him to carry on written conversations when he was in the company of others), "I am friendless and alone in the world." Many of his old friends and acquaintances had died or were moving away from Vienna. Also, many had lost touch with Beethoven deliberately, being unable to deal with his tendency to fly into terrifying rages for no apparent reason.

In 1815, Beethoven's brother Karl died. The two had been partially estranged because of Karl's wife. Beethoven loathed the woman, whom he referred to as the "Queen of the Night," after Mozart's personification of evil in *The Magic Flute*. It was Karl's dying wish that Ludwig take over the raising of his son; he did not feel that the boy's mother was morally capable of raising the boy properly. Apparently the courts of Vienna agreed, because after a lengthy legal battle, Beethoven was awarded custody of his nephew. The struggle, however, left Beethoven drained emotionally, physically, and financially, and young nephew Karl never adjusted to life with his irascible, deaf, genius uncle. Beethoven never married; his attempts at being a father were disastrous despite his good intentions. Karl was desperately unhappy, even to the point of attempting suicide.

In the late autumn of 1826, after a quarrel with his brother Johann, Beethoven returned to Vienna. He fell ill—his liver and kidneys were failing, the result of heavy alcohol intake over a period of many years. He struggled on for some months until March 26; he died during a storm. At about 5:00 PM, a violent flash of lightning illuminated his chamber. Beethoven opened his eyes, and raised his right hand with a clenched fist for several seconds. His face bore a threatening expression as though defying Death itself. When his hand sunk back to his side, he ceased breathing.

Beethoven, through the sheer force of his genius and the strength of his will, managed to transcend the obstacles of his life's struggle: his abusive childhood, the social struggle with a crumbling aristocracy which saw music as its servant, and his loss of hearing and consequent isolation and loneliness. In his own words, he decided to "seize Fate by the throat," rather than submit to its terrors. His life and his music are testimony to the ability of humanity to overcome its limitations; Beethoven himself changed the way Western civilization viewed music and musicians. As Luciano Berio pointed out, only after Beethoven did people begin to talk about music as an art rather than a craft.

Three Style Periods

Beethoven's works can be placed in three distinct style periods, cleverly known as Early, Middle, and Late. The composer and musicologist Vincent D'Indy has characterized those periods respectively as Imitation, Externalization, and Reflection.

Actually, it would seem that those three descriptions could describe the works of almost any creative artist. At the beginning of a career, an artist's works are mostly imitations of existing styles, or perhaps of the ideas of his or her teachers. Only as an artist attains real maturity can that person's creative individuality become truly externalized in his or her works. And, of course, toward the end of a life, there is more of a tendency to reflect on what has been accomplished rather than on what is to come. There is an increasing contemplation of the artist's mortality rather than his or her potential.

While this pattern could indeed apply to many artists, with Beethoven it is particularly appropriate—Beethoven went through three very distinct periods that can be delineated by specific dates and almost by specific opus numbers in his output. The reason that symphonies, string quartets, and piano sonatas were mentioned before as central to the understanding of Beethoven's musical development is that there are examples of each of these three types of works in each of his three periods. To understand Beethoven's development, one need only to examine examples from one (or all three) of these genres from each of the three periods and compare them.

Important Works from the Three Periods

Early (Imitation), to 1802, Op. 36

Symphony no. 1 in C, Op. 21
Symphony no. 2 in D, Op. 36
Six String Quartets, Op. 18
Piano Sonata Op. 13 in c, "Pathetique"
Piano Sonata Op. 27 no. 2, "Moonlight"
Piano Sonata Op. 31, no. 2 in d, "Tempest"

The works of the Early period are, as one would expect, a continuation of the style of Haydn and Mozart. Haydn's influence is more evident than that of Mozart. Beethoven was primarily a developmental composer rather than a lyric one; that is, Beethoven would normally base his works around a few thematic ideas, often short motifs rather than longer melodies, which he would then develop into his musical structures. He chose his thematic ideas more because of their possibilities for development than for their pure melodic expressiveness.

Even in this period, however, Beethoven's voice is distinct; his first published work was a set of three piano trios (a chamber ensemble consisting not of three pianos but of piano, violin, and 'cello) of which no. 3 in c minor is particularly wild. Haydn did not approve.

The most individual works of this period are the piano sonatas, which is not surprising for someone whose early reputation was as much as a piano virtuoso as a composer. Beethoven allowed himself greater freedom of innovation and experimentation in these compositions, written largely for his own performance. Interestingly, Beethoven seemed to be able to divorce himself from his personal circumstances when composing. The second symphony, which is one of his sunniest and happiest compositions, was composed during the same summer that produced the Heiligenstadt Testament.

Middle (Externalization), 1802–1812, Opp. 37–95

Symphony no. 3 in E-flat, "Eroica," Op. 55
Symphony no. 4 in B-flat, Op. 60
Symphony no. 5 in c, Op. 67
Symphony no. 6 in F, "Pastorale," Op. 68
Symphony no. 7 in A, Op. 92
Symphony no. 8 in F, Op. 93
String quartets Op. 59, "Razoumovsky"
String quartet in E-flat, Op. 74, "Harp"
Piano sonata Op. 53 in C, "Waldstein"
Piano sonata Op. 57 in f, "Appassionata"

Middle period Beethoven is the voice by which he is most widely known: this is the stormy, thundering titan, the defiant and heroic Beethoven. His works of this period are freer and more adventurous. He began experimenting with greater expansion of form and with richer harmonies and more unusual key relationships.

It is in this period that Beethoven's most famous piece of program music is found: the sixth symphony, known as the *Pastoral*. The work is a musical impression of a day in the country; it presents images of solitary walks and communion with nature along with the merry-making of villagers and a brief but violent storm. This particular work is an exception. Beethoven is seen historically as having brought the possibilities of absolute music to their greatest level of expression; he left no programmatic explanations of any of his major works except this one.

Nevertheless, many have found Beethoven's music so emotionally rich that it causes them to perceive some sort of extramusical image or images. Many of Beethoven's compositions have acquired "nicknames" because of this very quality; the names, incidentally, were more often supplied by the publisher than by Beethoven himself. It is interesting that Beethoven once commented to a friend that he often had such images in mind when he was composing. He never wrote any of these down, though, and considered the ideas rather childish. Given the importance that program music was to assume during the Romantic period, it would seem that the ideas were not childish, but merely unfashionable. It would be fascinating to find out what sort of images were passing through Beethoven's imagination when he was composing some of his "absolute" works.

Late (Reflection), 1812–1827, Opp. 96–135
Symphony no. 9 in d, "Ode to Joy," Op. 125
Five string quartets Opp. 127, 130, 131, 132, 133, 135
Five piano sonatas Opp. 101, 106, 109, 110, 111

The works of Beethoven's Late period were baffling to contemporaneous audiences; many, even among great musicians, felt that the composer had gone quite mad, having spent too many years in silence, and no longer had any idea what music really was. We now recognize these works as some of the most sublime and original compositions of all time and as generations ahead of their era. These works expand the standard structures of the Classical period almost beyond recognition.

The voice of the Late period is more contemplative and reflective than before; the heroic titan has now become a transcendent figure, concerned with thoughts of the celestial, the noble, and the sublime. The sense of struggle and triumph is not wholly absent, but it is usually balanced by more meditative passages.

In many ways, the most remarkable composition of the Late period is the lone representative of the symphony, the ninth symphony, called the "Choral" symphony, or sometimes the "Ode to Joy." The former designation refers to the fact that the work, in its last movement, adds both a chorus and four vocal soloists to the orchestra. The text for that movement is the poem *An die Freude (Ode to Joy)* by Friedrich Schiller.

Rhythmic Propulsion: Three Short Notes and a Long

The central characteristic of Beethoven's music is an explosive energy, an inexorable rhythmic propulsion. Certainly not all of his music is fast and energetic; he has his moments of tenderness, contemplation, and even humor. Yet even the gentlest passages of Beethoven are housed in a solid rhythmic pulse and formal framework. One of the most distinctive means Beethoven uses to create this quality is a recurring rhythmic idea: three identical short notes followed by a longer note.

This figure is found in what is possibly the most well-known theme in all of western art music: the opening theme of Beethoven's *Symphony no. 5*. In fact, that particular idea pervades the entire fifth symphony, in all four movements, and can be found again and again in Beethoven's works in prominent thematic or transitional material. It may seem that a simple idea such as this could be found regularly in any composer's work, but a study of any dozen of so of Beethoven's scores will show that, indeed, this particular composer uses that specific motif in prominent passages again and again—too frequently for it not to be deliberate.

The effect of the idea, or of any sequence of short notes leading into a long one, is to push the music forward, to provide a sense of rhythmic propulsion. Beginning music students often have a distressing tendency to play a group of short notes first, then stopping before going on to the longer one. The effect is like eliminating the last word of a sentence. The idea is not complete *until* the long note is reached; the burst of motion leading into that note simply makes the drive to it all the more powerful. For our examination of Beethoven's music, we will look at three works: a symphony in its entirety and the first movements of a string quartet and a piano sonata. All are from Beethoven's Middle period, and all use the three short notes followed by a long one as part of their important thematic material.

Symphony no. 5 in c minor, Op. 67

The fifth symphony was given its first performance on December 22, 1808, on a program that also included the sixth symphony (the *Pastoral*), the third piano concerto, a concert aria, a hymn for chorus, a *Sanctus* from a mass, a piano solo, and the *Choral Fantasia* for piano, orchestra, and chorus. That audience certainly got its money's worth!

The fifth symphony is Beethoven's most famous work, with the possible exception of the ninth symphony. It is also one of his most remarkable, with a taut construction based almost entirely on the opening motto of three short notes followed by a long. The work has a distinct sense of emotional progression: the opening movement appears to portray a terrific struggle; the slow movement that follows moves to a major key and a sense, however temporary, of repose and serenity; the third movement returns to the same mood of turmoil and struggle as the first, leading without pause into the final movement, which opens with three fortissimo C-major triads and an uninterrupted sense of victory.

Allegro con brio

The first movement is in sonata form as would be expected. The famous motif opens the work, and the long note is held for a bit before the motif is repeated, at a lower pitch. The first theme progresses by piling this idea onto itself, building an explosive sense of rhythmic energy.

The second theme, as would be expected, is more lyrical, and in Eb major, but even it is introduced by the three short notes and a long motif. It can be heard again in the 'cello and bass accompaniment to that second theme.

The development section takes the main motif and begins to fragment it, eventually reducing it to only two pitches, then to only a single pitch, alternately played by the winds and the strings. The energy and propulsion seem to fade, until the final bars of the development bring back the whole motif, hammering it repeatedly and building an incredible amount of tension until the recapitulation, where the opening motif is repeated in its original form.

The second theme is now in C major; as we come to the end of the recapitulation, it is evident that Beethoven is not bringing the work to a close but building up even more excitement. For Beethoven, the coda is not just a few bars designed to bring the work to a close, but an opportunity for greater development; the extended coda almost becomes another development section, and it is one of the most important characteristics of his Middle period.

By the end of the coda, we are brought back one final time to the opening motif, and it sounds as though Beethoven was repeating the recapitulation from the beginning. It is a deception, though—we now have only a few bars before the movement is complete.

Andante con moto

The second movement is an island of repose between the struggles and turmoil of the first and third movements. The form of the movement is a theme and variations; the theme itself is quite long, and there are only three variations. The movement is in the key of Ab major and opens with a quiet, lyric theme in the lower strings, played in dotted rhythms.

Beethoven cannot quite escape the sense of the heroic in this movement; the second half of the theme, which opens with the three short notes followed by a long motif, begins quietly, but the end of the theme is played *fortissimo*, for the whole orchestra and prefigures the ultimate triumph of the finale.

The first variation changes the theme to evenly flowing sixteenth notes; the second half of the theme is accompanied by thirty-second note arpeggios in the lower strings before building to the same climax. The second variation doubles the rhythmic motion of the theme, now being played in thirty-second notes.

After the climax of this theme, there is a long transitional section, in which the winds seem to be playing with each other.

The third variation begins in a minor key, with the same rhythmic character it had at the opening of the movement. Beethoven builds to the heroic theme one last time, before bringing the piece to a close.

Allegro (attacca)

The respite of calm is now over—it is time to return to the battle. The third movement is not specifically labeled "scherzo," though it is one in form and character. The scherzo and trio is identical in form to the minuet and trio, but is faster and more dramatic. After all, one can hardly imagine the courtly grace of the minuet being appropriate in a work such as this.

The movement begins quietly, but the mood is ominous rather than serene. A c minor chord is outlined in the 'cellos and basses, and it seems as though something is about to happen. And indeed it does: the French horns burst on the scene at top volume with (surprise!) three short notes followed by a long.

The movement progresses as a scherzo normally would, in two sections, with each repeated. The trio, in C major, begins with a positively humorous passage for the basses (which George Bernard Shaw compared to the image of elephants gamboling).

The theme passes through the rest of the orchestra, and eventually, as one would expect, we return to the main theme of the scherzo itself.

But now things are different; this is not a literal return. The notes themselves are the same, but now all is quiet. The blazing French horns are replaced by plucked strings and piccolo, all played *pianissimo*. Again the mood is ominous; Beethoven here intends to move into the finale quietly, almost by surprise.

The term *attacca* means that the orchestra is to go directly into the last movement without a pause. This in itself is quite unusual; usually, there is a specific conclusion to a movement, and a brief but distinct space of time before the next movement. Here, however, Beethoven links the two movements without a break. In order to do that, however, some things must be changed. The last movement begins in C major, *fortissimo*, so we must first pass through a transitional section, accompanied by three short notes and a long on the timpani while the music changes from c minor to C major, and from *pianissimo* to *fortissimo*.

Allegro

The sonata form finale opens with three rising C major *fortissimo* chords, establishing an uninterrupted mood of triumph to resolve the struggle of the first three movements. The exposition introduces some four separate thematic ideas, rather than the usual two themes. The first two are in C major, the second two in G major; the first of the G major themes is based on three short notes followed by a long.

It is not precisely true that the mood of triumph is uninterrupted. After the development section, Beethoven interrupts the victorious mood to bring back a direct quotation from the scherzo before entering the recapitulation. This unusual passage occurs for two reasons. The first is rather obvious when it is pointed out: the recapitulation is essentially a repeat of the exposition, and Beethoven originally came into the exposition directly from the scherzo, without a pause. The logical way to move into the recapitulation is the same way, from the scherzo.

Perhaps more importantly, however, is the sense of unity that this brief quotation achieves. As the works of 19th-century composers became longer and more complex, audiences had more and more difficulty following them without becoming hopelessly lost. Listeners in the preelectronic age had no way to study these pieces except in live performance, and composers were constantly seeking a means to unify large-scale compositions for an audience that might only hear a work once in a year's time. The recurring motif of three short notes followed by a long itself gives this symphony a strong sense of unity, but the direct quotation of material from a previous movement is even more helpful to the listener. The quotation of previously-heard material in a later movement is known as **cyclic technique**.

Once we are finally in the recapitulation, the rest of the movement progresses as one would expect, including an extended coda before the final eight (!) triumphant C major chords. The symphony is unmistakably at its end.

String Quartet no. 10 in E-flat Major, Op. 74, "Harp"

With the Middle period quartets, Beethoven effectively redefined chamber music as a medium of greater intensity and depth than it had been previously. The first set of quartets from this period, the three quartets, Op. 59, dedicated to Count Razoumovsky had already been charged with not really being music. The composer, in an uncharacteristically reserved response, simply told his accuser that the works were written for a later age.

Of course, throughout history, people have often said that any music they don't like or don't understand is "not really music." It would not be the first or last time such a charge was leveled at Beethoven.

These quartets are different, though: they are bigger, longer, grander, and more intense than any previous string quartet had ever dared to be. It often seems as though the works are not content with the limitations of chamber music, and are attempting to metamorphosize into symphonies.

The *String Quartet no. 10 in E-flat Major, Op. 74*, is in the same tradition as the *Razoumovsky* quartets. It was composed in 1809, while Beethoven was working on two other major works in the same key, the *Piano Concerto no. 5, Op. 73* and the *Piano Sonata no. 26, Op. 81a, "Les Adieux."*

Poco Adagio—Allegro

The work has an almost symphonic opening, with a slow introduction (you'll recall that Haydn was fond of this device in his symphonies). The passage is deeply expressive; its contemplative nature is interrupted by heavily accented chords followed by silences. Immediately after the fourth such silence, the first violin begins a gradual chromatic rise of slightly more than an octave. The other instruments move sometimes with and sometimes against that line, until, almost without realizing it, we are past the introduction and into the sunny *allegro.*

The first movement is a textbook example of sonata form. The nickname for the quartet, "Harp," comes from a transitional passage between the first and second themes, which is played *pizzicato*—plucked rather than bowed. First the 'cello and viola exchange plucks against a background of repeated chords in the two violins, then the pairs change places. With a bit of imagination, one can hear a harp behind those plucked strings. The second theme begins with the only reference to the three short notes followed by a long motif which occurs in this particular movement.

The development takes the thematic material of the exposition and fragments it (much as had happened in the first movement of the fifth symphony). The transition to the recapitulation makes use of the "harp" sounds again, with rising arpeggios in ever smaller rhythmic values until the players switch back to their bows to introduce the recapitulation.

That section is followed again by an extended coda. The recapitulation actually ends rather quietly; the players do not end the section as the exposition had done, but instead play sustained chords, reminiscent of the slow introduction. The upper strings begin to increase the rhythmic intensity by a repeated rocking motif, and then the first violin launches into a brilliant series of sixteenth-note arpeggios which is sustained almost until the end of the movement.

Meanwhile, the other instruments begin plucking the a variant of the "harp" motif. The second violin and viola begin trading statements of the same melody, and the 'cello finally switches from plucking to bowing, all building a terrific intensity until the final bars of the movement. This coda is one of the greatest passages in all of chamber music literature.

Piano Sonata no. 23 in f minor, Op. 57, "Appassionata"

The title of this work, however apt it may seem, was *not* Beethoven's idea. He was not pleased with the title, but it has stuck with the work, which is universally known as the "Appassionata." Beethoven felt it was the finest of all his piano sonatas when it was composed—before the remarkable final five works of his Late period. The mood here is really more tragic than passionate. The genial, humorous touches found in the "Harp" quartet are wholly absent.

Allegro assai

The first movement of the f minor sonata seems to have several references to the fifth symphony, until one realizes that this composition was completed in 1805 and published the following year, long before the first performance of the symphony. The first movement begins with much the same mood as the scherzo of the symphony: with a quiet outline of the tonic chord, creating an ominous mood.

Things remain quiet for some time; only the sounds of Beethoven's three short notes followed by a long, heard first in the bass, then in the treble, indicate the storm of sound that follows immediately.

The first theme is then repeated, but this time followed by crashing chords; the effect is electrifying, as though a current were being sent up one's spine. A series of repeated triplets introduces the second theme in c minor, before we hear a new idea in Ab major.

This is related to the initial theme in its rhythmic character, though the melody moves very differently. A third theme is introduced, again in f minor, before moving into the development section; there is no repeat of the exposition.

The development expands on the thematic ideas already introduced, bringing them to a climax with a return to the three short notes followed by a long motif. The recapitulation begins with the same material as the exposition but is accompanied by repeated triplets to give a heightened sense of rhythmic propulsion.

Again, the three short notes and a long motif are heard to make the transition to the explosive coda. As if exhausted by the effort expended, the movement ends *ppp*.

Symphony no. 9 in d minor, Op. 125: "Ode to Joy"

Beethoven's final symphony is not only his greatest symphony, but one that has taken on important symbolism for the world at large. True, that symbolism derives from the message of the poetry of Friedrich Schiller, the text of the last movement. But without the power of the musical setting, would that poem have nearly the same impact? And could it have reached beyond the German-speaking world without the universal voice of its music?

The work was completed and first performed in 1824. Beethoven conducted the work, despite being completely deaf (the orchestra was watching the concertmaster). After the performance, the audience applauded thunderously—even those who did not understand the work, and there were many, realized that they were in the presence of something titanic. At first, Beethoven did not acknowledge the applause because he could not hear it. One of the singers had to pull on his sleeve to get his attention so he could bow to the audience.

The first three movements are huge in scale, beyond anything heard to date. But the revolution was in the final movement, a setting of Schiller's *An die Freud (To Joy)* for chorus and four vocal soloists with orchestra. It was the first time in history that voice had been brought into the symphony.

As in the fifth symphony, Beethoven uses cyclic technique; because the scope of the work was so much greater than anything heard before, it was necessary. The last movement opens with a purely instrumental passage. After a pungent dissonance, the double basses play a passage that sounds like operatic recitative—more declamatory than melodic, though there is no text. The first movement is briefly quoted; the quotations are from the second and third movements, each separated by the double basses.

After those opening recollections, the basses enter with the main theme of the last movement, one of the world's most beautiful and well-known melodies. After the melody has passed through the rest of the orchestra, we hear a return of the opening chord, and the entry of the bass soloist. His first words are Beethoven's not Schiller's: "O friends, no more of these sounds. Let us sing more cheerful songs, more full of joy," and then we hear the first verse of the poem.

There is an alternation between chorus and soloists, and on the words *Vor Gott* (before God), the music changes key and mood. Percussion instruments introduce the "Turkish March" section, with tenor solo and chorus. After a fugal orchestral passage, the main theme is once again taken up by the chorus. An adagio section is heard with treacherously high notes for the chorus before the final, joyous utterance concludes the piece.

Beethoven's ninth has a message of the universal brotherhood of mankind, united by joy. It is no accident that the work is performed—it might be better to say invoked—at moments of greatest historical importance. When the Berlin Wall fell, an orchestra was brought together in Berlin with members from the Berlin, Bavarian, London, Paris, and New York orchestras; singers from the United States, Russia, Germany; an international quartet of solo singers; and conductor Leonard Bernstein. For the performance, Bernstein altered the text to replace *Freude* (joy) with *Freiheit* (freedom). The change was easy to make—the words are both two syllables, both begin with the same two consonants—and the effect was deeply moving.

Glossary

Cyclic technique: the use of a theme that has been heard earlier in a piece, as a means of unifying large-scale compositions

Heiligenstadt Testament: Beethoven's last will and testament, written in Heiligenstadt during the summer of 1802, in which he expresses his suffering over the loss of his hearing

References

Grout, Donald Jay. *A History of Western Music*, 3th ed. New York: W.W. Norton & Co., 1980.

Robbins Landon, H.C. (ed). *Beethoven: A Documentary Study*. New York: MacMillan, 1970, 55.

Tyson, Alan (ed). *Selected Letters of Beethoven*, tr. Emily Anderson. New York: St. Martin's Press, 1967.

THE EARLY ROMANTIC PERIOD (1809–1850)

To Express the Inexpressible

It seems convenient to divide the past into neatly defined eras with clear boundaries, but art resists such a simple understanding. Beethoven has certainly muddied the waters—his links to Mozart and Haydn are clear, but equally clear is how far away from the simplicity and restraint of the Classical ideal he ultimately came.

Making things even more complicated is the fact that Beethoven's music was so much more advanced that no one at that time was able to build on his music after his death; not until a generation had passed did someone come on the scene with the genius to continue that legacy: Johannes Brahms. This does not imply that music stopped developing; only that composers sought things new and different from what had gone before.

The new era is the Romantic Period—and we've encountered that term before. The Greek deities Apollo and Dionysus represented the complementary opposite aspects of art. Apollo represented order, logic, moderation; what we call Classic. Dionysus represented emotion, freedom, excess; what we call Romantic. In short, Apollo is form and Dionysus content. And both are essential for any work of art to communicate. Without some sense of order, the work becomes unintelligible. Without emotional content, the experience is dry and lifeless. Any given era will tilt toward one or other aspect, but any era must have a balance of the two. One cannot successfully exist without that balance.

Throughout history, each era has favored one or the other aspect: the Renaissance was a classic era, the Baroque a romantic one. The next two periods actually took the names Classic and Romantic. Beethoven unleashed the fury and transcended the moderation of the classic aesthetic. Subsequent creative figures ran with this new energy and freedom.

An Egalitarian Transformation

The American and French Revolutions may have been an outgrowth of the Enlightenment, but their impact was felt most strongly during the next century. Both marked the growing importance of egalitarianism in the West. And while when our founding fathers wrote "all men are created equal," they actually meant all white male property owners. They did not specify this. And that eventually led to the abolition of slavery, universal suffrage, public education—and the final dominance of representative governance replacing hereditary aristocracies.

In music, this also meant the emergence of the Artist, with a capital A, a solitary, heroic figure, whose most important characteristics were individuality and creativity. This is a great contrast to the 18th-century view that the musician is a servant, expected to provide entertainment to and uplift their employers, whether at court or in church, and that their style should conform to established norms without challenging or shocking.

Music: The Most Romantic of the Arts

All the artists of the day considered themselves and their age Romantic, but there was a common belief that music was the most Romantic of the arts. More so than the specific imagery of painting or literature, music does not and cannot express specific, universally identifiable images. Thus, in its capacity to express the inexpressible, it was most in keeping with the freedom of imagination that was the ideal of the Romantics. And in its ability to merge with other arts—with text or dance or visual settings—it was seen as the meeting place of the arts and as the heart of expression.

In a related development, the Romantic period saw the beginnings of printed aesthetic argument: music criticism. According to composer Luciano Berio, only after Beethoven did people begin to talk and write *about* music, as an art rather than as a craft. Some of the finest critics of the age were themselves great composers, and we'll learn about Hector Berlioz, Robert Schumann, and Richard Wagner in this and the next chapters.

The Romantics: Victory through Struggle

Unlike previous eras, the Romantics were self-aware. Baroque musicians did not know that term, and the Classical era was named by the next generation as well. But Romantic artists, whether in music, painting, literature, or any of the arts, were consciously romantic—they referred to themselves and their art as Romantic. Their interest was in the imagination, in distinctly individual styles, in self-expression, in innovation, and in experimentation.

Certain themes recurred throughout Romantic art. One was the **struggling and triumphant hero**, a figure battling tremendous odds and emerging victorious. *Ad astra per aspera* was the rallying cry: "to the stars through struggle!" The struggle may be artistic, it may be social, and it may even be physical. Mozart was in many ways the prototype, in his successful choice to forego the patronage system. But perhaps he was too gifted really to personify the struggle—Beethoven was clearly the real model. He struggled against an abusive childhood, against a hostile society, against the very loss of his hearing, and yet persevered and triumphed. He fought his alcoholic father by suing to be made head of his household at the age of 18. His attitude toward an aristocracy that demanded respect without earning it was "you are who you are because of an accident of birth; I am who I am because I am Beethoven." And, facing the isolation, the oblivion of deafness, was given courage by his art: "*I thought it impossible to leave this world until I had created all that I felt was within me.*"

This theme accounts for the frequency of references to the Faust legend in romantic art. The story of Faust is of a medieval scholar who was so frustrated with his inability to know all he wanted to know that he made a pact with Mephistopheles (one of the Devil's many names) to find this enlightenment . . . in exchange for his immortal soul. Depending on who is writing (or painting or composing), in the end Faust is redeemed, and the Devil defeated, by the perfect love of a woman. The image is clear—humankind's desire, our need, to transcend the limits of our existence.

Another such image can be seen in the Romantics' glorification of the virtuoso soloist. A virtuoso (the term has nothing to do with virtuous) is a musician, or anyone practicing an advanced skill, who has not only mastered the instrument technically, but who has simply transcended any and all challenges or difficulties the instrument presents.

And it was instrumental virtuosity that held the Romantics' fascination. Since the Baroque, vocal virtuosity had been common; the castrati were able to dazzle with all sorts of pyrotechnics. Not until the Romantic period, however, did instrumentalists take virtuosity as a goal. The violinist Niccolo Paganini brought the technical and expressive range of his instrument far beyond what any had before. He was an impressive figure, performing in black with sunken eyes and a mysterious air. The rumor circulated that he had made a pact with the Devil (lots of traffic in souls in this era) to give his soul for perfect mastery of his violin.

Actually, Paganini started that one himself . . . he had no dealings with the Infernal (though the rumor was persistent enough that he was denied a burial in consecrated ground after his death), but circulated the tale because he knew that any such scandal would increase the number of people who would pay to hear him play . . . and he needed the income, because he was often in heavy debt from gambling.

A young Hungarian pianist heard Paganini and decided to dedicate his life to expanding the possibilities of technique and expression on the piano. His name was Franz Liszt, and we will deal with him in greater detail later in this chapter.

Romantic Dualities

Other themes pervaded Romantic art, often in seemingly contradictory (but actually complementary) dualities. Romantics were fascinated with **Nature**, with a capital N—not the sort of ecological awareness, the scientific understanding of our times, but Nature as a metaphor, a symbol for absolute purity, for an uncorrupted existence.

And they were also fascinated by the **supernatural**. Romantic art is filled with demons, devils, and witches—people selling their soul to Satan in exchange for their deepest desires. This would never have occupied the artists of the Enlightenment. They were too, well, enlightened. But the Romantics were more concerned with imagination over logic, with a situation in which anything was possible.

The Romantics were also concerned with **exoticism**. Anything foreign was of interest. Images of Africa, the Far East, and the Americas were found frequently. Mind you, there was no particular desire for accuracy—an opera by Giacomo Puccini, *Manon Lescaut*, ends with the leading soprano dying of a respiratory disease (seemingly an odd choice for a singer's demise) in the vast desert just north of New Orleans.

And the Romantics were equally fascinated with **Nationalism**, which we will discuss at greater length in the next chapter. The egalitarian waves that swept Europe not only led to the formation of the modern states of Italy and Germany, it also awakened self-awareness in areas that had been out of the musical mainstream. Places such as Russia, Eastern Europe, Scandinavia, Spain, the United Kingdom—and, finally, the United States, Latin America, and Canada—all began to celebrate their own national and ethnic heritage in music.

The Romantics saw a revival of **spirituality**, with a particular fascination with the mystical aspects of the faith, a fascination with ritual and the miraculous. And, of course, amid all this freedom of imagination, all this challenge to social norms, a new freedom of exploration of **sensuality** was inevitable, including the celebration of this in the arts.

The Music of the Romantics

If one word could be used to describe Romanticism in music, it would be **expansion**. Musicians sought ways to exceed their limitations, and in the process, things got bigger.

- The **orchestra** expanded. Beethoven's fifth symphony was the first to use trombones and piccolo. Big deal. By the end of the period, Gustav Mahler wrote his eighth symphony, using extra strings, harps, organ, six each of the woodwinds, eight each of the brass, an offstage brass orchestra, eight vocal soloists, and three choirs. The work is known as the *Symphony of a Thousand*, though it only needs about 750 people to perform.
- The **piano** expanded its range at the top and the bottom, and it used an iron frame instead of the wood of the lighter 18th-century fortepiano. It was taken up by scores of great virtuosos and became the favorite solo instrument of the day.
- **Dynamics** expanded. It was not uncommon to see *ffff* or *ppppp*—beyond a certain point, this is hyperbole; it just indicated as loud, or soft, as possible.
- **Harmony** expanded. Dissonances were more widely used, changes of key were more adventurous and complex, and chords were richer and more complex. Where before, chords were mostly triads, with occasionally an extra note added, during this era, chords consisted of five, six, or even seven different pitches.

- **Rhythm** expanded. Subdivisions were more complex, tempo changes more frequent, and extremes of tempo were often encountered. The Romantics make more use of *rubato*, an expressive device in which the player speeds up some passages, slows others down, or perhaps hangs on to a note longer than its written value would indicate. While this was universally practiced in any era, 19th-century musicians used it more often and to a greater degree than those in earlier times.

Romantic dualism even applies here—among all these tendencies toward expansion we find a corresponding interest in **miniatures**—short pieces, usually with only a single theme. Short pieces for piano or guitar, dances, or character pieces were popular, especially among amateur musicians (another dualism—in an age with a fascination with virtuosity, home music making by amateurs was still wildly popular).

And this was also a golden age of the **song**. While that term is popularly used for any piece of music, it strictly means a work for a solo singer with a single instrument accompanying. That seems like it should be the normal means of music making, the core in any age but, surprisingly, that's not the case. The last big flourishing of song was the Elizabethan lute song at the end of the Renaissance. The Baroque was so consumed with opera that standalone songs were rarely encountered; though Haydn and Mozart both wrote songs, neither considered them a particularly important part of their work. Art songs (so called to distinguish them from popular songs and folk songs, though the distinction is often quite blurry) were so numerous in German-speaking countries that they are often called *Lieder* (German for songs [the singular is *Lied*]).

Program Music

One of the most important new directions in the 19th century was **program music**. We encountered the idea of program music earlier in the music of Vivaldi, specifically his *Four Seasons*. This was a set of four violin concertos, each a musical depiction of images from sonnets describing the four seasons. The use of music to portray nonmusical ideas (or, better, extra-musical) is not new—obviously, some Baroque composers worked with the idea, and even in the Renaissance there were attempts. What is new for the Romantics is the wide fascination with program music.

Two things account for this interest. The era considered music to be the most Romantic of all the arts; in light of this, it was a natural route to take to explore music's ability to portray visual or literary images through sound—and through pure sound, instrumental music. The presence of text in vocal music already includes an extra-musical element. The Romantics were intrigued by the capacity of pure, instrumental sound to suggest images and ideas without any concrete limitation.

Another aspect that caused the Romantics to pursue the possibilities of program music was the overwhelming force of the music of Beethoven. Particularly in his Late period, Beethoven was writing music beyond the comprehension of many. Some simply assumed that his prolonged deafness had left him mad, unable to write comprehensible music because of that madness.

But the finest musical minds, though they may have been unable to comprehend fully his innovations, knew that he was writing music that was profound, sublime, and beyond the capacity of any to follow. The conviction was widespread that Beethoven had achieved perfection in **absolute music**—the opposite of program music, music that only existed as pure sound. And, as perfection cannot be improved, the future of music needed to be found in a new direction. That direction was program music.

Further Romantic Dualism: Revolutionary versus Reactionary

Not all Romantics were alike. Indeed, such a unified conformity would be antithetical to the movement. There were revolutionaries, to be sure (several banded together, proclaiming their work to be the Music of the Future), but there were also conservative voices whose work was grounded in tradition. We'll begin with two such figures who are most famous for their orchestral works, and we'll start with the revolutionary.

Early Romantic Orchestral Music

figure 8.1

The large Romantic orchestra. © JupiterImages, Inc.

Hector Berlioz (1803–1869)

Frenchman Hector Berlioz is a fascinating iconoclast. After an ill-advised attempt at medical school (where he had enrolled to please his parents—when he ran screaming from the room when asked to dissect a cadaver, it was evident that medicine was not in his future), Berlioz began study at the Paris Conservatory. His rebellious and innovative nature was evident even then, and he often antagonized his teachers and the administration.

He is almost unique for his era in that he never mastered an instrument. He played guitar and a bit of the flute, but was never a performer on either. His major skill was his mastery, his understanding, of the nature of *all* instruments. We call this *orchestration*; Berlioz knew how each instrument worked, how they could blend (or contrast) in ensembles, and how to mine their special capabilities. His striking abilities can be understood at least partially in that his creative imagination was not bound by a particular instrumental technique.

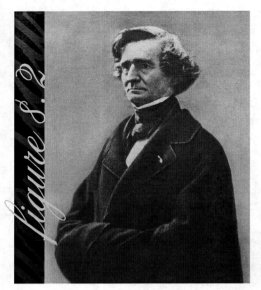

Hector Berlioz. © JupiterImages, Inc.

How does a musician make a living if he doesn't play an instrument? Berlioz pursued three directions: **composer**, **conductor**, and **critic**. His compositions are prized as among the finest of the era, and his music criticism—remember, this was the first era in which aesthetic argument about musical matters was seen as important—has also survived in some excellent translations. Unfortunately, we have no way to experience his conducting, though his autobiography, *The Memoirs of Hector Berlioz*, is fascinating, witty, and an excellent portrayal of Berlioz the artist and man.

Even though he was writing just after Beethoven, his music seems at least a full generation in the future. His works are characterized by:

- Bold, imaginative use of orchestral colors;
- Unusual harmonies and striking modulations;
- Irregular phrase structure; and
- Formal experimentation.

Most importantly, his instrumental music is almost entirely programmatic. He was fascinated with the use of pure instrumental sound to tell a story, to convey specific feelings and emotions. His love of literature was deep, and his appreciation for the greatest of authors and poets insightful. Some of literature's greatest figures—Shakespeare, Virgil, Lord Byron, Goethe—provided inspiration for his music.

As a lover of literature, he became one of the greatest writers. We have already mentioned his *Memoirs*; his music criticism has been collected in a delightful translation called *Evenings with the Orchestra*, written from the viewpoint of a professional orchestra. He also wrote one of the earliest, and still one of the finest, textbooks on orchestration: his *Treatise on Orchestration*.

Symphonie fantastique

Berlioz' most famous work is programmatic, but in this case, the program is not from literature but from his life. It reflects a combination of actual events and fantasy.

The facts: at the age of 28, Berlioz was already well-developed as a composer. He was also well-developed as a passionate eccentric. He saw a production of *Hamlet*, with an actress named Harriet Smithson. He was so taken by her performance that he fell madly, obsessively in love with her (without having actually met her). He deluged her with flowers and passionate letters. She initially dismissed him as a disturbed young man, with considerable justification. In real life, Berlioz and Smithson did finally meet, and were married (it was a disaster, as one might expect), but initially she rejected him, and he turned this rejection into this magnificent work of art.

The *Symphonie fantastique* is a **program symphony**, patterned after the same formal arrangement that Haydn, Mozart, and Beethoven had used, but with each movement organized around a story. Berlioz wrote the story himself:

Prologue:

A young musician with a vibrant character and an extraordinary imagination has fallen in love with a woman who seems to him the ideal of femininity. His despair has caused him to nearly poison himself with opium. In his sickened state, his beloved is transformed into a musical theme, a fixed idea (idée fixe), that is heard each time she comes to mind.

I. Reveries, passions

First, he is haunted by a feeling of melancholy, a desire for which the fulfillment has not yet been met. Then he sees his beloved for the first time, and as the idée fixe is played, his unfocused desires become a flow of passion . . . he feels the anger of jealousy, a return of tender forgiveness, and finally the strength of his faith.

II. A Ball

He finds himself at a ball, a noisy, festive party, with his beloved in attendance.

III. Scene in the Country

He is haunted by the fear that his beloved may be unfaithful and seeks to find some peace by spending a day in the country. The pastoral setting, with shepherds calling to their flocks and the gentle voice of the wind in the trees, cannot calm his soul. He hears a distant sound of thunder before silence overcomes all.

IV. March to the Scaffold

In his tormented confusion, he dreams that he killed his beloved in a fit of blind jealousy, has been convicted, and is led off to his execution. Heavy steps are interrupted by a brilliant march as he is led to the guillotine. His last thought is of his beloved, and the **idée fixe** *is heard once more before the axe, and his head, fall.*

V. Dream of a Witches' Sabbath

All is not over . . . after his execution, he awakens to find himself at a Witches' Sabbath, surrounded by demons, monsters, and other horrible creatures. He hears distant cries and responses to them. The **idée fixe** *is heard once more, but it has been changed . . . its noble, demure character has been lost, and it is now only a trivial dance tune, grotesque and mocking. It is* **she** *who comes to the Sabbath! A shout of joy greets her arrival, and she joins in the orgy. It is midnight, and the funeral bells sound, a parody of the* **Dies Irae** *. . . then the dance of the witches begins, joining later with the Dies Irae.*

Berlioz: *Symphonie fantastique: I, V*

The work is a fascinating achievement. It is a five-movement program symphony that follows the standard pattern of the sonata cycle, with the only exception that it has an extra scherzo, so there is one before and after the slow movement. It explores many of the Romantic ideas: sexual passion, the supernatural, and the expansion of the orchestra.

A technique was alluded to in the description of the *Dream of a Witches' Sabbath*, when the *idée fixe* became a "trivial dance tune, grotesque and mocking." The technique is called **thematic transformation**, by which a theme is altered in such a way that it is not only different, but performs a different function. In this case, the original pitches remain the same . . . and that's enough to recognize the theme. But the theme was first heard in the first violins, with a specific rhythm. When it recurs in the last movement, it is heard on a squeaky clarinet, and a bouncing, jerking rhythm. It symbolized the transformation of his beloved into a figure of horror.

A similar process is heard with the **Dies Irae**. This is an ancient plainchant melody, part of the Requiem Mass. It means "Day of Wrath," a horrific vision of the final judgment, and the melody has long been used to conjure images of death. Here, the notes of the first phrase are heard three ways: first in long, solemn notes in the low brass; then twice as fast, in the high brass; and finally *six* times faster in the woodwinds—actually in the same sort of sound into which the *idée fixe* had been distorted. And then the second and third phrases of the *Dies Irae* are given the same treatment. The result is quite horrifying.

Surprisingly, the *Symphonie fantastique* is an early composition, dating from around 1830—yet it uses sounds that Beethoven had never conceived.

Other Works by Berlioz

If you are intrigued by this work, you may want to explore others by Berlioz:

Romeo et Juliet is another program symphony, but far more innovative than the *Symphonie fantastique*. It uses two choruses and three vocal soloists; interestingly, it portrays the deepest, most romantic scenes only with the orchestra.

Harold en Italie is a cross between a program symphony and a viola concerto, based on the work by Lord Byron. It was written for Nicolo Paganini to play on his newly acquired Stradavarius viola, though he never performed it.

Of Berlioz' choral works, *L'Enfance du Christ* (*The Childhood of Christ*) is a gentle, beautiful oratorio. His *Requiem* is a wilder, more dramatic work, which uses two off-stage brass ensembles.

The opera *Les Troyens* (*The Trojans*) is perhaps his greatest achievement, a huge, gloriously beautiful setting in two parts of Virgil's *The Aeneid*, the story of the fall of Troy and the conquest of Carthage. It was never performed, in its entirety, during Berlioz' lifetime.

Felix Mendelssohn. © JupiterImages, Inc.

Felix Mendelssohn (1809–1847)

When Felix Mendelssohn was a boy, when other boys his age might be given toy soldiers, or girls given dolls, his parents bought him an orchestra. A real one.

"Hired" would be more accurate than "bought." This is not as self-indulgent as it may seem . . . Mendelssohn was a remarkable child prodigy, on the level of a Mozart (and he was composing better music earlier than Mozart). The orchestra was hired so he could practice his conducting in the rehearsal hall at the back of the estate, where the family regularly hosted concerts.

The Mendelssohn family was quite wealthy. Mendelssohn's grandfather was Moses Mendelssohn, a famous Jewish philosopher, generally recognized as the father of Zionism. His father was not particularly famous but was a successful banker, who used to comment that, "when I was growing up, I was the son of my father . . . now that I'm grown, I'm the father of my son."

Although the family was Jewish, Felix was raised as a Protestant—at that time, Germany had a variety of laws that prohibited Jews from engaging in certain professions and activities—but the conversion did not protect him from attacks from some notorious anti-Semites such as Richard Wagner. The family adopted the name Bartholdy, and Felix is still occasionally referred to as Mendelssohn-Bartholdy.

The Mendelssohn home was very happy and well-adjusted. He was very attached to his equally talented sister Fanny (later Fanny Mendelssohn Hensel), who was herself a gifted composer. Some of her works were published under Felix' name—not because he was trying to take credit, but because that was the only way a publisher would accept the work of a woman.

Fanny Mendelssohn Hensel, like Nannerl Mozart, was not only sister to a great musical prodigy, she was herself a great musical prodigy. Unlike Nannerl, however, she was given some opportunity to develop her gifts, though not much encouragement to pursue a career. Even her adoring brother Felix cautioned her against such ambitions, feeling that they were unrealistic . . . after all, had there ever been a woman composer (there had, though he didn't know of them)? It was Fanny's husband, the painter Wilhelm Hensel, who was sufficiently free thinking that he encouraged her compositional activities.

Apart from an oratorio, her entire output consists of songs, piano solos, and chamber music. For an excellent example of her abilities, listen to her *Piano Trio in d minor, Op. 11*. This work is as fine a composition as any for this combination of instruments, by composers of either sex. The only way to explain why it was neglected until fairly recently is the prejudice against women as creators of anything but children.

example

Fanny Mendelssohn Hensel: *Piano Trio in d minor, Op. 11*

I. Allegro molto vivace.

The family encouraged their children to achieve all that they could, and Mendelssohn became astonishingly skilled and versatile. He was not only a composer; he was a pianist and organist, a teacher, writer, and critic, a conductor, a painter, and a musicologist.

A musicologist is one who studies the history of music (you are currently in an introductory musicology course). Prior to the 19th century, no one was particularly concerned with the music of the past. Music was the product of servants, and its place was to entertain the aristocracy (or even the lower classes) or to enhance the liturgy of the Church. But after Mozart, after Beethoven, the power of music, the strength of genius, changed this role. People began to treat music as an art, something more significant than entertainment; they began to discover that there had been many great works of art from the past that had not been heard since they had fallen out of fashion.

Mendelssohn is credited with the rediscovery of Johann Sebastian Bach—specifically in the revival of one of Bach's greatest choral works, his *St. Matthew Passion*. The masterwork had been unperformed since its premiere in 1729. Mendelssohn restored and modernized the score and conducted a performance of the work almost exactly a century after it had last been heard. This event, as much as any, started the Bach revival, which continues to the present.

Mendelssohn is unusual among the Romantics—he was generally happy and well-adjusted, in an age populated by neurotics. Because his life was substantially without struggle (unless one counts overwork), his music tends to be the least successful when portraying emotions of turmoil and stress. It is happy music, graceful, elegant, and serene, and the closest of all the Romantics to the music and style of Mozart.

example

Mendelssohn: *A Midsummer Night's Dream: Overture*

A good example of Mendelssohn's music, and of his abilities as a prodigy, can be heard in this overture. It is part of a set of pieces knows as **incidental music**—music to accompany a stage play; in this case Shakespeare's *A Midsummer Night's Dream*. Such music (which you can think of as equivalent to a film score) was often used in plays; we've long known that music can intensify the dramatic experience. It may be used to set songs called for in the play, or to facilitate scene change, or to accompany some action that uses music, like a march.

Or, in the case of an overture, to introduce the play. The work opens with delicate chords, to evoke the enchanted forest where the action takes place. The rapid melody in the strings evokes the faeries that inhabit the forest, and a later theme evokes the Athenian lovers. Another represents the comic tradesmen; there is even the sound of a braying donkey, when Bottom the Weaver has had his head transformed into that of an ass. This is program music at its finest. It is also in sonata form. Mendelssohn's music, as was mentioned earlier, is closest in sound to the music of Mozart, and he never abandoned the forms he inherited from the Classical period composers.

Another thing to know when you listen to this: it was composed when Mendelssohn was he all of 17 years of age.

Other Works by Mendelssohn

Mendelssohn is best known now for his orchestral works. His greatest include:

- *Symphony no. 3 ("Scotch")*
- *Symphony no. 4 ("Italian")*
- *Symphony no. 5 ("Reformation")*
- *Violin Concerto in e minor, Op. 67*
- *Incidental Music to A Midsummer Night's Dream*
- *Hebrides Overture*

His chamber music is equally fine, including:

- *String Octet* (composed at the age of 16)
- *Piano Trio in d minor*

His piano music includes several pieces he called *Songs Without Words*: lyric, graceful, single-movement works with such lovely melodies that they seemed actually to be songs, but without a singer or text.

Early Romantic Piano Music

Since the mid-18th century, the piano had been the favorite solo instrument of Europe. Any household with enough money had a piano, and many in the middle and upper classes played with varying levels of skill. There was a considerable market for music for these amateurs, ranging from simple dance music to arrangements of the hit tunes from popular operas.

But this was also the golden age of the piano virtuoso—almost a symbol for the age. These were towering figures, striving alone against the challenges of making music on this huge, difficult, yet rewarding instrument. During most of the century, and in the previous one, concerts tended to be rather long and rather diverse. One might hear a movement from a symphony, followed by some chamber music, an aria or two, a piano sonata, a concerto, and then the rest of the symphony. They often ran several hours, but sustained interest by their variety. But these piano virtuosos did not want to share the attention, and began to perform

© Losevsky Pavel, 2010. Used under license from Shutterstock, Inc.

solo recitals—just the piano, just the pianist. That developed during the Romantic period and became so popular that today, anyone getting a degree in music performance must perform an entire recital (or more than one) on their own.

We'll consider the music of three composers here, each of which was a specialist in the piano to some degree: Robert Schumann, Frederic Chopin, and Franz Liszt.

Robert Schumann (1810–1856)

Robert and Clara Schumann. © JupiterImages, Inc.

Robert Schumann was the son of a bookseller. From an early age, he had a love for and sensitivity to great literature; not surprisingly, he became one of the century's greatest music critics and song writers.

He began his musical career as a highly gifted pianist, studying with one of the greatest teachers: Friederick Wieck. Wieck was a highly methodical, demanding teacher. He was impressed by Schumann's talent, but was disturbed by his lack of discipline and his resistance to the sort of technical training that's necessary for any musician.

That impatience led to the end of Schumann's potential as a performer. He tried to develop a device that would have been a short cut, a spring-loaded device attached to the fourth finger of his hand (the weakest and least independent). The device exerted extra pressure against the natural motion of the finger—rather like a runner who trains with weights on his ankles, so that when the weights are removed, he can run faster.

Unfortunately, the repeated use of this device over time caused nerve damage (or, according to some sources, the device malfunctioned and broke his finger). He could still play, but without the technical mastery needed for a performance career. He turned his attention to composing, and we are richer for that. He also turned his attention to his teacher's daughter.

Clara Weick was nine years old when Robert began studying with her father. He took no notice of her at that point, beyond her obvious talent (see text box). But as she matured into a young woman, the two bonded and fell in love.

Her father was alarmed; he thought that Robert was unstable, and at first forbade Clara to see him. All his efforts, legal and otherwise, failed to keep them apart, and when Clara reached the age of consent, they were married, and it was a happy union.

Clara Wieck Schumann

While Wieck found Schumann impossible to mold, that was not the case with his daughter. He was extraordinarily controlling, not only as her teacher but especially so as her father; until she was married, he wrote the entries in her diary. As a pianist, he saw her as a test of his pedagogical theories and controlled her practice to the finest detail.

Luckily, his pedagogical principles (as opposed to his parenting skills) were sound. Clara developed into one of the great pianists of her age. She also demonstrated considerable skill as a composer and left a legacy comparable to that of Fanny Mendelssohn. That she didn't compose more is due in part to the prejudices of the age—she was never free of self-doubts—but perhaps more from her priorities. She was more interested in performing, and in particular championing the works of her husband, than composing. At one point, she described herself as a pianist first, a mother second (she and Robert had seven children), and a composer third.

Like Fanny Mendelssohn Hensel, she composed a single piano trio, the **Piano Trio in d minor**, that remains her most popular instrumental work, along with several songs. There is also a remarkable piano concerto, which was later orchestrated by her husband. That she sought his assistance is understandable, as she composed the work when she was 13 years old.

Clara Wieck Schumann: *Piano Concerto in a—III*

Eventually, Schumann patched things up with his father-in-law, and together they founded the *Neue Leipziger Zeitschrift fur Musik* (*The New Leipzig Journal for Music*—a publication that still exists, though they have dropped the "New" from the title). This became one of the most influential journals of music criticism of its day, and Schumann was its chief writer.

Schumann's writing style was a fascinating one, consisting of conversations among various alter egos: Florestan, the extrovert; Eusebius, the dreamer; and Meister Raro, the mediator. Some have taken this to be evidence of his later decline into mental illness, though this ignores the fact that this writing style—argument by imaginary dialogue—had been common since Plato, and was at this time, though it is more rare today.

As a critic, Schumann had an extraordinary ability to detect genius at first sight—he introduced Chopin to the musical world with the famous quote, "Hats off, gentlemen—a genius." Later he introduced Johannes Brahms to the world in equally prophetic, and accurate, language.

Schumann did, however, suffer from mental illness. From 1850–1853, when he was music director for the city of Dusseldorf, he began displaying increasing signs of mental instability. After an unsuccessful suicide attempt in 1854, when he tried to drown himself by diving into the Rhine river, he was confined to an asylum for the rest of his days, with only a few lucid intervals. His only visitor during that time was Johannes Brahms. Clara was not allowed in. Asylums of that day were just barely this side of dungeons and were considered inappropriate for women.

Schumann's Music

Schumann's style has strong elements of classicism, but his most typical quality is a mercurial shifting of mood and thematic material, seemingly with little thought as to transition and overall structure. Consequently, he is least successful in his large-scale works based on the sonata cycle and most successful in works that consist of strings of miniatures. These works are bound together by their own internal logic; while hardly obvious or conventional, there is a definite sense of structure and form, though not according to classical formal principles.

He also tended to compose in a single genre for great lengths of time. His first 30 opus numbers are almost entirely for piano. After that, a year and more of nothing but songs (not coincidentally, just after he and Clara were married). Then he turned to chamber music, then orchestral works. This last group is somewhat less highly regarded. They tend to suffer from muddy orchestration—though the right conductor can bring the works off successfully.

He was not, then, a piano specialist, though he began as one, and it is in that context we will hear his music.

Papillons is Schumann's Op. 2, his second published work, written at about the age of 20. In it he establishes a pattern that he will follow in many of his piano works. He essentially ignores standard formal organization, and instead takes inspiration from an extra-musical source, and that is what dictates the form.

The source is a novel by Jean Paul (1763–1825), *Flegeljahre (The Awkward Age)*. In one of the scenes, set at a ball, two brothers are competing for the attention of a girl. One of the brothers is an extrovert, a forceful personality, while the other is more of a dreamer—of course, an exact parallel of Florestan and Eusebius, Schumann's two alter egos. The party swirls into the night, finally breaking up as the clock tolls 6 and dawn is near. The twelve dances, mostly waltzes, each originally bore titles that corresponded to events in the novel, though Schumann removed them from the final publication. He did, however retain the initials F and E, concluding each section, depending on whether the personality of Florestan or Eusebius was dominant. See if you can tell which one in each of the parts.

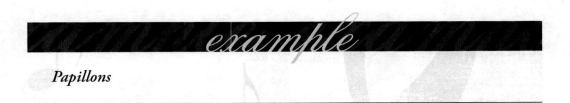

example

Papillons

Other Works by Schumann

If you enjoyed *Kinderszenen*, you may like some of Schumann's more virtuosic piano pieces, including:

- *Papillons*
- *Carnaval*
- *Fantasy in C*

Schumann was one of the great *Lieder* composers. You may enjoy his song cycles (to be discussed under Schubert):

- *Dichterliebe*
- *Frauenliebe und Leben*

His finest orchestral works are his:

- *Piano Concerto in a*
- *Symphony no. 3 in Eb, "Rhenish"*

Franz (Ferenc) Liszt (1811–1886)

. . . It was in Berlin that "Lisztomania" swept in. The word was coined by Heine {not Ken Russell—if any of you are perverse enough to be Russell fans}. The symptoms, which are odious to the modern reader, bear every resemblance to an infectious disease, and merely to call them mass hysteria hardly does justice to what took place. His portrait was worn on brooches and cameos. Swooning lady admirers attempted to take cuttings of his hair, and they surged forward whenever he broke a string in order to make it into a bracelet. Some of these insane female "fans" even carried glass phials about their persons into which they poured his coffee dregs. Others collected his cigar butts, which they hid in their cleavages. The overtones were clearly sexual. Psychologists may have a wonderful time explaining such phenomena, but they cannot change the facts: Liszt had taken Berlin by storm, and for a pianist this was unprecedented. Liszt remained in Berlin for ten weeks. His feat of playing eighty works in twenty-one concerts has been noted. In no other city did he make so many appearances in so brief a time. (Walker)

The hysteria that met Liszt the performer, while not unwelcome at the time, has been quite detrimental to his long-term reputation. Too often he is thought of as a composer of flamboyant yet ultimately vacuous piano works designed simply to show off his technique and to mesmerize the female members of his audience, with whom he would then copulate freely.

This reputation needs to be reexamined because in the light of fact, such images dissolve. He was born 30 miles from Vienna, to an Austrian mother and a Hungarian father (though he proudly touted his Hungarian ancestry, he never learned to speak the language), who was in employ of the Esterhazy family, Haydn's employers. He studied with Salieri and Czerny, and traveled to Paris to study at the conservatory.

He was denied entry into that institution; in fairness to the admissions officer who made that decision, at that time Paris was a mecca of piano study, and the demand for admission was tremendously intense. The Conservatoire made a decision to limit admission to French nationals.

Liszt was inspired by Paganini's example of transcendent virtuosity and determined to develop the most astonishing technique on the piano that the world knew. In Paris, it seemed that there were more virtuoso pianists than prostitutes, and each had his or her special tricks (the pianists, not the prostitutes), Liszt outshone them all, with a few special tricks of his own.

Liszt's early career became associated with the concept of spectacular, but empty, virtuosity. His recitals were indeed spectacles. Indeed, he is credited with being the first to give solo recitals—usually with two pianos on stage in case he broke a string. This emphasis on spectacle has led to the unfortunate notion that his music tends to be flamboyant but empty. Even conceding this as partially true of some works, one must ask oneself how any young man in his early 20s would react to the sort of public adulation that Heinrich Heine (*not* Ken Russell) dubbed Lisztomania.

Such an impression also ignores the fact that Liszt retired at the age of 37 and lived another 38 years, never playing again for his own benefit (though he would occasionally for the benefit of others). It ignores the fact that he later dedicated himself to the Church, that his teaching was done for free, based only on the talent and dedication of his students, and it ignores the long history of generosity and civility from Liszt to others.

Franz Liszt. © JupiterImages, Inc.

Even his reputation as what the modern press would call a "womanizer" seems suspect. Liszt in reality was attracted to women for their intellectual qualities, not their raw physical charms; note that in an age during which composers were constantly dropping like flies, mostly because of complications from venereal disease, Liszt lived a long, healthy 75 years. He was either very lucky, very careful, or perhaps the reputation is not wholly deserved.

Most importantly, the assumption that Liszt was all empty virtuosity ignores the fact that his greatest works have an undeniable depth, beauty, and substance—some are still blazingly virtuosic, but with the goal of using that virtuosity towards the goal of great music.

One such work—or, more precisely, set of works—is his twelve *Transcendental Etudes*. All music students know etudes. The word means exercise, or study, and all students play pieces that are designed to build technique and expressiveness. What to make, then, of these works, which are more demanding than any student could hope to play?

The key word here is *transcendental*. These are works for the virtuoso, for the musician who has transcended all difficulties, mastered all challenges, of the piano. They run the gamut of expression and challenges.

Even the idea of the concert etude—an etude with sufficient musical quality that it was intended for public, professional performance—was new. Liszt was the first to develop this (the honor is usually given to Frederic Chopin, but there are three versions of these etudes, from 1826, 1838, and 1852; the earliest predates those of Chopin). All but two of these compositions are programmatic. At least, as presented in the 1852 version, which was the only one of the three to add descriptive titles. We will hear no. 11, *Harmonies du soir* (*Harmonies of the night*), a work that combines infinite tenderness with overwhelming grandeur.

example

Liszt: *Transcendental Etude no. 11, Harmonies du soir*

Liszt, like Schumann, did not restrict himself to piano compositions. Among his innovations was the **symphonic poem**, a one-movement programmatic orchestral work. The concept is a simple one; it's rather amazing that none developed the idea before Liszt. Nearly all orchestral composers after Liszt used the form.

Other Works by Liszt

Liszt's greatest piano works include his:

- *Sonata in b minor*
- Transcendental etudes
- Nineteen Hungarian rhapsodies
- *Annees de Pelerinage* (*Years of Pilgrimage*)
- *Harmonies poetique et religieuse*
- *Mephisto Waltz*

His orchestral works include:

- *Faust Symphony*
- *Les Preludes* (symphonic poem)
- Two piano concertos

During his final years as a lay priest, Liszt turned to sacred choral works. His oratorio *Christus* is relatively unknown, but incredibly beautiful.

Frederic Chopin. © JupiterImages, Inc.

Frederic (Fryderyk) Chopin (1810–1849)

Chopin was born in Poland. His father was French and had fled to Poland to avoid military conscription; his mother was a Polish aristocrat. Chopin left Poland in 1831 and moved to Paris. At that time, his unique style was fully developed; unlike Beethoven—indeed, unlike nearly all composers—there is no detectable stylistic difference between works of 1831 and those of 1849. It is not that he failed to grow, but that his genius revealed itself early and fully.

Chopin became a product of Paris society: he played mostly in private salons before invited guests, as was then fashionable. He performed only a few major public concerts in his lifetime—and he was terrified before each performance.

However, those private gatherings were different. Chopin was comfortable in the setting, and those were remarkable. Paris was the major cultural center of Europe at that time, and at any given evening, the greatest creative minds may be present: musicians like Liszt, Berlioz, and Rossini; painters like Delacroix; authors like Dumas or Hugo.

It was at one of those gatherings that Liszt (Chopin's friend, despite their utterly different temperaments) introduced him to Aurora Dudevant. She was a writer, who used the *nom de plume* Georges Sand. It was not unusual at the time for a woman writer to adopt a masculine pen name in order more readily to get her works into print. It *was* somewhat unusual for the same woman to cut her hair short, dress as a man, and smoke large, smelly cigars, as Sand did. She was the temperamental opposite to Chopin, who was as effeminate as Sand was masculine. Chopin was small (never weighed more than 100 pounds in his life), both sickly and hypochondriacal, and tended to dress with meticulous attention to recent fashion—a bit dandified, actually.

At first meeting, Chopin and Sand repelled each other. They were naturally destined to become lovers; for nearly the rest of Chopin's life, she was a combination of lover, best friend, mother figure, and muse. They separated two years before Chopin's death over family disagreements revolving around Sand's two children. Chopin later died of tuberculosis, under the care of his sister.

Chopin's Music

Chopin and the piano are inseparable. Unlike Schumann and Liszt, Chopin never wrote anything that did not include piano. There are songs for voice and piano, concertos for piano and orchestra, and chamber music for piano. And there are lots of solo works for piano. These include:

- Stylized dances, like mazurkas and polonaises from his native Poland, and the popular waltzes;
- Works based on the sonata cycle; and
- Single-movement solo piano compositions, with titles like *nocturne*, *ballade*, *scherzo*, and *impromptu*. Some of these originated with Chopin and never came to have a universal meaning. Other composers, for instance, wrote *ballades*, but they bore little resemblance to Chopin's; the titles are evocative rather than specific.

Chopin believed that the voice was the most beautiful musical instrument, and his music tries to emulate that. He emphasized a singing, legato line (all the sounds connected), and his works have a distinct use of rubato. And all of his music was **absolute music**.

The last characteristic is especially interesting. He had no interest in program music. Chopin, that most romantic of Romanticists, disliked Romanticism. He thought the music of Berlioz and Liszt was vulgar, he did not understand the music of Beethoven, and he disliked the work of romantic writers and painters. He acknowledged only three influences: Bellini (an opera composer we'll discuss below), Mozart, and Bach. He rejected the idea that the future of music lay in its interrelationship with the other arts. The performer of Chopin, therefore, must understand the underlying classical foundation of this music to create a musically successful performance.

example

Chopin: *Twenty-four Preludes, Op. 28*

Some pianists present excerpts from the set; it would not be surprising if any of you who had piano lessons had played one or two of them. As a set of miniatures, they can be quite delightful. But taken as a unit, they form one of the most remarkable **single compositions** for piano of the entire Romantic Era—and Chopin did conceive them as a single work. The cycle contains one prelude in each of the 24 keys, an idea he may have borrowed from his idol J. S. Bach, who had written two sets of preludes and fugues in every key. Indeed, he may have even borrowed the name of the pieces from Bach . . . though it hardly seems appropriate, as these preludes are not a prelude to anything but the next prelude. The set creates a series of contrasting moods and techniques that adds up to quite more than the sum of its parts.

- No. 1 in C, *Agitato*: like an improvised toccata, similar to the openings to the Liszt *Transcendental Etudes*
- No. 2 in a minor, *Lento*: strange, asymmetrical, even grotesque, with a sense of depression rather than the brightness of no. 1
- No. 3 in G, *Vivace*: bright and graceful, the antithesis of no. 2
- No. 4 in e minor, *Largo*: overplayed by students, but exquisitely poetic nonetheless
- No. 5 in D, *Allegro molto*: a happy arabesque of arpeggios
- No. 6 in b minor, *Lento assai*: also overplayed, yet "It precipitates the soul into a frightful depression" (Georges Sand); the feeling is intense yet restrained
- No. 7 in A, *Andantino*: perhaps the simplest of the preludes, mazurka-like; yet among the most difficult to bring off interpretively
- No. 8 in f-sharp minor, *Molto agitato*: anxious, agitated, yet without reaching a real frenzy
- No. 9 in E, *Largo*: echoes of Beethoven, prefiguring of Brahms, in the cross rhythms and dark coloration
- No. 10 in c-sharp minor, *Allegro molto*: "Ruins and eagle feathers" (Robert Schumann); a brief flash of darkness and color, only a fleeting impression
- No. 11 in B, *Vivace*: equally brief, but conversely sunny
- No. 12 in g-sharp minor, *Presto*: more emotional upheaval; a technically difficult piece, with rising chromatic lines and harsh chords
- No. 13 in F-sharp, *Lento*: mood of the nocturnes, restful and serene
- No. 14 in e-flat minor, *Allegro*: parallel octaves, with an alien turmoil
- No. 15 in D-flat, *Sostenuto*: the only prelude with a contrasting theme, in c#; called "Raindrop" because of the repeating dominant pedal throughout; ". . . the shades of dead monks seem to rise and pass the hearer in solemn and gloomy funereal pomp" (Sand)
- No. 16 in b-flat minor, *Presto con fuoco*: glittering scales against a broken accompaniment
- No. 17 in A-flat, *Allegretto*: tranquil, suave, sweet
- No. 18 in f minor, *Allegro molto*: fiery recitatives, muscular and dramatic
- No. 19 in E-flat, *Vivace*: murmuring grace, widely-spread harmonies, displaced rhythms
- No. 20 in c minor, *Largo*: remarkable work, simply a chord progression with the character of a funeral march; "contains more music than all the trumpetings of Meyerbeer" (Sand)
- No. 21 in B-flat, *Cantabile*: nocturne-like, with an ecstatic melody, chromatic accompaniment
- No. 22 in g minor, *Molto agitato*: bold dissonance, like no. 18 but with more rhythmic drive
- No. 23 in F, *Moderato*: delicate, half dance, half etude
- No. 24 in d minor, *Allegro appassionato*: the most tragic, dramatic, and virtuosic of the preludes, proud and scornful, ending with hammered single bass notes. Romanticism is not pretty!

Other Works by Chopin

If you enjoyed the preludes, you will like his other solo works:

- Waltzes
- Mazurkas
- Polonaises
- Impromptus
- Ballades
- Scherzos

You may also enjoy his larger works:

- Piano Concertos no. 1 in e minor, no. 2 in f minor
- Piano Sonatas no. 2 in bb minor, no. 3 in b minor

Early Romantic Vocal Music

Franz Peter Schubert (1797–1828) and the *Lied*

Franz Schubert. © JupiterImages, Inc.

Schubert, with Mozart and Mendelssohn, was one of history's great prodigies. His early musical training was largely instinctual—teachers (including Salieri) felt they could teach him nothing, that he absorbed music on his own with little help or direction needed from them.

He was trained as a school teacher, as his father had been, but while teaching (in Vienna it was a branch of government service, complete with uniforms) was a stable profession, it afforded him the same degree of pleasure as, say, sticking sharp objects into his eyes. Schubert knew that creating music was his reason for being. He once said that, "I have come into this world for no other purpose than to compose," and felt the state should support him. The state declined. He was supported by giving lessons, sales of his music (often sold for a fraction of its worth), and often by the generosity of a circle of friends in Vienna.

This circle of artists and intellectuals would frequently meet for "Schubertiads," evenings at local coffee houses or homes, devoted to listening to the latest that little Franz (nicknamed "Schwamerl"—Little Mushroom—by his friends) had composed in chamber music, piano music, and songs.

There was always something new to listen to at these Schubertiads: in his brief 31 years, Schubert was amazingly prolific. His output includes 10 symphonies (3 in varying stages of completion), 22 piano sonatas and numerous shorter works for piano, 35 chamber works, 6 masses, and 17 operas. Schubert longed to be an opera composer, to no avail. All were dismal failures. Schubert seems to have had the bad luck to try to set to music libretti so appallingly awful that no amount of high quality music could save them. He is most noted, however for having written over 600 *Lieder* (German for "songs").

His most important musical characteristic is melodic invention: a convenient skill for a *Lieder* composer. Schubert's skill as a melodist is so profound that, in his instrumental music, he often leaves the superficial analyst feeling that he is weak on the process of development. A quick examination of most of his mature works will easily set that to rest, but the impression comes from the fact that when another composer, such as a Beethoven, would develop existing material, Schubert simply will write another melody.

Schubert had only one major public performance of his works in his lifetime. He died at 31 of typhoid fever and was buried at his request next to Beethoven. His epitaph reads "Music has here buried a rich treasure, but still fairer hopes."

Schubert and the Art Song

The Romantic period coincided with the golden age of German poetry, and musicians responded to that by making it the golden age of the **Art Song**. The term is used to distinguish an Art Song—a setting of a poem sung by a single singer with instrumental accompaniment, usually a piano—from a Folk Song. These are usually associated with a particular ethnic or national heritage; the original composers of Folk Songs have been lost to history.

The term is also used to distinguish Art Songs from Popular Songs, and here the distinction can be muddy, if not essentially artificial. There are certainly pop songs that have become classic, have outlived the audience for which they were written and continue to be heard long after that generation has passed. And there are more than a few Art Songs that are of little or no interest to an audience, regardless of how distinguished the composer was.

Schubert composed over 600 Art Songs, usually known by their German name, *Lieder*. Among the 600, there are a few that are less than stellar, but very few. Schubert was one of

A *Lieder* performance in someone's living room. © JupiterImages, Inc.

the most consistently fine song writers of all history, and the first since Dowland to see the importance of this sort of music.

Schubert's predecessors, Haydn, Mozart, and Beethoven (all, with Schubert, collectively known as the First Viennese School), wrote *Lieder*, but none gave the form much importance. And none demonstrated the kind of sensitivity to every nuance of text that Schubert does. None, also, gave the piano such attention. Prior to Schubert, most songs in any language used the piano for simple harmonic support, but Schubert makes the piano another character, an equal contributor to the artistic goal.

The Song Cycle: *Die schöne Müllerin*

Among his *Lieder*, Schubert left two authentic **song cycles** (a third work, a set published by his brother after his death, is not a real cycle). A song cycle is a set of songs, intended to be performed in order, that is unified musically and/or textually. Schubert's two cycles, *Die schöne Müllerin* (*The Lovely Maid of the Mill*) and *Die Winterreise* (*The Winter's Journey*) are both narrative (they tell a story). Both have text by the same poet: Wilhelm Müller. Both seem to be about the same person, though the protagonist is not named in either.

Die schöne Müllerin is the story of a young man. A miller by trade, he is currently, as they say, in between jobs. He starts out walking in the woods, a pastime he enjoys like most of his fellow Austrians.

example

Schubert, *Die schöne Müllerin: Das Wandern (Hiking)*

Hiking is the miller's joy, hiking!
He must be a miserable miller,
Who never likes to hike

We've learned this from the water,
It does not rest by day or night,
It's always thinking of its journey,

We see this also with the wheels,
They don't like to stand still,
And go all day without tiring.

The stones themselves, heavy though they are,
They join in the cheerful dance,
And want to go yet faster.

Oh, hiking, hiking, my joy,
Oh, Master and Mistress,
Let me continue in peace, and hike!

Here, the jaunty sounds of the piano perfectly describe his joy in a brisk walk. He even suspects he might find a stream in the woods; and, as streams are used to power the wheels of any mill, he may find a job opportunity on his excursion.

In fact, he finds just that: a brook flowing briskly through the woods. We can tell the young man is a bit unstable, because he immediately starts to talk to the brook. This is a conversation he will keep up for the rest of the cycle.

figure 8.10

A traditional German mill. © JupiterImages, Inc.

example

Schubert, *Die schöne Müllerin: Wohin? (Where to?)*

I hear a brooklet rushing
Right out of the rock's spring,
Down there to the valley it rushes,
So fresh and wondrously bright.

I know not, how I felt this,
Nor did I know who gave me advice;
I must go down
With my wanderer's staff.

Down and always farther,
And always the brook follows after;
And always rushing crisply,
And always bright is the brook.

Is this then my road?
O, brooklet, speak! Where to?
You have with your rushing
Entirely intoxicated my senses.

But why do I speak of rushing?
That can't really be rushing:
Perhaps the water-nymphs
Are singing rounds down there in the deep.

Let it sing, my friend, let it rush,
And wander joyously after!
Mill-wheels turn
In each clear brook.

From http://www.gopera.com/lieder/translations/schubert.html. Translation by Celia Sgroi. Reprinted by permission of Celia Sgroi.

He asks the brook where he should go and chooses to follow it on its path. The gentle piano arpeggios are a perfect imitation of the flowing waters. And, sure enough, the brook does get rather larger, and a few kilometers down, is the source of power for a mill. The young man asks the brook if he should enquire about a job at the mill, but before the brook can answer, he sees the owner's daughter. She is the loveliest lass he's ever seen, and he decides it would be an excellent idea to get work here.

He tries to impress the girl with the quality of his work, but isn't strong enough. He lays flowers at her door, but she doesn't know who sent them. Finally, he gets her to agree to go out with him.

Now, a hot date in those parts consists of sitting out by the brook and looking at reflections in the water. The lady is decidedly underwhelmed, and at one point, looks up at the cloudless sky, remarks that it's about to rain, and she should get inside.

The young man fails to get the hint . . . he's ecstatic, and he's just had a date with the girl of his dreams. His next song is full of triumph and joy!

example

Schubert, *Die schöne Müllerin: Mein! (Mine!)*

Little brook, let your gushing be!
Wheels, cease your roaring!
All you merry woodbirds,
Large and small,
End your melodies!
Through the grove,
Out and in,
Let only one song be heard today:
The beloved millermaid is mine!

Spring, are all of those your flowers?
Sun, have you no brighter shine?
Ah, so I must be all alone
With my blissful word,
Incomprehensible to all of Creation!

From http://www.gopera.com/lieder/translations/schubert.html. Translation by Celia Sgroi. Reprinted by permission of Celia Sgroi.

If this were the end, all would end happily. It is, however, only the halfway point. Sure enough, trouble: a hunter emerges from the woods. He is not only more manly than the youth, he is wearing the girl's favorite color: green. She runs off with him, leaving him to mourn and accuse for the remainder of the cycle. As he nears acceptance, he contemplates the flowers she gave him, now wilted and dead, and predicts that they will grow again in spring . . . coming from his grave, when she recalls his true love for her.

example

Schubert, *Die schöne Müllerin: Trockne Blumen (Dried Flowers)*

All you little flowers, that she gave me,
You shall lie with me in my grave.

Why do you all look at me so sadly,
As if you had known what would happen to me?

You little flowers all, how wilted, how pale!
You little flowers all, why so moist?

Ah, tears will not make the green of May,
Will not make dead love bloom again.

And Spring will come, and Winter will go,
And flowers will grow in the grass.

And flowers will lie in my grave,
All the flowers that she gave me.

And when she wanders past the hill
And thinks in her heart: His feelings were true!

Then, all you little flowers, come out, come out,
May has come, Winter is over.

From http://www.gopera.com/lieder/translations/schubert.html. Translation by Celia Sgroi. Reprinted by permission of Celia Sgroi.

The young man has been somewhat unstable from the beginning, but all this causes him finally to snap. In the penultimate song, "The Miller and the Brook," the brook starts to talk back. In the final song, the Miller is silent and the brook sings. The song is "The Brook's Lullaby"; it seems the young man has committed suicide in his despair, drowning himself in the brook. The brook softly sings to him, promising to rush over him to block the painful sounds of life, like hunting horns, to keep him safe until that time when all shall wake.

example

Schubert, *Die schöne Müllerin: Des Baches Wiegenlied (The Brook's Lullaby)*

Good rest, good rest, close your eyes!
Wanderer, tired one, you are home.
Fidelity is here, you shall lie by me,
Until the sea drinks the brooklet dry.

I will bed you cool on a soft pillow,
In the blue crystal room,
Come, come, whatever can lull,
Rock and lap my boy to sleep!

When a hunting-horn sounds from the green forest,
I will roar and rush around you.
Don't look in, blue flowerets!
You make my sleeper's dreams so troubled!

Away, away from the mill-path,
Hateful girl, that your shadow might not wake him.
Throw in to me your fine handkerchief,
That I may cover his eyes with it!

Good night, good night, until all awake,
Sleep out your joy, sleep out your pain!
The full moon climbs, the mist fades away,
And the heavens above, how wide they are!

From http://www.gopera.com/lieder/translations/schubert.html. Translation by Celia Sgroi. Reprinted by permission of Celia Sgroi.

This description may sound a bit flippant; this poetry is somewhat overly sentimental for modern tastes. But be assured, Schubert took the poetry seriously, and he lavished the story of this tragic young man and his watery friend with some of the loveliest, most affecting music ever written.

Song recitals are a special art form. They will never be as popular as opera or orchestra concerts, in much the way the poetry readings are not as popular as plays. In the latter experiences, there is some level of spectacle; details of what is being sung are provided with the settings, costumes, and acting. In a song recital, you have to provide these in your own imagination.

Song recitals, to appreciate properly, need concentration. You will normally be given a copy of the translations of the texts; to understand and enjoy what is being sung, to appreciate the nuances of composition and interpretation, you must follow that text and listen actively.

Too many people are unwilling to put out that sort of effort. We are used to our entertainment being brought to us on some sort of televised screen while we sit, motionless and uninvolved. But for those willing to put out the effort, the rewards are considerable, particularly if the songs are by Franz Schubert.

Other Works by Schubert

Schubert's works were not kept in any careful order in his short life, and only a few were published, so the use of the *Opus* designation is of little use. His works were cataloged by musicologist Otto Erich Deutsch, so you will sometimes see a D. followed by a number, to indicate the order of the works (like Köchel's Mozart catalog, Deutsch arranged the works in chronological order rather than by genre). If you enjoyed *Die schöne Müllerin*, you may like:

- *Die Winterreise*, the sequel to *Die schöne Müllerin*
- Any of the remaining songs, which are too numerous to mention only a few

Of his instrumental works, you might explore:

- *Symphony no. 8 in b minor, "Unfinished"*
- *Symphony no. 9 in C, "Great"*
- *Quintet in A, "The Trout"* (this is not a piece for five fish, but for piano, violin, viola, 'cello, and double bass, the fourth movement of which is based on Schubert's song, *Die Forelle* {*The Trout*})
- Impromptus (these are for solo piano, in two sets of four each, Op. 90 and Op. 142)
- *Wanderer Fantasie* for piano

The Vienna Opera House. © Lazar Mihai-Bogdan, 2010. Used under license from Shutterstock, Inc.

Early Romantic Opera

Opera remained wildly popular in 19th-century Europe. Indeed, this was the pop music of its day and, like modern pop music, many works were performed, were popular, and then were forgotten. Only the greatest have survived.

By this point, operatic traditions were not only well-developed in Italy but also in France and in the German-speaking countries; each had its particular character.

Carl Maria von Weber. © JupiterImages, Inc.

Germany: Carl Maria von Weber (1786–1826)

After Mozart's *Magic Flute* and Beethoven's sole operas *Fidelio*, one person dominates German opera: Carl Maria von Weber.

Weber (who was the cousin of Mozart's wife) is an underappreciated composer. His works are not limited to opera, and his symphonies, concertos, chamber music, and piano works deserve to be performed more often. Several of his operas are still in the repertory, and his masterpiece *Der Freischütz* (literally, the Free Shooter, which in German conveys the idea of an enchanted marksman) is often thought of as the first romantic opera. That work, like most German romantic operas, uses spoken dialog instead of recitative, but this is no *singspiel*. In fact, it (and Beethoven's *Fidelio*) has almost no comic elements.

The story revolves around a rural community. The most beautiful girl in the village, Agathe, is being given in marriage to the winner of a shooting contest (as rational a means of picking a spouse as many others). The leading contender is Max, the greatest sharpshooter in those parts. Unfortunately, Max (who is Agathe's choice anyway) is experiencing something like shooter's block. He can't seem to hit his target. Led on by one of the darker members of the community, he makes a deal with The Dark Hunter. The Dark Hunter is Samiel, the Devil, and Max sells him his soul for seven enchanted bullets. Six bullets are charmed and would behave rather like a cruise missile, going precisely where they were aimed; the seventh belonged to Samiel, and would (unbeknownst to Max) ultimately be lodged in the heart of his bride. The *Wolf's Glen*, in which the transaction is made, scene is a real masterpiece of weird scenic and sonic effects.

As would be expected at the time, the Devil is foiled; the bullet goes into the man who brokered the deal, and Max is redeemed by the pure love of his lady. The overture is itself a masterpiece, a full sonata-form movement with a slow introduction.

example

Weber, *Der Freischütz: Overture*

France: Grande Opera and Giacomo Meyerbeer (1791–1864)

France in the 19th century was absolutely mad about *Grande Opera*. The form was directed toward the newly affluent French bourgeoisie, emphasizing grandness and spectacle: large casts, chorus, dance, and massive state effects. Though many such works were composed, the most popular was the result of a three-way partnership between **Louis Veron**, director of the Paris Opera, **Eugene Scribe**, librettist, and **Giacomo Meyerbeer**, composer.

Dance was especially important. The public demanded dance, whether it was relevant or not. And it had to be in the second of three acts, so the public could enjoy a leisurely dinner, arrive late, enjoy the second act dance, and depart early. Berlioz' *Les Troyens* was not a success in France because he insisted on presenting the dance in the first act where it was dramatically relevant.

figure 8.13

The Paris Grande Opera. © Anton Hlushchenko, 2010. Used under license from Shutterstock, Inc.

The works are rarely given today, in part because of economic factors. It costs a small fortune to assemble all the required artists, workers, and stage paraphernalia. But another factor is that the works are often more involved in their spectacle than in their dramatic coherence. Most successful examples are not to be found in Meyerbeer (though his works *Le Prophete*, *Robert le Diable*, and *L'Africaine* are still occasionally performed), but by such figures as Berlioz (*Les Troyens*), Rossini (*Guillaume Tell*), or Verdi (*Don Carlos*); those masterpieces are all successful settings that merge grandeur with deep emotional involvement.

Italy: Bel Canto

Gioacchino Rossini, **Gaetano Donizetti**, and **Vincenzo Bellini** are *not* the owners of Three Guys Pizzeria in Brooklyn; they are the three composers most closely associated with the style of *bel canto*.

Bel canto means beautiful song or beautiful singing in Italian. One would think that would apply to all opera, but it is used for a specific style. While some have seen the tradition as originating with Handel and passing through Mozart to the three composers discussed here, most consider it as an Early Romantic style. It is characterized by:

- Light, agile voices;
- Vocal virtuosity used as a metaphor for emotional intensity;
- Farcical comedies in the style of Mozart;
- Dramatic works throwbacks to *Opera seria* (Rossini) or with a dramatic intensity prefiguring Verdi (Donizetti, and to a lesser degree, Bellini);
- A pairing of *cavatina/cabaletta* aria form; and
- Weak or incomprehensible libretti.

The *cavatina/cabaletta* aria form is something that began in the works of Mozart. The *cavatina* is a slow, lyric aria; the *cabaletta* is faster and more distinctly rhythmic. Each section was preceded by an orchestrally accompanied *recitative*, and there were often other minor characters or choruses included. It was, in effect, an independent scene, the structure of which made it possible to cover a great deal of emotional and dramatic ground. It was common, particularly in the *cavatina*, to introduce the melody with a woodwind instrument playing a solo: the woodwinds were perfectly suited to the light, agile character of *bel canto* singing.

Interestingly, *bel canto* opera was supplanted by the heavier, more dramatic (and, frankly, louder) styles that followed, and singers lost the special technical abilities needed to perform it. Much of the music was ignored until the 1950s, when singers like Maria Callas and Joan Sutherland returned to the style and mastered the formerly lost techniques.

Gioacchino Rossini (1792–1868)

Rossini was the most popular of the three. He wrote over 40 operas, and his fame was so great that if you asked most of Europe who was the greatest living composer, the answer would more frequently be Rossini than Beethoven. He is best remembered now for his comedies, such as *Il Barbiere di Siviglia* (*The Barber of Seville*), *La Cenorentola* (*Cinderella*), and *L'Italiana in Algeri* (*The Italian Girl in Algiers*). In his time, his serious operas were greatly celebrated, such as *Semiramide*, *Tancredi*, and *Otello*. His trademark quality was building tremendous intensity through the use of an orchestral crescendo (he was known in the trade as *Il Signor Crescendo*, Mr. Crescendo). His opera overtures are frequently performed in concert, separately from his operas, and they are very effective.

His operas were so successful that by the age of 37, he found he had more money than he could spend for the rest of his life, and so he retired. He decided to compose one last opera, and to make it to please himself rather than to please his audience. The result was *Guil-*

laume Tell (William Tell), one of the greatest and most moving *grande operas* about the 13th-century Swiss revolutionary.

He then moved permanently to Paris and spent the rest of his days with his mistress, the singer Isabella Colbran. His only compositions from these years were some sacred compositions and a series of pieces whimsically titled *The Sins of My Old Age*. He was something of an expert chef: the dish *tourne-dos Rossini* was invented by him.

As glorious as is *William Tell*, Rossini's *The Barber of Seville* is his most beloved opera. We have met the barber before: he is Figaro, the same one as in Mozart's *Marriage of Figaro*. Mozart's work was the second of a set of three plays by Caron de Beaumarchais. This is the first. It had already been set by Paisiello, and that composer's fans cruelly disrupted the opening night. But no one paid them to disrupt the second performance. That was a triumph, and today only musicologists remember Pasiello's opera.

We'll hear the overture (from Mr. Crescendo) and Figaro's opening aria, "Make way for the barber of the city," in which Figaro celebrates, well, Figaro!

Tournedos Rossini. © Monkey Business Images, 2010. Used under license from Shutterstock, Inc.

example

Rossini, *The Barber of Seville*: Overture; *Largo al factorum*

Gaetano Donizetti (1797–1848)

Donizetti was the most prolific and most uneven, of the group, which is why only one of his works is frequently performed now, along with perhaps five others that are irregularly presented. He is known for tragedies, and was particularly drawn to works from English history and literature. His most famous work is *Lucia di Lammermoor*, based on Sir Walter Scott's *The Bride of Lammermoor*. Other English works include *Anna Bolena* (Anne Boleyn) and *Roberto Deveraux*, named for Queen Elizabeth's reputed lover).

His comedies are in the style of Rossini, and the best of them are only slightly less popular. These include *L'Elisir d'Amore (The Elixir of Love)*, *Don Pasquale*, and *La Fille du Regiment (The Daughter of the Regiment)*. His dramatic works at their best have an intensity which prefigures Verdi, who will be discussed in the next chapter.

Vincenzo Bellini (1801–1835)

Bellini was the least prolific of the group, with only 13 operas, but his works have a consistently higher quality. All of his operas are works that are serious and dramatic. He lived in Paris, where it was said that he would declaim his libretti aloud to determine the right melodies for the text. His trademark style was an aria with long, arching phrases over a simple, arpeggiated accompaniments; the melody was often introduced first by a solo woodwind.

His major works include *Il Puritani (The Puritans)*, *Il Pirata (The Pirate)*, and *La Sonnambula (The Sleepwalker)*; his most important masterpiece is *Norma*.

Norma illustrates one of the problems with *bel canto* librettos. The setting is in pre-Christian Gaul (what is now France). The population is under the control of an occupying Roman army, and Norma is the Druid Priestess to whom the people look for guidance. She is secretly in love with the Roman Centurion commanding the occupying army, and has somehow managed to bear him two children without anyone noticing.

However absurd the premise is, the situation is made believable by the strength of the music. Disbelief is readily suspended in the face of Norma's opening aria: her call to prayer to the chaste Goddess of the Moon. This is an excellent example of the *cavatina/cabaletta* structure. After her opening *cavatina*, she tries to calm the anger of her people and keep them from active resistance, while longing for the return of her Roman lover in the *cabaletta*.

example

Bellini: *Norma—Casta diva . . . Ah, bello a me ritorna*

Glossary

Dies irae: *a medieval plainchant* (Latin: *Day of Wrath*) that is part of the text of the Requiem, Mass, the Mass for the dead; it portrays a horrifying vision of the final judgment, and is frequently quoted by Romantic composers to conjure an image of death

Idee fixe: in Berlioz' *Symphonie fantastique*, the theme used to depict the composer's beloved

Miniature: a short piece, usually for piano, guitar, harp, or chamber ensemble, and usually monothematic

Program music: music that is based on an extra-musical source—this might be some work of literature; a depiction of an event, historical or otherwise; a painting; a geographical location; specific to instrumental music, since in vocal music there is already an extra-musical element: the text (the opposite is *absolute music*)

Symphonic poem: a one-movement, orchestral work of program music

Thematic transformation: the transformation of a theme so that it makes a different emotional effect; the *idée fixe* in Berlioz' *Symphonie fantastique* is a good example

Reference

Walker, Alan. *The Virtuoso Years*. New York: Cornell University Press, 1988.

Tear-Out No. 3

Identify the following musical examples as music of the Classical Period or of the Romantic Period.

1. _____

2. _____

3. _____

4. _____

5. _____

The information in this table may help you:

	CLASSICAL	ROMANTIC
Harmony	Simple, clear, and balanced	More intentionally dissonant, varied
Orchestra	Smaller, lighter	Expands, adds extra instruments like trombones and harps
Melodies	Regular phrases, tuneful and simple	Longer, more complex phrases, richer harmony
Instrumental music	Sonata cycle works: symphony, string quartet, piano sonata	Program music, form determined by program rather than preexisting outline
Aesthetic ideal	Balance, clarity, emotion contained in form	Individuality, creativity, emotion, freedom

Listening Exam

LATE ROMANTICISM (1850–1910)

A New Cast of Players

The Late Romantic period (1850–1910) is not actually recognized as a separate period in music history. There were no changes of style or aesthetic emphasis, and the same trends that were begun during the early part of the period are continued during the latter. This course separates the two eras only to facilitate study. Yet there is *one* aspect of the period that can legitimately be seen to be divided into early and late periods: the fact that so many of the prominent figures of early romanticism were dead or creatively inactive after 1850. Rossini had retired, Berlioz was consumed with unsuccessful attempts to achieve a performance both parts of his opera *Les Troyens*, and Donizetti, Bellini, Schubert, Schumann, Chopin, Mendelssohn, Weber, and Beethoven were all deceased. In fact, the only figure who was active throughout both parts of the era was Franz Liszt. Therefore, it is possible to view the late Romantic period as a separate era in that it is a continuation of previous ideas by a different cast of players.

We began our study of the Early Romantic period by contrasting two composers who specialized in orchestral music: one revolutionary and one conservative. We will do the same with the Late Romanticism, though this time, we'll start with the conservative.

Johannes Brahms (1833–1897)

Throughout the 19th century, indeed throughout history, there has been a conflict between the conservative and the progressive, between the reactionary and the radical. The very nature of Romanticism naturally tends to emphasize such tensions. Among the conservative figures of the era, the name of Johannes Brahms stands as perhaps the last great musical classicist.

Brahms was a conscious continuation of the aspects of classicism exemplified in works of Haydn, Mozart, and, especially, Beethoven. The titan from Bonn was Brahms' specific standard against which he measured his own work. When Beethoven died, there was no one to follow in a "Beethoven School," not because his work was out of fashion, but because no one was capable of continuing the miraculous innovations of his Late period—no one, that is, until Brahms.

He was the son of a Hamburg lower-middle-class family. His father was a double bass player, which is probably where Brahms got his love of the darker, deeper colors of the orchestra, the family placed a great deal of importance on education. Johannes was encouraged to get as much training as he could; as the family lacked the funds to finance it, he had to work his way through his education. He did this as a pianist.

He had begun as a very promising concert pianist—so much so that he was given lessons for free by Eduard Marxsen, Hamburg's finest teacher. He later repaid Marxsen by dedicating his *Second Piano Concerto in Bb, Op. 83* to him. Unfortunately, at this time, Germany was overrun by promising concert pianists, and Brahms ended up as a barroom/brothel pianist. This was, of course, a rather unhealthy environment for an impressionable teenager, and Brahms' memory of the scenes of the exchange of money for sex colored his view of the opposite sex for the rest of his life.

chapter nine

Brahms as a young man.
© JupiterImages, Inc.

His big break came in 1853, when he met Joseph Joachim, one of the greatest violinists of the age, who was to become a lifelong confidant, and Robert and Clara Schumann. Robert immediately took the young composer under his wing and published a glowing article in the *Neue Zeitschrift* proclaiming Brahms the "Young Eagle" and the "Musical Messiah for which the world had long been waiting." His efforts as mentor established Brahms' career internationally, and he never forgot the debt he owed the older composer.

At that same meeting, Brahms began to fall hopelessly in love with Clara. This produced a terrifically frustrating situation, in which Brahms was unwilling, even long after Robert's death, to sully the memory of his mentor by establishing sexual relations with his wife—and yet, Clara represented to him a feminine ideal, the polar opposite to the prostitutes of his youth, and Brahms never found a replacement for her on the pedestal. Though he had numerous love affairs, Brahms lived and died a bachelor.

In 1862, he settled in Vienna and lived a singularly uneventful life thereafter, except for his composing. He was recognized as one of the world's greatest composers. Even criticism from the radical press was couched in respectful terms.

Brahms' Music

Though Brahms is described as the last great classicist, his music does not sound like that of Mozart or Haydn—or Mendelssohn, for that matter. He is classic in his utter lack of interest in program music and in his devotion to the formal arrangements and techniques of the classical masters. The following are some characteristics of his music.

- All his instrumental works are absolute music.
- His music is extremely self-critical and is at a highly consistent quality level.
- There is a richness of scoring: dark colors and doubling of melodies at third and sixth.
- There are broad, sweeping—mostly diatonic—melodies.
- There is a free use of rhythm.

example

Brahms: *Symphony no. 1 in c minor, Op. 68*

IV. *Adagio-Piu andante-Allegro non troppo, ma con brio-Piu allegro*

Brahms didn't compose his first symphony until after the age of 40 . . . actually, that's not entirely accurate. He didn't allow a symphony he had written to be published until that time, though he made several attempts . . . and destroyed them all. By this point, Brahms was both a mature and a famous composer, and was identified by the public as Beethoven's heir. His first symphony was called, by some critics, Beethoven's Tenth. The critique was intended to imply a lack of originality, but was totally misguided. This work could never be mistaken for one by Beethoven, despite an intentional reference to the last movement melody from the Ninth symphony.

The movement title is bewildering, but it only lists various tempos, each for a separate section. Brahms often used tempo changes as structural delineations. The opening is, frankly, strange, with odd dissonances to convey a sense of disarray, instability . . . but all is resolved when the *Allegro non troppo* arrives. The harmony stabilizes, and a warm, beautiful melody emerges. Like Beethoven's Fifth symphony, also in c minor, this work ends in C major; the mood here is more joyful than triumphant, but equally satisfying.

---

example

Brahms: *String Sextet no. 2 in G, Op. 36*

I. *Allegro non troppo*

Some listeners find Brahms' symphonies so rich that they are put off by the sounds. They might enjoy his chamber music more—it has the same rich language, but because it is for a smaller ensemble, with one player to a part, there's an enjoyable transparency to the sound.

Brahms wrote two string sextets, for two each of violins, violas, and 'cellos (sextets are not particularly common, and there is no standard instrumentation). The second has an interesting story. Brahms had just broken off a love affair with one Agathe von Siebold. The break was amicable . . . she just wasn't Clara. He offered her a memorable gift in the first movement. It's in the expected sonata form, and Brahms crafted the second theme from her name: A-G-A-(t)H-E. In German practice, the note B-natural is called H. B in German means B-flat.

Other Music by Brahms

Because Brahms destroyed anything he didn't think could stand comparison with the music of Beethoven, nearly any of his works will be rewarding. His piano music is especially interesting and beautiful. Early in his career, he wrote large-scale, virtuosic sonatas and variations, but at the end of his life, he wrote shorter, lyrical masterpieces, most of which he designated intermezzos or capriccios.

Piano:
- *Sonata no. 3 in f minor*
- *Variations and Fugue on a Theme by Handel*
- *Variations on a Theme by Paganini*
- *Intermezzos and Capriccios*

Orchestral:
- Four symphonies
- Two piano concertos
- Violin concerto
- Double concerto for violin and 'cello

Chamber music:
- Piano quintet in f minor
- Piano trio in B major
- String sextets in Bb and G
- String quartets in a minor and c minor

Choral:
- *German Requiem*

Brahms at the piano. © JupiterImages, Inc.

Piotr Ilych Chaikovsky on a coin. © Andreas Guskos, 2010. Used under license from Shutterstock, Inc.

Piotr Ilych Chaikovsky (1840–1893)

Chaikovsky was born in a remote section of Russia. You will usually see his name spelled Tchaikovsky, though he is filed under the letter C in the U.S. Library of Congress. Indeed, you'll often see differing spellings of Russian composers because Russia uses the Cyrillic Comment on spelling difficulties between Cyrillic rather than the Roman alphabet, and there is no consistent correlation between the two.

Chaikovsky was trained for civil service and came late to music. He didn't even begin formal training until the age of 23. He studied at newly formed Moscow Conservatory, joined its faculty after graduation, and worked there for 12 years.

After this time, he was contacted by a rich aristocrat, Nadezhda von Meck, who considered Chiaikovsky to be one of the world's most gifted composers. She felt he should be supported so that he could devote all his time to composing instead of being consumed by teaching duties and arranged to send him a monthly stipend. The situation was not analogous to the 18th century patronage system under which Haydn served, since von Meck made no attempt to control Chaikovsky's musical output or direction.

Although Chaikofsky and von Meck carried on a lengthy correspondence, they never actually met. This was partially because of von Meck's insistence, which may have been based on the Victorian custom that public discussion of financial matters was thought to be in poor taste. But it was also because of Chaikovsky's preference: he was terrified of ever meeting his benefactress face to face.

Chaikovsky stands out in the era as one of the most neurotic figures in an age filled with them. He was self-critical to an almost pathological degree and was tortured any time one of his works was first performed. At one point, he wrote to a friend how he loathed the sound of the piano trio and felt it was the most hideous sound ever concocted by mankind. Chaikovsky watchers will realize that, at that time, he was already engaged in composing his own *Piano Trio in a*, one of the most beautiful chamber works of the whole era.

He was married to a former student for about a week, after which they legally separated. The young lady was herself terribly unstable and had pursued her teacher obsessively, but his marriage was an unsuccessful attempt to cover up his homosexuality and pederasty (he was infatuated with his young nephew Ivan).

His fears were well founded. Certainly during the "enlightened" 20th century, homosexuality still finds persecution; in 19th-century Russia, public exposure could have meant banishment or imprisonment. During that time, he wrote to a friend of the "ghastly spiritual torture" he was undergoing, and shortly thereafter attempted suicide by the novel method of wading into the Moscow River in the middle of winter, attempting to contract pneumonia. He did not get the disease, but recovered, only to die later after from drinking untreated water during a cholera epidemic. This has been seen as a suicidal act, and there is some evidence that he was coerced into the act by leaders of the Moscow musical community to avoid scandal.

Chaikovsky's music has an undercurrent of suffering and despair, yet it avoids being depressing by his skill as a melodist: he managed to express his own sense of sadness into some of the most sublime melodies of any composer. Melody is his strong point, almost to the exclusion of other qualities. He does, admittedly, lack the profundity and depth of a Beethoven, Brahms, or Mahler, but his melodies have made him one of the most popular composers of all time.

Chaikovsky's Music

Chaikovsky's operas are very popular in Russia, but few singers outside of that country are trained to sing in Russia, so they are not often performed in the West. He is best known for his orchestral works. He composed:

- Six symphonies, of which the fourth, fifth, and sixth are particularly fine
- *Violin Concerto in D*
- *Piano Concerto no. 1 in Bb minor*
- Several symphonic poems, including *Romeo and Juliet* and *1812 Overture*
- Ballets: *Swan Lake*, *Sleeping Beauty*, and *The Nutcracker*

His innovations in ballet are particularly important; prior to Chaikovsky, ballet music was of little importance and only rarely made any attempt at overall musical unity. He was the first to treat a ballet score with the kind of depth and structural integrity of the finest of orchestral music, and his scores to *Swan Lake*, *Sleeping Beauty*, and *The Nutcracker* remain the most popular of all time. For each of the three, various suites of the most popular pieces have been compiled, and are frequently performed without the dancers.

example

Chaikovsky: *Suite from The Nutcracker*

- *Overture*
- *March*
- *Dance of the Sugarplum Fairies*
- *Chinese Dance*
- *Dance of the Reed-flutes*
- *Arabian Dance*
- *Russian Dance*
- *Waltz of the Flowers*

Nationalism

Chaikovsky is often associated with the movement known as Nationalism, though he is actually more as a mainstream European composer, no more Russian than Brahms was German or Rossini was Italian. While he surely was identifiably Russian, he made no attempt specifically to reflect this heritage. There were others, however, who did consciously set out to achieve this goal.

Nationalism refers to the celebration in art of one's national or ethnic heritage. It can take one of three manifestations:

- Quotation of folk song;
- Imitation of folk song or dance; or
- Celebration of patriotic theme or national hero.

It is an extension of the movement toward egalitarianism that was so important in the Romantic period, and it is usually found outside of Germany, France, and Italy. Those countries had defined the musical mainstream for so long that they had little real need to celebrate heritages that were already celebrated. But countries outside that mainstream felt that they had something to celebrate as well, and one finds nationalism showing up in places such as Russia, Eastern Europe, Scandinavia, England, Spain, and the United States.

Russia: The Mighty Five

The Russian name is *Kushka*. It translates poorly; you can find it as *The Mighty Five*, *The Fistful*, or even simply *The Clique*. They were five composers dedicated to the establishment of a specifically Russian style of music: **Mili Balakirev** (1837–1910), **Cesar Cui** (1835–1918), **Alexandr Borodin** (1833–1887), **Nikolai Rimsky-Korsakov** (1844–1908), and **Modest Mussorgsky** (1839–1881).

Chaikovsky was not a member; he was too much of a loner, and besides, they were centered in St. Petersburg (known as Leningrad during the Soviet years), as opposed to Chaikovsky's Moscow. They rejected academic training as too strongly based on European models, and all but Balakirev were amateurs—Borodin was a chemist and Mussorgsky a civil servant.

St. Isaac's Cathedral, St. Petersburg. © JupiterImages, Inc.

Their intent was appropriate; they believed that formal training would destroy their essential "Russianness"; in fairness, Russian music education at that time taught students to compose like Germans. But despite Pink Floyd's assertion that "we don't need no education," there is a need for mastery of one's craft. Eventually, Rimsky-Korsakov obtained formal training, and both Mussorgsky and Borodin sent their works to him to correct technical flaws.

Mussorgsky is arguably the most interesting and original of the five. Many of his works are better known in "corrected" versions by Rimsky-Korsakov; his originals, however, may sound less slick, but have an earthy power about them that many prefer. He is best known for three works, the opera ***Boris Godunov***, the piano suite ***Pictures at an Exhibition***, and the symphonic poem ***Night on Bald Mountain***.

example

Mussorgsky: *Pictures at an Exhibition* (excerpts)

Promenade
Gnomus
Promenade
The Old Castle
Baba-Yaga
The Great Gate at Kiev

This work is perhaps better known as an orchestral transcription; there are several, the most popular of which is by Maurice Ravel (we heard his *Bolero* earlier). It has also been arranged for other instrumentations, including rock band (Emerson, Lake, and Palmer) and classical guitar. But the original is for piano.

The composition is a suite of pieces that depicts, well, pictures at an exhibition. The artist Viktor Hartmann was a friend of Mussorgsky, and after his death, there was a posthumous exhibit of his works. Mussorgsky was so moved by the art works that he immortalized many of them in individual movements, liked by a recurring theme he labels the *Promenade*. That piece is in an irregular meter (11/4) and features modal harmonies. Those weren't encountered since the late Renaissance, but they persisted in the music of the Russian Orthodox Church and in Russian folk music.

Eastern Europe: Antonin Dvořák (1841–1904)

Dvořák (the character ř in Czech is pronounced with an "rzh" sound) was the son of a butcher and innkeeper. He left home at 16 to study music in Prague; his early music was discovered and championed by Brahms, as Brahms had been championed earlier by Schumann. With such support, he was quickly recognized as the leading nationalist composer in Eastern Europe.

His fame was such that in 1892 he received an offer from New York to become the director of the National Conservatory, at an annual salary of $15,000. That was roughly 20 times his annual salary at the Prague Conservatory. Having been made an offer he could not refuse, he came to America. He was, unfortunately, terribly homesick. He used to spend summers in Spillville, Iowa, which was populated mostly with Czech immigrants (and which hosts an annual Dvořák Festival every summer).

His homesickness did not translate into any dislike of the United States. Indeed, he was impressed with American music and encouraged local composers to establish their own national school. An interview in the *New York Times* quoted him:

Dvořák on a Czechosolovakian stamp.
© Route66, 2010. Used under license from
Shutterstock, Inc.

" *In Negro songs, I have found a secure basis for a new national music school. America can have her own music, a fine music growing up from her own native soil and having its own character—the natural voice of a free and great nation.* "

After three years, he could stand his homesickness no longer, and in 1895 he returned to Czechoslovakia, rejoined the Conservatory, and six years later became its director.

This homesickness will surprise no one who loves Dvořák's music. It is beautiful, joyous, touching, and deeply steeped in the sounds of his homeland. Interestingly, he rarely quotes identifiably Czech sources, but often will imitate the melodies and rhythms of folk song and dance.

His important works are mostly orchestral, though his chamber music is second only to that of Brahms. There are nine symphonies (four originally were suppressed; unlike Brahms, he didn't destroy his works but merely withheld them from publication. You will still see different numbering on older recordings); three concertos, one each for piano, violin, and violoncello; symphonic poems and overtures; and sixteen Slavonic dances.

example

Dvořák: *Slavonic Dance Op. 46, no. 8: Furiant*

Dvořák's *Slavonic Dances* are what first got the attention of the musical public. They were originally written for piano four-hands (that's a term for two players at the same piano), but were better known in his own arrangements for orchestra. The first set of eight was published as Op. 46 and were so popular that his publisher urged him to write another set. That was published as Op. 72. They are, as the title indicates, dances popular with Slavonic peoples. There are polkas, skocnas, furiants, dumkas, mazurkas, sousedskas . . . each with its own tempo and rhythmic character. The last dance of the first set is a furiant, characterized by alternation between 6/8 and 3/4 meters, and major and minor tonalities.

Spain: Isaac Albéniz (1860–1909)

Isaac Albéniz. © JupiterImages, Inc.

Albéniz was a remarkable child prodigy as a pianist. He passed all his exams to be admitted to the Paris Conservatory at the age of 6, but he was playing with a rubber ball while the admissions jury was deliberating and broke a mirror. It was decided to give him some more time to mature.

To escape an abusive father, he ran away to Latin America, where he supported himself for many years as a tavern/brothel pianist. When he returned to Europe, he studied with Franz Liszt and made a career as pianist and composer. He is known primarily from his works for piano, nearly all of which are nationalist. He unfortunately spent much of his time writing operas on libretti by an extremely bad English writer, Francis Money-Coutts, who hired him to set his (and only his) words to music. He accepted the agreement for the financial security involved, but all the music was essentially wasted.

Much of his output consists of piano miniatures, but his masterpiece is *Iberia*, a set of 13 piano pieces describing, well, Iberia, the Latin name for Spain.

example

Albéniz: *Iberia—Triana*

If you enjoy Albéniz music, you should explore that of his compatriot **Enrique Granados** (1867–1916), who also wrote mostly nationalist piano music.

Scandinavia: Jean Sibelius (1865–1957)

In some ways, Sibelius was not really a nationalist; his music has little influence from folk *music*, but his tone poems are often based on folk *lore*. He stopped composing after 1921 because of alcoholism and the frustration of his music being ignored as apart from the various developments during the early 20th century.

His most important works are orchestral. There are seven symphonies: his *Violin Concerto, k* and several symphonic poems, including *Tapiola*, *Finlandia*, *En Saga*, and *Oceanides*. His *Four Legends from the Kalevala* can be thought of as a symphony, though the composer presented it as a set of four symphonic poems.

example

Sibelius: *Four Legends from the Kalevala*

IV. *Lemminkäinen's Return*

The *Kalevala* is the Finnish national epic. It dates from ancient times and recounts the story of the hero Lemminkäinen. In the fourth movement, he is returning from *Tuonela*, the land of the dead. It may not surprise you to learn that, in Finnish mythology, Hell is cold.

Another Scandinavian nationalist worth discovering is **Edvard Grieg** (1843–1907).

United States: Louis Moreau Gottschalk (1829–1869)

The United States took some time to establish its own artistic voice. Most early attempts were pale imitations of European models. There is, to be sure, a string trio by Benjamin Franklin, which is a dreadful piece of music, but it's by Ben Franklin, so you do hear it occasionally.

Gottschalk was America's first great virtuoso pianist. He traveled to Paris early in his career and was refused entry into the Paris Conservatory on the grounds that anyone from the New World had to be a barbarian. But he made some powerful friends on this journey in Frederic Chopin and Hector Berlioz, who helped him start a concert tour. He returned to the New World and spent the remainder of his career as a touring pianist, traveling through the United States and Latin America.

His music cannot be considered great by any stretch of the imagination, but it is lots of fun, and there's always room for that. *The Banjo* is filled with the sounds of his native New Orleans; you can even hear the sounds of *The Camptown Ladies* at the beginning and the end.

example

Gottschalk: *The Banjo*

Nationalism in the 20th Century

The nationalist movement, though essentially romantic in its origins and egalitarian essence, did not end with the end of the Romantic period. Indeed, it continues through the Revolutionary Age and beyond, and in many quarters is still flourishing. Let's consider the contributions of three more figures, respectively from England, Spain, and Argentina.

England: Ralph Vaughan Williams (1872–1958)

Ralph Vaughan Williams worked mainly in the 20th century, but his roots are firmly affixed in the Romantic musical language; he is arguably the strongest example of English nationalism.

His music ranges more widely than some of his fellow nationalists (whose gentle voices are often referred to as the English Pastoral School), and he was quite prolific. He wrote operas, songs, great choral works, nine symphonies, and many symphonic poems. In his *Fantasia on Greensleeves*, we find Vaughan Williams' most British voice.

example

Fantasia on Greensleeves

Spain: Joaquín Rodrigo (1901–1999)

Joaquín Rodrigo's life outlines the entire 20th century, but his musical style never went far beyond its Romantic roots—the main thing that identifies him as a composer of the Revolutionary Age is his fondness for adding an extra half step to a chord. The effect is rather like sprinkling already spicy food with an extra dollop of salsa piquante.

His most famous composition is a concerto for guitar and orchestra, the *Concierto de Aranjuez*. Indeed, the work is so popular, it is the most frequently performed concerto written in the 20th century, for any instrument. Rodrigo did not play guitar, and has written for all other media, including piano works, orchestral, songs, even *Zarzuelas* (a Spanish opera with spoken dialogue instead of recitative). But this work, along with many works for solo guitar and four other guitar concertos, is the work that has captured the imagination of the world.

example

Concierto de Aranjuez

Allegro con spirito; Adagio; Allegro gentile

The outer movements of the concierto are lively (and highly virtuosic) Spanish dances. Rodrigo has achieved a nearly impossible feat of putting a guitar with an orchestra and allowing it to be heard. He does so with absolutely brilliant orchestration. The guitar is rarely heard against the entire orchestra, but alternates with it, or is paired with solo wind or string instruments. Indeed, this was a set of three guitar concertos composed in 1939 (the other works were by Mario Castelnuovo-Tedesco and Manuel Ponce), when such works had not been composed since the early 19th century. The long gap was necessitated by this same problem of balance. Only by

figure 9.7

The gardens at the Royal Palace, Aranjuez, Spain.
© 2011, JupiterImages, Inc.

that date had sound reproduction improved that a guitar could be amplified with a microphone without losing a natural quality of sound.

The second movement, *Adagio*, is one of the most heart-rendingly beautiful melodies ever composed, and it has a very personal meaning for Rodrigo. He lost his sight at the age of three, and was married to concert pianist Victoria Kahmi, who long assisted him in setting his compositions to paper. The second movement was inspired by a tragedy—the loss of their first child at the time of its birth, a difficult moment that almost took the mother's life as well. The steady chords in the guitar, and the pulse of the bass line, represent Victoria's heartbeat. The florid melody of the guitar was Rodrigo's prayer that she, and the baby, would be saved. The prayer was only partially answered, and the final ascending melody and harmonics in the guitar represent the child's soul ascending to heaven.

Argentina: Astor Piazzolla (1921–1992)

Nearly all Latin American composers have some elements of nationalism in their music, however modern and abstract it becomes. Many operate comfortably in the poorly defined border between cultivated and vernacular, classical and popular, traditions. Argentine Astor Piazzolla is such a composer. He is a champion of the *nuevo tango*, an Argentine tradition that takes traditional tango music and combines it with more sophisticated compositional and harmonic techniques. The Tango remains the favorite dance of Argentines, especially the *Porteñas*, as the inhabitants of the port city of Buenos Aires are known (there is at least one 24-hour Tango Channel on Buenos Aires cable TV), and Piazzolla has taken it to a much higher level than any had previously.

figure 9.8

The Argentine Tango. © 2011, JupiterImages, Inc.

Still, his music retains the character of popular music. He doesn't fully orchestrate most of his music, since it would be played by whomever was handy—a combination of percussion, guitar, violin, and the *bandoneon*, a type of accordion that was Piazzolla's main instrument—and the arrangement and the precise realization of a given piece might include extensive amounts of improvisation. Such is the case in this example, which includes the composer on bandoneon, along with those instruments mentioned.

example

Primavera Porteña

Primavera means Spring in Spanish (and in Italian); this is from a set of four pieces called *The Four Seasons of the Porteñas*, one of his most popular compositions.

The Nationalist Heritage

If this music appeals to you, spend some time investigating the works of the nationalist composers. There are some great delights to be had from them. For many, in the last part of the Romantic period, the tendencies toward expansion were actually getting somewhat out of hand. Many late Romantic works seem to some listeners to be not so much expansive as overripe. But the nationalist composers, by infusing their music with the simplicity and vitality of their native folk music, brought back a sense of honesty and directness which music desperately needed.

And, as we saw with Sibelius and Vaughan Williams, nationalism does not end with the Romantic period . . . it continues as a vital movement to the present.

Late Romantic Opera

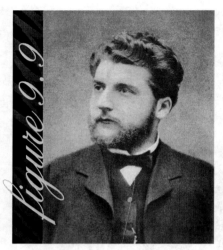

Georges Bizet. © JupiterImages, Inc.

Opera during the late Romantic period is dominated by two giant figures: one from Italy and one from Germany. We will, however, begin in France. And we begin there because one of the most popular operas of all time is *Carmen* by Georges Bizet (1838–1875).

Carmen is an ***opera comique***, the French term for an opera with spoken dialogue instead of recitative. It is set in **Spain**, and shocked listeners when it premiered because of its subject matter, treating violent passions of the common people instead of the aristocracy or historical/mythological figures. Since its composition, it has become among the most popular of all operas—all because of its concise, believable action, its intensity of emotion, and its plethora of great music.

Carmen is a Gypsy girl with a sexual magnetism that causes any male who comes within 10 meters of her to lose his capacity for rational thought. At the outset, we meet Carmen working in a Seville cigar factory (an actual place, now part of the University of Seville). She gets in a knife fight with one of her coworkers and is promptly arrested and carted off to jail.

At Army headquarters, Carmen starts to sing to herself, unaccountably making plans to spend the time drinking and dancing at Lila's Pastia's Tavern. It would seem to most observers that she's going to be in jail, but fortunately, her arresting officer, Don José, is male, and he's in that 10-meter danger zone. She seduces him with promises to meet later, and he releases her.

© Veronika Vasilyuk, 2010. Used under license from Shutterstock, Inc.

---

example

Bizet, *Carmen*: Seguidilla, "Pres des ramparts de Seville"

She did, in fact, intend to meet him, but he ended up being demoted to private and spent the time in jail himself. Don José does finally join with Carmen, leaving behind his family and his sweet fiancée Micaela, and deserting the Army. Carmen is as fickle as she is passionate, and she eventually leaves Don José for a bullfighter, Escamillo. The climactic scene takes place outside of the Bullfight Arena. Inside, Escamillo is gored to death by the bull, and Carmen is stabbed to death by a jealous Don José. Bodies are everywhere . . . no wonder the work is so popular.

Now, on to the giants.

Italy: Giuseppe Verdi (1813–1901)

Giuseppe Verdi (whose name does, in fact, mean Joe Greene) almost singlehandedly constitutes the history of Italian music after Donizetti. His output is almost entirely dramatic opera—the second and the last were comedies, but the rest were serious, tragic works. In 1836, he married Margarita Barezzi, who bore two children. Both died in infancy, and his wife died in 1840—perhaps these early tragedies gave him an essentially tragic outlook on life. In any case, the theme of a tragic father/daughter relationship is a recurring one in his operas.

Another recurring theme is that of a people suffering under a tyrannical rule of either government or church (Verdi was a devout atheist, and saw the Church as an oppressive, not a liberating, force). Not coincidentally, Verdi was strongly sympathetic with the Italian struggle for unification and independence from the Austro-Hungarian Empire.

Italy was not Italy until around 1861, after a long struggle. During that violent time, one often saw the expression **VIVA VERDI**! scrawled on walls. This was not written by an opera fan; it was an acronym for the revolutionary slogan **Viva Vittorio Emanuele, Re D'Italia**! Victor Emanuele was indeed the first president of the united Italy, and Verdi was elected to the first Italian Parliament despite the fact that he was not running—a technique that perhaps should be tried in this country.

Verdi's early career was not promising. He failed his entry exam into the Milan Conservatory: "Piano inadequate, abilities in composition insufficient." In fairness, his early works are rather crude. Nevertheless, throughout his career, he gradually refined his technique, his sense of stagecraft, and his expressiveness until by the end of his career, his last few works verge on perfection. Throughout his career, all his works share one prominent characteristic: **emotional intensity**. Constantly in his correspondence with his librettists, he encourages them to provide him with situations of the most intense, violent emotional conflicts—plausibility was no object. He would make situations plausible by the power of his music.

His early works met with limited success until three works of 1851–1853: *Rigoletto, Il Trovatore*, and *La Traviata*. These firmly established Verdi's reputation as the leading composer of Italy. From this time forward, he worked more slowly and more carefully. Though Verdi had excellent literary sources for his libretti (Shakespeare, Hugo, Dumas, Schiller), he never got a first-rate libretto until the end of his career.

Giuseppe Verdi. © JupiterImages, Inc.

Otello

At this point, Verdi had retired from composing and from his brief, unwanted career in politics and was tending an olive farm in northern Italy. He was coaxed out of retirement to set libretti by writer/composer Arrigo Boïto, based on Shakespeare: *Otello* (written at age 74) and *Falstaff* written at age 80). These two works represent perhaps the most perfect union of word and music ever achieved in opera.

Falstaff is based on the character Sir John Falstaff from *The Merry Wives of Windsor*. It is a delightful comedy, written with such a sure touch that it seems Verdi had always written comedy.

Otello is a different matter. Based on Shakespeare's *Othello*, the work is a dark tale of what evil can be capable of destroying. Othello is a General in the Army of Venice, the ruler of the Venetian colony of Cyprus. He is married to Desdemona, the daughter of a wealthy and prominent Venetian aristocrat; she loves him with all her heart, as he does her. Othello enjoys the peak of success: he is wildly popular with his people, who regard him as a great war hero and a just ruler, and he has all the wealth, power, and love one could ask from life.

Yet he is vulnerable. Othello is black and from Africa. He is a black man living in a white world, never completely a part of it. For all his strengths, this remains his one point at which he can be attacked.

Enter Iago. Some literary scholars describe Iago as the most perfect villain ever created. He is a lieutenant in Othello's army, and was recently passed over for a promotion he felt he deserved. In his bitterness, he broods, and he sees a way he can destroy his commander. If he can plant the seeds of distrust in Othello and convince him that Desdemona is unfaithful to him, he can use that deception to bring about Othello's downfall.

Iago can do this because Othello does not have total confidence in himself and his place in this world. Iago carefully maintained an image of himself as "Honest Iago," the one who can be trusted above all else, the one to go to when in need of counsel.

Iago's methods are subtle and careful. He plants the seeds of suspicion slowly, seeming unwilling to say anything. Eventually, Othello is driven almost to madness. He kills his wife by suffocation, just before Iago's deception is discovered, and then stabs himself to death over the body of Desdemona.

Just two excerpts can demonstrate Verdi's capacity to convey emotions in music. At the close of Act I, after Othello's triumphant return from battle at sea, Iago crafts a fight to break out between two of Othello's trusted assistants, one of whom will be framed as Desdemona's supposed lover. Othello comes on the scene to restore order, commands both to lay down their swords, and then clears the town square, leaving himself alone with his wife. The ensuing duet is achingly beautiful, and one can hardly imagine anyone or anything coming between them.

It is not necessary to reproduce all the dialogue here, but one passage is taken directly from Shakespeare. Othello recounts many of the struggles he has passed through, captivities and defeats later turned to victory. He sings to her, ". . . and you loved me for the pains I had to endure; and I loved you that you did pity them."

Verdi: *Otello, Act I: Gia nella notte*

Much of the strength of Boïto's libretto comes from the fact that he had sufficient understanding to let the power of Shakespeare's words speak for themselves. Many passages are simply taken directly from the original and translated into Italian. But Iago's Act II aria is Boïto's invention, though it is perfectly consistent with Iago's character.

It is a soliloquy—sung alone, the characters thoughts expressed aloud to the audience. After sending a friend on an errand, he sings to himself a parody of the Catholic Mass. The third part of the Ordinary is the *Credo*, the Nicene Creed: *I believe in one God, Maker of Heaven and Earth* . . . But instead, Iago sings *Credo in un Dio crudel . . . I believe in a cruel God . . .*

Verdi, *Otello: Act II: Credo in un Dio crudel*

Germany: Richard Wagner (1813–1883)

Wagner was born the same year as Verdi, in Leipzig. He was in a theatrical family: his stepfather and two sisters were actors, and a third sister was an opera singer. He originally intended to become a poet and playwright, but at the age of 15, he became acquainted with the music of Beethoven. The experience was overwhelming, and at that point he decided to devote his life to music.

He had only six months of formal music education, after which he taught himself by studying scores. He embarked on a career as a composer/conductor. Like Berlioz, he never mastered an instrument (much of what we know of Wagner's early life comes from Wagner himself; we also know that he was not above inflating his own story, so some details are suspect).

Wagner's early years were spent composing and conducting, and also drinking, dueling, gambling, and freely copulating. He shamelessly lived off of other people and accumulated huge debts which he never repaid. Eminent musicologist Joseph Kerman describes him as a "sponge." He worked in Paris, Leipzig, and Dresden, usually leaving town just ahead of his creditors.

After 1851, he sought and received asylum in Switzerland, where he remained, writing not music but prose—opera libretti, and treatises on art, opera, and socialism (Wagner, unlike Verdi, was an *active* revolutionary, though whether his socialist ideas were born from an authentic sympathy with the working class or just a novel way of outrunning his debts is unclear).

In 1864, Wagner received an invitation from the court of King Ludwig of Bavaria to come to Munich. Ludwig was an 18-year-old who had just attained legal age to rule and was fanatically devoted to Wagner's music. He thought Wagner was the greatest genius the world had ever known (Wagner, needless to say, agreed). His castle, which forms the model for the castle at the center of Disneyworld's Magic Kingdom, was decorated throughout with scenes and characters from Wagner's operas.

Ludwig put the resources of the Bavarian treasury at Wagner's disposal, which can charitably be described as an error in judgment. These funds, plus much additional fund raising, led to the building of the opera house at nearby **Bayreuth**, a house which is still in the hands of Wagner's descendants and is still devoted only to the performance of Wagner's operas. It is open only during the summer.

figure 9.12

Artificial cave in Ludwig's castle. © Leonardo_da_gressignano, 2010. Used under license from Shutterstock, Inc.

The project was not as indulgent as it may seem. In fact, Wagner had a conception of opera that went beyond what was technically possible in any opera house then in Europe. He needed a facility with special features in order for his vision to be realized.

Ludwig was eventually declared insane by his ministers because of his financial extravagances and was ultimately found drowned in one of the castle pools—whether it was murder or suicide was never determined. Wagner was also out of favor in Munich because of his personal scandals. He was living at the home of the conductor Hans von Bülow and repaid his hospitality by having an affair with his wife, Cosima (herself the illegitimate daughter of Franz Liszt). She bore Wagner two children before von Bülow would consent to a divorce.

Wagner was an unsavory character who gives lie to the mistaken belief that beauty of artistic creation is related to beauty of personality. He combines great musical genius with utter selfishness and absolute ruthlessness. He believed his genius should be supported and that it gave him the right to live in luxury at the expense of others; he would let nothing get in the way of what he set out to acquire or accomplish.

Wagner was a rabid German nationalist ("I am the most German of beings—I am the German Spirit") and violently anti-Semitic (he was the author of an anonymous pamphlet denouncing the music of Mendelssohn because of his Jewish roots, and he claimed that all the troubles in the world were the fault of the Jews, the Jesuits, and the French). He was, not surprisingly, influential on the philosophy of Adolf Hitler, who once said "If you are to understand my thought, you must know the music of Wagner." Yet despite this, his contribution to the development of music is too great to be ignored.

Bayreuth Opera House. © Heller Joachim, 2010. Used under license from Shutterstock, Inc.

Wagner brought the essence of Romantic expansion to its ultimate conclusion. In harmony especially, he expands the resources of tonality as far as they can practically go: long stretches of his music are so chromatic that it is no longer clear what the tonal center is at all. The 20th century felt that he had exhausted the possibilities of tonal harmony and the future lay only in a total rejection of that basis.

Wagner felt that his works, conceived as a *Gesamtkunstwerk* (**Universal Works of Art**), were so different from the operas which preceded them that they shouldn't be called operas. He termed them **music dramas**, and their primary distinction is in their rejection of the so-called number opera style, replacing it with an unending flow of melody from the beginning of each scene to the end—the old distinctions of recitative and aria are no longer applicable.

Much greater importance is given to the orchestra, which is larger and more powerful than the traditional orchestra (this is one of the main reasons Wagner needed a new facility built to his specifications at Bayreuth). Singers needed less agility and more pure power. He even called for a particular kind of tenor, called a **heldentenor** to supply this need. *Held* in German means *hero*; a *heldentenor* has a particularly powerful, ringing voice. An authentic heldentenor is a rare find; only a few may be heard in any generation.

Perhaps the most interesting thing about Wagner's music is his use of the **leitmotif**, a musical idea that represents a person, object, place, action, or a concept. It is similar in concept to Berlioz' **idee fixe**, but in Berlioz, the melody is added on to the musical structure, not as a part of the thematic development. In Wagner, the leitmotifs *are* the musical development and in a given work there are hundreds of them. In this technique, he manages to combine the Romantic fascination with program music with Beethoven's techniques of thematic development.

Wagner exerted as close to total control of his vision as could be imagined. He not only composed the music, he wrote his librettos, conducted the performances, and even did the architectural design of Bayreuth. He coached the singers in singing and acting; he might have sung roles himself if he had the voice to do so.

The Ring of the Nibelungs

We will only study one of Wagner's works, but that one consists of four music dramas. *The Ring of the Nibelungs* took Wagner almost a quarter of a century from beginning the librettos to the premiere. It consists of four works:

- *Das Rheingold (The Rhine Gold)*
- *Die Walküre (The Valkyrie)*
- *Siegfried*
- *Götterdämmerung (The Twilight of the Gods)*

At Bayreuth, the works are generally given over a five-day period, with *Rheingold* on one day, *Walküre* the next day, a day off for singers and audience to recover, then *Siegfied* and *Götterdämmerung* on the next two days. Intermissions are long to enable audiences to enjoy some of the fine Bavarian pastry sold at nearby establishments. All the music together takes just under 20 hours to perform.

For all that, the work is amazingly unified. It can be argued that there isn't a wasted note in the entire cycle. It's based on Germanic and Scandinavian mythology, and the players include the Norse gods Wotan (Odin) and his wife Fricka, Loke the trickster, Donner (Thor) the god of thunder, and Freia with her golden apples.

There are other beings here. Some are divine, some are mortal, and among the mortals there are others besides man. There is the race of the Nibelungs, the dwarfish miners who live underground. There are the Giants, and there are half-divine humans who are the offspring of a god and a mortal.

The story is too complex to be recounted here, but let us get enough background to make sense of the Forging Scene from *Siegfried*.

The gold in the Rhine River is central. It is magical, and whoever possesses it and makes a ring from it can rule the world. However, that power will only come to one who has renounced love. It is guarded by the Rhine Maidens, whose only delight is to swim around the gold in the river and enjoy the sight of it.

The gold is stolen by a vile and disgusting Nibelung named Alberich who's not likely to get any love anyway (see the vile and disgusting part). The gold is then stolen from him by Wotan and Loke, who use trickery to fool him. They now have the gold, but Alberich puts a curse on it. Wotan uses it to pay for the construction of Valhalla, the god's new home, by two giants, Fasolt and Faffner. On receiving the gold, Faffner kills his brother (see the curse part).

We'll skip *Die Walküre* except to identify the Valkyries. These are women warriors, daughters of Wotan, whose duty is to fly winged horses into battles to pick up fallen soldiers and return them to Valhalla . . . or, according to some accounts, back to battle after they have been healed, so they can get killed again. Wotan's favorite is Brünnhilde, but she defies his orders in a battle and is punished by being set on a rock, asleep, to belong to the first man who finds her and kisses her awake. In one last kindness, Wotan agrees with her request to be surrounded by impenetrable fire, so only the bravest man would come through and possess her.

Siegfried was not translated because it is a proper name. Siegfried is a young man who is immensely strong, handsome, and utterly fearless. He was orphaned at birth and was raised by a Nibelung named Mime. Mime, like most of his kind, is vile and disgusting, but he has always told Siegfried that he is his father. Siegfried has noticed that all the forest creatures look like their parents and has realized that Mime can't possibly be his father.

Mime finally tells Siegfried the truth. His mother died in childbirth; she had left her husband and run off with her brother and lover, whom she had never known because they had been separated from birth (both, however, were children of Wotan with a mortal woman). Her gift to her son, whom Mime promised to raise, was an enchanted sword that had been broken in battle and was waiting to be reforged. Mime, for all his skill as a smith, was never able to do the job.

But the sword belongs to Siegfried, and he has both the right and the skill to do the job. The Forging Scene is filled with Siegfried's song as he mightily pumps the bellows of the fire and hammers the blade into shape. His final goal is to confront Faffner, now turned into a dragon and hoarding the magic gold, slay him, and take the gold.

Siegfried's music is interrupted periodically with Mime's whining voice. He plots for two outcomes. If Siegfried is slain, he will be rid of this annoying, disrespectful, and ungrateful teenager for good. If he does kill Faffner . . . well, then, he'll be *hungry* after his battle. And old Mime will have made him some delightful soup to regain his strength . . . until the poison takes effect.

Siegfried successfully reforges his sword, named *Nothung* (Needful); before taking it to Faffner's lair, he tests it be slicing Mime's anvil into two halves.

example

Wagner: *Siegfried, Act I: Forging Scene*

Siegfried does indeed kill the dragon. In the process, he tastes some of the dragon's blood, which allows him to understand the song of one of the forest birds. He is warned of Mime's plot and is also told of a rock nearby atop a high hill where a beautiful maiden lies in enchanted sleep, surrounded by impenetrable fire.

Wagner's Other Music Dramas

Wagner wrote three other works he designated Music Dramas. Two were written and premiered when he was working on *The Ring*, and the third was his final composition:

- *Tristan und Isolde* (1859)
- *Die Meistersinger von Nuremburg* (1867)
- *Parsifal* (1882)

Tristan und Isolde is based on a Medieval Irish legend. Tristan is a loyal soldier for King Mark and is sent to bring back the King's future bride, Isolde, from her home. Along the way, both are given a magic potion that causes them to fall deeply in love. The work centers on the tensions between powerful erotic desire and inescapable duty. It contains some of Wagner's darkest and most powerful music, and in many ways it marks the end of the Romantic Period—some 50 years before it is finally exhausted. No other work, for a full half century, stretches the resources of harmony so far; no other work sustains tensions for such an extended time before they are finally, blissfully resolved.

Die Meistersinger von Nuremburg (*The Mastersingers of Nurnburg*) is Wagner's only work that has no dependence on magic or myth. It is his most human work, and his only comedy. It is set in Renaissance Germany, at a time when tradesmen were forming guilds to promote trade, and when the guild of the Mastersingers—songwriters with great devotion to their art—flourished among that society.

Parsifal is based on a Medieval French tale of Percival and the Holy Grail. It revisits a recurring theme in Wagner: the conflict between the sacred and the profane and the capacity of love to transcend all. Its overtly Christian themes may seem odd in light of Wagner's life, but he linked that faith, particularly German Protestant faith, with German identity and German superiority. Had he lived, his next project would have been a music drama, *Jesus of Nazareth*.

Glossary

Absolute music: instrumental music that refers only to itself; the opposite of program music

Bandoneon: an Argentine instrument, a type of accordion, used especially in the nuevo tango

Bayreuth: the city in Bavaria, Germany, where Wagner built an opera house specifically designed for production of his works; still under the control of the Wagner family, open only in summers, and devoted exclusively to Wagner's works, with the sole exception of Beethoven's Symphony no. 9

Heldentenor: a tenor with a particularly strong, dark sound (from the German Held, meaning hero); usually given lead roles in Wagner's music dramas

Leitmotif: a musical idea that represents something: an object, idea, action, person, or place

The Mighty Five: Five Russian nationalist composers based in St. Petersburg, devoted to creating a truly Russian style of music: Modest Mussorgsky, Alexandr Borodin, Nikolai Rimsky-Korsakov, Mili Balakirev, and Cesar Cui

Music drama: Wagner's mature works; he thought they were so different from traditional operas that they should be known by another name

Nationalism: the reflection of a composer's national heritage in music; perhaps by the celebration of an important historical event, or the quotation of a folk song, or the imitation of the style of folk song or dance

Nuevo tango: an Argentine tradition that takes traditional tango music and combines it with more sophisticated compositional and harmonic techniques

Universal work of art: in Wagner's thought, the ultimate goal of his operas/music dramas, a synthesis of all aspects of art—music, visual arts, literature, dance, architecture; while this had always been the goal of opera, in Wagner, all is under the control of one central artistic genius, his own (sometimes known by the original German term, Gesamtkunstwerk)

POSTROMANTICISM, *VERISMO,* AND IMPRESSIONISM
The Golden Sunset of Romanticism

Postromanticism

The transition into the 20th century is, like the transition from Classicism to Romanticism, difficult to follow. After Wagner, the essence of Romanticism continued in the music of several composers who continued the expansive language of Romanticism into the 20th century. There were many who can be considered a part of that group, including Sibelius and Vaughan Williams, who were discussed in the previous chapter. They are loosely connected by the influence, to one degree or another, of the music of Wagner, and their conviction that the language of Romanticism was still viable.

Gustav Mahler (1860–1911)

Mahler was born in Iglau in Bohemia to Jewish parents. He did not at first intend to become a musician. When, at the age of 8, he was asked what he wanted to be when he grew up, he answered "a martyr." Many who worked under him later wished his early ambition had been realized because Mahler was best known in his time as a conductor, and a rather tyrannical one at that. He demanded perfection and displayed little patience when his orchestras fell short. In fairness, he was just as demanding on himself, and his musicians respected him as much as they feared him.

Gustav Mahler. Library of Congress, Prints and Photographs Division, Reproduction Number: LC-USZ6-878.

The path at that time to a career in conducting led through opera houses. Just as in any city in the United States that has any cultural ambitions likes to have a symphony, in Europe at that time, any city would have its own opera house. He worked his way up until he became director of the Budapest Opera, the Hamburg Opera, and finally the Vienna Opera. He took that last post despite Austrian laws that banned a Jew from serving as the director. He briefly converted to Catholicism for the post, though he was never devout as Jew or Christian. From 1907 until just before his death, he was the conductor of the New York Philharmonic and the Metropolitan Opera.

The schedule of a conductor leaves little time for composing, but then as now, there is a concert season from mid-fall through spring. Summers were off-season, and Mahler liked to spend them at a country home where he could compose in peace. Perhaps because of this, his output is limited to only two types of compositions: **Symphonies (9½)** and **Orchestral Song Cycles**.

The alert reader presumably wonders how one composes half of a symphony. In Mahler's case, one dies while working on the composition. Mahler was a brilliant man, widely educated in many fields, but he was also superstitious. He took quite seriously the idea, widely held at the time, that no one could compose more than nine symphonies, because that's all Beethoven composed.

Mahler was not the only one to think this. Anton Bruckner, who was not discussed earlier, renumbered his symphonies starting with no. 0 and he died half way through his ninth symphony that was actually his tenth. Mahler was more successful at avoiding fate. After his eighth symphony, he titled his next work *Das Lied von der Erde* (*The Song of the Earth*). It was an orchestral song cycle but distinctly in the form of a symphony, just without the designation. Mahler followed with his ninth symphony, and died when he had completed two movements of his tenth.

Mahler was a passionately intense man, and his music is also passionate. His works tend toward the monumental, in length and in performing forces. His orchestras are large, and in four of his symphonies he includes singers. Mahler was the composer of the *Symphony of a Thousand* mentioned in the introduction to Romanticism in Chapter 8. However, he avoided the temptation, too often succumbed to by late romantic composers, to overindulge in great gouts of sound. While other composers will use all their forces for most of the piece, Mahler

Figure 10.2

St. Anthony of Padua. © JupiterImages, Inc.

uses his forces sparingly, a few at a time, like a constantly changing chamber ensemble, and only a few times in a piece will all the forces be brought into use.

An excellent example of this, and of the influence of vocal music even in purely instrumental pieces, can be heard in the scherzo movement of his *Symphony no. 2 in c minor, "Resurrection."*

The "Resurrection" of the title is from the final movement, which includes two vocal soloists and a chorus. It is a setting of a Klopstock poem, *Auferstehung* (*Rise again*). The vision of the Resurrection is more Pantheist than Christian . . . at the end of times, all that has lived will rise to join all that is living and return to the Divine. That glorious finale is hinted at toward the end of the scherzo, when things build to an earth-shatteringly dissonant chord. It is the very chord that begins the final movement, and its purpose is, indeed, to wake the dead.

But this movement is of simpler stuff. It is, in fact, an arrangement of a song with orchestra Mahler had composed earlier, to a bit of German folk poetry collectively known as *Des Knaben Wunderhorn* (*The Youth's Magic Horn*). This particular poem is *St. Anthony of Padua Preaches to the Fishes.* In the poem, the great Saint goes to the riverbank to preach his Sunday sermon to the fishes. The pike, the carp, and the perch all listen and say what a wonderful sermon it was. Then they go on their way; the pike are still greedy, the carp are still lazy, and the perch are still thieves, but they all agree on what a fine sermon it was.

Notice that Mahler, despite having a large orchestra at his disposal, only uses a few instruments at a time. One hears only half of the first violins in some spots, or a single wind; and, until that huge chord, only a few places use most of the orchestra. It's like hearing a chamber ensemble that keeps changing its instrumentation.

example

Mahler: *Symphonie no. 2 in c minor: III*

Richard Strauss (1864–1949)

Some listeners find Strauss' music to be more noisy than expansive, but many find him among the greatest of the Postromantics. His earliest works owe much to Brahms, but he flirted briefly with some of the extremely dissonant music that was emerging in the early part of the 20th century. He was an astute business-man, always conscious of his public reception, perhaps too much so to travel that experimental path.

And also, perhaps because of his willingness to ally himself to whomever was in power, he became publicly loyal to Hitler's regime. Though this was more out of professional expediency than because of any philosophical common ground, he still had to go through a de-Nazification process after World War II.

Strauss' output centers around three areas: **Symphonic Poems** (he preferred to call them Tone Poems (such as *Till Eulenspiegel*, *Also Sprach Zarathustra*, and *Don Quixote*); **Operas** (his first two are his most modern: *Salome* and *Elektra*. He shrank from that abyss—the near breakdown of tonality—and his next work remains his most popular: *Der Rosenkavalier*); and **Lieder** (many of which were arranged for orchestral accompaniment by Strauss, and some were originally intended for orchestra *Four Last Songs*).

Richard Strauss. Library of Congress, Prints and Photographs Division, Reproduction Number: LC-B2-3747-11.

---

example

Strauss: *Till Eulenspiegel*

The full title in translation is "Till Eulenspeigel's Merry Pranks." The figure in German folklore dates to at least as early as 1300, and the music depicts his capacity to cause trouble. He is represented by a horn theme and another on clarinet, each of which recurs throughout the piece. After upsetting merchant's shops, flirting with young ladies, and ridiculing stuffy professors and hypocritical clergy, the authorities finally catch up with Till, and he is sentenced to death by beheading for blasphemy. He cannot, try as he might, talk himself out of this situation, but after the axe is heard to fall, we hear his theme once more . . . either he managed to escape, or his spirit of defiance cannot be killed.

Sergei Rachmaninoff (1873–1943)

Rachmaninoff was one of the century's greatest pianists. He was born in Russia but immigrated to the United States for most of his life. His music is deter-minedly Romantic in the face of all the century's rejection of that very ethic—at least, the rejection of many musicians. Audiences never outgrew Romanticism, and as performer and composer, he is among the most popular.

Apart from his three symphonies, his most important works are for piano. These include four piano concertos, the *Rhapsody on a Theme by Paganini*, and many works for solo piano. He adored Chaikovsky and shared a bit (only a bit, mercifully) of that composer's self-doubt. He reached a particular crisis after the poor reception of his first symphony. He went into a deep depression and wrote nothing for several years. But in 1900, he entered psychological hypnotherapy and was given the suggestion that his next composition would be a masterpiece. That next composition was his second piano concerto, and all agree that it is a masterpiece.

Sergei Rachmaninoff. Library of Congress, Prints and Photographs Division, Reproduction Number: LC-USZ62-103112.

Rachmaninoff: *Piano Concerto no. 2 in c minor*

I. Moderato

Arnold Schoenberg (1874–1951)

If you have any music background, you may be surprised to see the name Arnold Schoenberg here. Certainly, he is best known for his groundbreaking work in **atonality**, music without a tonal center. That music is considered by many to be the antithesis of Romanticism (though we will see in the next chapter that the truth is quite different).

But Schoenberg's earliest musical hero was Brahms, and then he fell under the spell of Wagner. His early compositions are distinctly in the Postromantic style. Important works of this period include *Gurrelieder*, *Pelleas et Melisande*, *Verklärte Nacht* (*Transfigured Night*), *String Quartet no. 1*, and *Chamber Symphony no. 1*.

We'll deal with Schoenberg in greater detail later, but for now, let's hear the orchestral opening of his massive work, *Gurrelieder*. The story of the work, based on Danish mythology, is something like Wagner's *Ring*, but for now, just let the music describe the magical setting.

example

Schoenberg: *Gurrelieder*, opening

Opera: *Verismo*

Postromantic opera is probably best seen in the works of Richard Strauss, the master of the form. But there was another movement in Italy called *verismo* (realism), that shares with the Postromantics the richness and intensity of musical language. Wagner is certainly felt here, though the voice of Verdi is even stronger.

The name *verismo* may strike you as odd, but "Realistic Opera" is not an oxymoron. It refers to a style of Italian opera that follows Verdi and leads into the 20th century. There are elements of the philosophy in works by Bizet and Massenet, but the movement is at its root an Italian one.

In *verismo* opera, everyday people are portrayed in ordinary situations reacting violently under the influence of powerful emotions. You may see something in common with what are now referred to as "soap operas"—daytime (or, for a time, evening) dramas that were called "operas" because of their intensity of emotion (and "soap" because such companies often sponsored the shows).

That the works are not always logical bothers their audiences little. The sentimental yet powerful stories, rich harmonies, beautiful melodies, and colorful orchestration have made these works among the most popular of all operas.

Interestingly, with the exception of Puccini, most composers of *verismo* are famous for a single work. They composed many, but only one was a major success. Of these, the most popular are a pair of one-act operas, both composed as entries in a one-act opera competition.

They still represent their composers' finest work and are frequently paired in performance, as each is too short for an evening's performance but together they are perfect.

Ruggiero Leoncavallo (1858–1919): *Pagliacci*

Pietro Mascagni (1863–1945): *Cavelleria rusticana*

Giacomo Puccini (1858–1924)

The most popular of the *verismo* composers was **Giacomo Puccini**. He composed a series of works, all still wildly popular:

- *Manon Lescaut*
- *La boheme*
- *Madama Butterfly*
- *Tosca*
- *Turandot*

Giacomo Puccini. © JupiterImages, Inc.

La boheme means "The Bohemians." This does not refer to expatriates from the Czech Republic but was then a slang term for young, artistic types who lived a carefree, money-free existence, making up the rules for themselves rather than conforming to social mores. The cast includes several of these: Rodolfo, the poet; Marcello, the painter; Colline, the philosopher; and Schaunard, the Musician. In the first act, the troupe goes off to find some dinner, but Rodolfo is delayed when he meets his neighbor, Mimi. She has dropped her key and cannot find it; the matter is complicated when the lights go out and only moonlight remains. She introduces herself in the aria *Mi chiamano Mimi*.

Puccini: *La boheme, Act I*

Mi chiamano Mimi

Impressionism

If Germany and Russia had their Postromanticism and Italy had *verismo*, France had Impressionism. The musical style borrows its name, and its aesthetic, from corresponding movements in visual arts (**impressionist painting**) and literature (**symbolist poetry**).

Monet: *Parliament.* © JupiterImages, Inc.

In impressionist painting, the artist was less concerned with the literal representation of an object or scene than with the impression made from the play of light on it. Works often made of pinpoints of light and color that only coalesce into recognizable images at a distance. Painters such as Claude Monet, Pierre-Auguste Renoirs, and Camille Pissarro are associated with this movement.

In **Symbolist poetry**, suggestion rather than depiction is emphasized. Stephan Mallarme, one of the greatest of the symbolists, once said "To name an object is to suppress ¾ of the enjoyment of a poem—the dream is to suggest it." Even his use of the word "dream" (rather than the object or the goal) is typical of the symbolists.

Similarly, in music, impressionism involves a blurring of outlines, in form, color, harmony, and rhythm. Characteristics include the following:

- Delicate, muted, and shimmering orchestral colors;
- Fluidity of rhythm;
- Use of unusual scales, such as pentatonic or whole-tone;
- Use of unresolved dissonances; and
- Use of parallel streams of chords.

To the nonmusician, some of this may mean little. The reference to the scales, for instance, cites pentatonic and whole-tone scales. The classic pentatonic scale is the same as the major scale, but with the fourth and seventh notes omitted. If you recall from the beginning of the class, those are the notes that are one-half step away from their neighbor, rather than a whole step. And it is the half step that helps to define harmonic motion most strongly. If you don't have those half steps, harmony is more ambiguous and less clearly defined. A whole-tone scale consists entirely of whole steps—no half steps at all, with a similar result.

The part about unresolved dissonances was really unusual. Musicians study for years to understand how dissonances can be, and should be, resolved in traditional musical language. But what if you didn't resolve them? What if the dissonance just sat there, not moving as expected? Again, the result would be to blur expectations.

How about those parallel streams of chords? The key word here is parallel. We learned earlier that in any given key, there were triads made from the diatonic scales of the key, and that those came in a particular order. But if the stream of chords is parallel—all major, all minor, or all the same type of seventh chord—it's as if we are constantly changing the key, moving between different tonalities. Again, expectations are thrown completely off balance.

Two prominent composers are most often paired as impressionists, although its influence has been felt by almost every composer of the century to one degree or another. They are Claude Debussy and Maurice Ravel.

Claude Debussy (1862–1918)

Debussy studied piano at the Paris Conservatory, where he got bad grades because he insisted on his own personal style even during his student days. Despite fighting with his professors, he won the Prix de Rome, a prestigious scholarship that allowed two years of free study in Rome. He was appalled to find that Rome was full of Italians, with very few French persons, and he later claimed to have learned nothing. One of his early positions was as tutor for the children of Nadezhda von Meck, Chaikovsky's patron.

Like everyone in his age, he was initially fascinated by Wagner. Unlike most, he came to be repelled by him, and said of *The Ring*, "My God! How unbearable these people in skins and helmets become by the fourth night!" Though his music is based largely on Wagner's innovations, its basic character is that of a reaction against Wagner.

His life was one of a series of financial and personal crises. The suicides of two women associated with Debussy shocked Paris, which was notoriously difficult to shock. His long-time mistress shot herself when he left her for Rosalie Texier, his first wife—and she in turn shot herself when he left her for Emma Bardac, his second wife.

His late works are increasingly nationalistic, with an even more specific rejection of Germanic domination. He took to signing his compositions "*musicien francais.*" He died of cancer in 1918 when the Germans were shelling Paris during World War I.

Claude Debussy. © JupiterImages, Inc.

example

Prelude: a l'apres-midi d'un faune

Debussy's earliest mature orchestral work was the *Prelude: a l'apres-midi d'un faune* (*Prelude: to the Afternoon of a Faun*). In this case, the Faun is not a baby deer, but a mythological creature, half-man, half-goat, also known as a satyr, and possessed of an insatiable sexual appetite.

It is based on a poem by Mallarme, and it suggests a scene that begins with the Faun playing his flute (actually, Pan pipes) languidly in the afternoon heat. He tries to recall whether he actually carried off two beautiful nymphs earlier that day and had pleasures with them, or whether he just imagined it. The effort exhausts him, and he falls asleep in the warm, fading sunlight.

Other Music by Debussy

Orchestral

- *La Mer*
- *Nocturnes*

Piano

- *Preludes, Books I and II*
- *Pour le Piano*
- *Suite bergamasque* (the famous *Claire de Lune* is in this)
- *l'Isle joyeaux*

Maurice Ravel. © JupiterImages, Inc.

Maurice Ravel (1875–1937)

Ravel is superficially similar in style to Debussy, but with a touch of neo-classicism (to be discussed later). Musicians often use images from sight to describe sound. One such case is the observation that Debussy shimmers, while Ravel glistens.

He was born near the Spanish border, and his music has some influence from Spanish folk sounds. He is one of history's greatest orchestrators, and in that capacity, we have met him before. He was the composer of *Bolero*, a piece that is totally dependent on orchestration to make its mark; he was also mentioned as the orchestrator of Mussorgsky's *Pictures at an Exhibition*. He even orchestrated many of his own piano works.

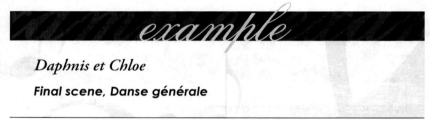

example

Daphnis et Chloe

Final scene, Danse générale

Debussy's *Prelude: a l'apres-midi d'un faune* was originally an orchestral work, but it was later choreographed for performance by Vaslav Nijinsky, who also danced as the Faun, in a production by the *Ballets Russes*, which will be discussed much more in the next chapter. Ravel's *Daphnis et Chloe* was written originally as a ballet.

It can be argued that Ravel's music was not entirely impressionist, but this work is a total realization of the impressionist aesthetic and a masterpiece of sensuality. The entire score is filled with exquisite music, but the closing six scenes are often excerpted as *Suite no. 1* and *Suite no. 2* for purely orchestral performances.

The story of the ballet is simple. Daphnis and Chloe are lovers, but are separated when Chloe is kidnapped by brigands. They are finally reunited with the aid of the Great God Pan (himself a satyr, and the creator of the Pan pipes). The final scene is the *Danse générale*, in which the lovers are joined by nymphs and satyrs in a frenzied Bacchanale.

Two things stand out in the music. The meter, for the most part, is asymmetrical, 5/4, grouped as 3+2. And halfway through, Ravel introduces a wordless chorus, whose moans of pleasure leave no doubt as to what's happening.

Glossary

Impressionism: in music, a style of French music, a transition between Romanticism and the Revolutionary Age, characterized by delicate, shimmering orchestral colors; unresolved dissonances; unusual scales

Pentatonic scale: a scale consisting of only five notes, typically scale degrees 1, 2, 3, 5, and 6; this type of scale will have no half steps, and creates ambiguity in harmony

Post-romanticism: music, primarily German, that continues the essential style of Wagner into the Revolutionary Age—often using large-scale works for outsized orchestra and high levels of chromaticism without leaving tonality entirely

Verismo: as style of opera, primarily Italian, that focuses on ordinary people in extraordinary situations that cause them to react with extreme emotions

Whole-tone scale: a scale consisting of seven whole steps, no half steps; used often by Impressionist composers

Other Music by Ravel

Ravel's music is some of the most sensual, sexiest music ever composed. It's surprising to learn that he never had a lover of any gender that can be confirmed. His sensuality seems to have been solely in his musical world.

You'll notice several duplicate titles listed in both orchestral music and piano music. That's not a typo. Ravel orchestrated several of his own piano works.

Orchestral

- *Bolero*
- *Rhapsodie Espagnole*
- *Pavane pour une Infante defunte (Pavane for a dead Princess)*
- *Tombeau de Couperin*
- *Ma Mere l'Oye (Mother Goose)*
- *La Valse*

Chamber music

- *Piano trio in a minor*
- *String Quartet in F*

Piano

- *Pavane pour une Infante defunte (Pavane for a dead Princess)*
- *Tombeau de Couperin*
- *Ma Mere l'Oye (Mother Goose)*
- *La Valse*
- *Gaspard de la nuit*
- *Sonatine*

Vocal

- *Chansons madecasees* (for voice, piano, and flute)

THE 20TH CENTURY
The Revolutionary Age (1910–1970)

A New Approach

This chapter represents a new approach to understanding the music of the last century; it is an approach that represents the thoughts of the author, and, at this point, only the author. Although informal consultations with colleagues have found considerable sympathy for this viewpoint, it has not been published in a peer-reviewed setting and does not yet represent any scholarly consensus.

Essentially, music historians have long referred to the music of the 20th century as 20th-century Music . . . the age did not have a descriptive name, like Baroque or Romantic, largely because we were still in it. What was perceived as the latest (one hopes not the last) era of music history might receive such a name, but that would be for someone in the future to coin. As of the time of this writing, it is the year 2011 C.E. We can no longer speak of the most recent music as 20th-century Music because we're now in the 21st century.

Moreover, we now have sufficient distance from the music of that era to notice that there is an actual date after which there was a significant change. It is possible to date that era from 1910 to 1970, and I will call the era, until someone comes up with a more satisfying description, the **Revolutionary Age**.

That period was marked with an astonishing amount of change, and things developed and shifted at a rate exponentially faster than anyone had seen in the past. Whereas in the past, it may have taken a century or more for a particular stylistic movement to exhaust itself, now movements are arising, flourishing for a decade or so, and finding a new movement arise which is a rejection of it . . . and the rejection is often equally short-lived.

There are reasons for this, and those will be discussed below. But the essential nature of the music of The Revolutionary Age was, well, revolution. Many believed that the voice of Romanticism was exhausted, and the future lay in something radically new.

Just what that new direction should be was not always agreed on. As is too often the case with political revolutions, this artistic revolution knew what needed to be destroyed, but didn't have a clear idea of how to proceed after the destruction.

Even the swinging pendulum between the Classic and the Romantic had lost any equilibrium. Music that was essentially Classic has coexisted with music that is essentially Romantic, and those have existed with music not clearly allied to either camp. By the 1950s and 1960s, movements were in progress that explored extremes of either aesthetic, attempting to function without the balance of the other. Thus, it can be argued that, by the 1970s, music had explored extremes in all directions. At that point, anything was possible; everything had been explored.

And *from* that point, composers for the last 40 years have most often taken the attitude that, while anything is possible, not everything is desirable. An eclectic approach has reigned for some time—any composer writing at this point will take those styles, movements, and techniques that he or she finds most congenial, most personal, and will simply ignore other directions.

Apart from that, since the 1970s, no identifiable movement in the cultivated musical tradition has emerged. It is too recent for there to be any need for, or ability to, christen this time (and "The Eclectic Age" is just too prosaic).

Thus, the student should realize that this particular approach is not universally accepted; it is the product of the author's analysis of the direction of music in the most recent times. The student should also realize that this newly coined term does not actually affect our understanding of the music of the past century, but it does offer one person's take on the progress of music in time.

The Revolutionary Age

During the years surrounding the beginnings of the 20th century, profound changes were taking place in European society. The expansive freedoms of the Romantic era had begun to degenerate into a kind of overripe decadence; the overwhelming sense of romantic optimism and the belief in the ultimate triumph of humankind's struggle were losing hold and were to be replaced by a resignation to human mortality. The collapse of the romantic ideal led to a total redefinition of all types of artistic expression: music along with art, dance, drama, poetry, and literature. Visual art was freed from the need to represent recognizable objects and moved to abstract images; dance and drama were liberated from their dependence on conventionalities of movement and plot; literature and poetry ranged ever farther from traditional expectations. And music followed natural trends in harmonic development and abandoned tonality entirely.

The century saw a revolution that, in music, is as important as any in history, including the shift from unaccompanied melody to harmony at the end of the Middle Ages. And, as has been the case with many revolutions, the past has often been overthrown without any clear idea as to what will actually replace it. Nevertheless, the feeling that "anything is possible" is exhilarating and rather frightening. Artists of the 20th century have faced what has been called the "abyss of freedom" and have had to create their own rules. Each has had to choose how deeply he or she will explore that abyss.

Every era tends to think of itself as unique, but our own century is different in two important areas. The **technological revolution** of the 20th century has become almost overwhelming, changing every aspect of our lives. In addition, at no time in the past has the gap between classical and popular traditions been so pronounced.

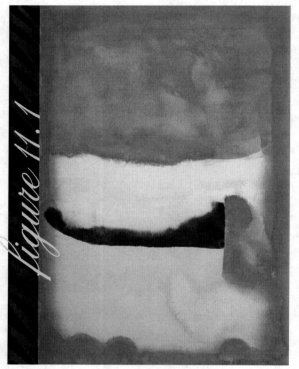

Mark Rothko: *Yellow and Pink on Red.*
© JupiterImages, Inc.

The Technological Revolution

When one contemplates the important historical events that have shaped civilization during our century (and consequently the art of that civilization, as humanity seeks to express what it has become), the prevalence of war is the first thing to come to mind. Whether or not the century has seen *more* war than any other time is debatable; what is unarguable is that those wars have a greater capability for destruction than humanity has ever known. We have fought two World Wars—conflicts that have included so many nations spread over so many continents that they can actually be considered global.

The reason we have never had such a conflict before is not because humanity lacked the urge to destroy itself on such a scale: we lacked the technological means to accomplish such a task. To coordinate forces of destruction on such a scale demands means of transportation for manpower and machinery over global distances, as well as some efficient means of communication to coordinate those forces. Until the 20th century, we simply lacked such technology.

We also lacked the technology of destruction with which to wage a truly global war. During the 20th century, that technology increased to terrifying proportions. And, after the close of World War II, we now have the power to destroy all life on the planet, apparently several times over. This is unique in human history. Military forces of previous centuries may have been able to invade a neighboring country and murder all men, women, children, and livestock, while burning the crops and salting the fields, but *eventually* life would return, as nature would reclaim its own. The horror of total annihilation is unique to our time.

Ironically, however, many of the *positive* aspects of technology have been products of war efforts—when the war is over, the innovations remain and can be put to peaceful use. Many of the developments in transportation, communication, and medical care of our century have come from research during wartimes.

Imagine, for instance, what music history would be like if air travel had been available to Haydn—if he were not stuck at the Esterhazy estate, but could instead hop on a flight to London, Paris, or Rome, and be back the next day for his duties. How would his music have been different? Imagine also what would have happened if modern medical care were available to some figures of the past. Many of the major composers of the Romantic era dropped dead before their fortieth birthday, many of complications from diseases that can now be cured by a quick shot of penicillin. How would history be different if Mozart had lived past 35 years, or Schubert past 31 years, or Chopin or Mendelssohn past 40 years?

The most significant developments, from the standpoint of the art of music, have taken place in communication technology. The ability to store a musical performance electronically, and reproduce it at will, is as profound a change in music as the development of music notation was a millennium ago.

Prior to the 20th century, anyone who wanted to experience music had to do so through live performance. Now, musical performances can be broadcast electronically, by radio, television, or even computer network, and can be experienced by millions simultaneously. A performance can also be recorded and stored, by means of a vinyl disc, magnetic tape, computer-encoded compact disc, DVD, MP3 or MP4 audio file—and who knows what will be next. Anyone with the devices to reproduce this material can have access to the finest performances of the greatest music of the century. The very existence of a course like this would be impossible without the use of 20th-century recording technology.

That technology has changed the very nature of musical performance. Music prior to the 20th century existed at a specific point in time: the moment of performance; that moment could not be preserved or repeated, except in the imagination. With recording, though, an artist or ensemble can work in a studio until the precise qualities that are sought have been achieved. The audience, then, does not see a work in progress but a finished product. The recording musician, then, works more like a painter, sculptor, novelist, or poet.

This has also changed audience expectations of live performances—the modern audience, used to the technical perfection that can be achieved in a studio, demands a higher level of that perfection in live performance. For many, this technical finish has led to a lower level of spontaneity and imagination in live music; however, for better or worse, modern conservatories and universities are now training student musicians to compete at this level of technical excellence.

Classical and Popular Traditions and the Musical Canon

The second way in which our century is unique is in the divide between so-called classical and popular musical traditions (sometimes referred to as *cultivated* and *vernacular*, respectively). These terms are difficult to define clearly; it is arguable that the distinctions are actually more artificial than real. Generally, it can be said that popular music is composed for the entertainment of a specific audience, and when that audience no longer exists, the music is of no interest to others. Classical music (some of which admittedly arises from popular traditions), however, possesses a *transhistorical* quality: it speaks powerfully to its intended audience but can somehow transcend that audience and its era. A "classic" has a quality of universality and has stood the test of time.

This last element is the problem of modern music. How does one know, during the era in which music is made, whether it will stand the test of time? The unfortunate answer is, one does not know. Only time itself will truly tell.

Of course, some such divisions have always been present in history. During some eras, the split has been between sacred and secular traditions, or between the music of the aristocracy and that of the common people, or between written and oral traditions. Often, the popular music of the past has been lost because much of it was never preserved in written form.

But at no time in history has so much veneration been given to past composers, while those of our own era are so sadly neglected. The modern composer Arthur Honegger once said, "The public doesn't want new music. The main thing it demands of a composer is that he be dead."

Before the Early Romantic period, there was virtually no interest in listening to music that was more than 10 years old. No one would have thought to offer a course like this at that time. Occasional exceptions like Mozart's *Don Giovanni* only served to prove the rule.

Even during the 19th century, the bulk of attention was given to contemporary composers—who, by and large, *were* the popular musicians of their era. The operas of Weber, Rossini, Donizetti, and Verdi were huge successes; the recitals of Liszt created the same hysterical enthusiasm that can be found in some, but not all, modern rock concerts. Though the music was often intended for a cultivated audience, the sweeping egalitarianism of the 19th century made concerts open to all levels of society.

But also, during this time, something started to emerge. Perhaps we can credit Mendelssohn, who began the revival of the music of J. S. Bach, with establishing the idea that certain music from the past can and should be preserved, enjoyed, appreciated, and even venerated. Perhaps some credit also goes to Mozart and Beethoven, who forced a reevaluation of the position of the musician in society as artist rather than servant.

There is, in the arts, literature, and philosophy, this notion of a **canon**, a set body of works that, by virtue of their high quality, are worthy of preservation and study. The canon in visual arts, and in literature and philosophy, has been around for some time, but music, for whatever reason, didn't begin to establish a canon until the 19th century. Because it came late, the musical canon has been more flexible, with works being added as awareness increased of lost traditions or unrecognized masterworks. This notion of a body of Classical music is an expression of this canon.

So what has happened during our time? Several factors have contributed to the deepening split. Both the spread of technology and new techniques of marketing, geared more toward the greatest and quickest profit rather than to sincere artistic expression, have contributed to the divide. Likewise, we will see that composers were perhaps more ready for the 20th-century revolution than audiences were. Yet, there has developed an overriding conviction among modern musicians: it is more important for a composer to present an honest vision or his or her imagination than to create what will please the widest audience. This has often meant that a composer must pay a price of financial neglect in exchange for artistic integrity.

New Aspects of Music

The Revolutionary Age was marked by a rejection of the conventions of the past and by the creation of new conventions. This means nothing less than the redefinition of the art of music itself; it will not surprise you to know that there was never any agreement as to how that redefinition should be manifest or whether it was necessary at all. While certain generalizations of past eras, regarding aspects such as rhythm, harmony, texture, and the like are not only possible but easy to detect, this is not easy with music after 1910.

Certain aspects are evident, while hardly universal. **Rhythm** becomes more of a foreground element, more complex and varied. One even finds works scored entirely for non-melodic percussion instruments. Ballet becomes more important than opera as a meeting place of the arts. The age found more in common with the pulsating sounds of a factory or urban traffic than the murmur of a brook. **Melodies** are more angular and less songlike; there is a conscious attempt *not* to be lyrical. **Form** explores new ways to organize musical material that have no relation to the sonata cycle. And after thousands of years, a new family of instruments arises: **electronic instruments**.

Nowhere are changes as profound as in harmony. The shift was profound and did not happen overnight. It had been stirring all through the Romanic period as composers' music became more complex and used dissonant notes ever more freely. The **Impressionists** contributed to the breakdown of harmony when they started using unusual scales and unresolved dissonances.

Others discovered that music can be created that centers on more than one tonal center, called **polytonality**. Perhaps a piano piece can put the right hand in D major and the left in Ab major, or an orchestral work can have strings in one key and winds in another.

Composers also found that they could create new effects by using traditional musical materials in an untraditional way. This was called **pandiatonicism** because the "traditional musical materials" were often the diatonic scale, arranged not as expected but in new combinations. For instance, traditional chords were built using the interval of a third. But if one builds a chord using the interval of a fourth—called **quartal harmony**—a new sound is heard.

After all this stretching and pulling, the composer **Arnold Schoenberg** was the first to make the final leap into the abyss, writing music without any tonal center at all: **atonal music**. Schoenberg was unhappy with the term, though it has long been standard, because it described what the music was not rather than what it was. He preferred **pantonal**, which is actually more accurate: "pan" means "all," and in this system, all notes are used equally, none dominates as the music's center.

Harmony had also, in the past, been the turning point for two of the other three seismic shifts in music, occurring roughly every 300 years:

- 1000 C.E.: Notation arises, and composition replaces memory and improvisation.
- 1300 C.E.: Harmony arises for the first time, as modal polyphony replaces monophony.
- 1600 C.E.: Tonal harmony replaces modal.
- 1900 C.E.: Atonality arises, with the intent to replace tonality.

Indeed, the expectation of those who pioneered atonal music was that it was the music of the future and would replace tonal music as surely as tonal music had replaced modal harmony. That did not occur, though neither did atonal music stop being written. It remains an option that is used by those composers who choose to do so (John W. Duarte has said that atonality is the 25th key . . . 12 major keys, 12 minor, and atonality).

Whither Music? The Battle to Determine the Direction of the Revolutionary Age

As we saw in the last chapter, the collapse of Romanticism was not immediate. The Postromantic composers extended the Romantic language and aesthetics well into the new century. The Impressionists were the first to make a conscious break with the past in their new treatment of harmony, form, and tone color. New developments would follow, restructuring and even redefining the language of music into something for a new age.

After the first decade of the new century, it was clear to most musicians that a new era was dawning, one during which a new kind of music would be made. The question was, what kind of music would that be? If the swinging pendulum was to be on schedule, it would seem that the 20th century was due for a return to another age of classicism. Other figures felt that the Romantic language was moving in a particular direction, *beyond* the Postromantic era to a brand new sort of musical language, which would obey totally different organizational rules.

The stage was set for a battle between two towering geniuses, each with his own unique vision of the future of music: Igor Stravinsky's **neoclassicism** and Arnold Schoenberg's **serialism** (both of which will be discussed subsequently). To a great extent, every composer of the first half of the century became allied with one camp or the other.

Neither Stravinsky nor Schoenberg, of course, began their careers with what was to become their most important contributions. Both grew gradually toward these goals, and both made other significant contributions during their early periods: Stravinsky in his early nationalistic works and the **primitivism** of *The Rite of Spring* and Schoenberg in his early Postromantic works and his subsequent **expressionist** period.

Igor Stravinsky (1882–1971): Nationalism and Primitivism

Igor Stravinsky. © Marvin Koner/Corbis.

By the estimation of many, Igor Stravinsky was the most important composer of the 20th century. He was born near Petrograd (St. Petersburg, known as Leningrad during the Soviet era), the son of musicians—his father Feodor Stravinsky was a bass with the Russian Imperial Opera. His parents, who loved him, felt that music was too insecure a profession and encouraged him to study law. As a law student, he was a disaster and even once paid another student to take one of his finals for him.

Law school was profitable for his musical future, for one of his schoolmates was the son of Nicolai Rimsky-Korsakov, one of the members of the group of Russian nationalist composers who called themselves the Mighty Five. Stravinsky began taking private lessons in composition with Rimsky-Korsakov in 1907, continuing until the older composer's death the following summer. Not surprisingly, most of Stravinsky's earliest works are strongly influenced by Russian nationalism.

Paris and Diaghilev

In 1909, Stravinsky left Russia (never to return permanently, as it turned out) and came to Paris. There, he made the acquaintance of another Russian expatriate, **Sergei Diaghilev**, director of the *Ballets Russes* (Russian Ballet). Diaghilev had a vision for ballet similar to that which Wagner had for opera: he saw it as a Universal Work of Art, a synthesis of all aspects of artistic expression into a single medium.

The difference in Diaghilev's vision and that of Wagner is that Wagner wanted to unify his work under the guidance of a single artistic genius—his own. Wagner wrote the librettos for his works along with the music, he created the staging for them, designed the building in which they could best be performed, and probably would have sung all the parts if he had not been busy conducting the orchestra.

Diaghilev, on the other hand, brought together specialists in their particular areas to create his ballets. The music was composed by the world's finest composers (in addition to Stravinsky, Diaghilev also commissioned works from Ravel, Debussy, and Prokofiev), the dances created by the greatest choreographers (such as Ballanchine and Folkine), danced by the greatest dancers (such as Nijinsky), and had sets designed by the world's leading figures in the visual arts (such as Picasso). In taking this approach, Diaghilev may have come closer to the ultimate ideal than Wagner himself.

Stravinsky enjoyed a long association with Diaghilev, and his first three major works for the *Ballets Russes* remain his most popular works. The first two, *L'Oiseau de feu (The Firebird)* and *Petrouchka*, are both based on Russian folklore and are strongly influenced by Russian nationalism and the brilliant colors of Rimsky-Korsakov's orchestration. Both also make use of **polytonality**, the use of two or more tonal centers simultaneously, and *Petrouchka* has a new rhythmic character, with a powerfully driving quality over repeated harmonies. Neither of these works, however, prepared the public (or Diaghilev) for what was to come next.

The scenario for *Le sacre du printemps (The Rite of Spring)* was suggested to Diaghilev by Stravinsky one day when the two were doing lunch. The ballet would be set among prehistoric Slavic tribes, who would gather each year to celebrate the end of winter and the reemergence of life in the spring. The "rite" of the title refers to a ritual, ceremony, or sacrifice. The proceedings would culminate with a human sacrifice: a virgin would be chosen from the tribes and would be given the dubious honor of dancing herself to death to guarantee the success of the next season's crops.

Diaghilev was fascinated by the idea and encouraged Stravinsky to get right to work. He expected the completed work in a few months, but to his dismay it took Stravinsky almost two years to complete the work. The composer collaborated with choreographer Vaclav Nijinsky and set/costume designer Nicholas Roerich (who was also an archeologist who specialized in prehistoric Slavic tribes—the original costumes were based largely on authentic artifacts). The final result was unlike anything Diaghilev could have imagined.

Stravinsky felt that the scenario for this ballet, describing the ultimate primitive horror of ritual human sacrifice, demanded a new musical language. *The Rite of Spring* has been described as an expression of **primitivism**, an outgrowth of a related movement in the visual arts that portrayed and glorified images of primitive society, in somewhat cruder techniques than the gentle, sensuous images of impressionism. In music, primitivism is manifested in harsh dissonances, powerful, driving rhythms, and simple melodic motifs with a limited range and an imitation of primitive folk song.

The Rite of Spring, like its two predecessors, uses polytonality—though here those sounds are more deliberately harsh than those in *The Firebird* or *Petrouchka*. *The Rite* also uses unusual combinations of instruments and orchestral colors. It is in rhythm, however, that *The Rite* is most revolutionary. In addition to the overwhelming rhythmic energy of the work, Stravinsky also uses **polyrhythms**, several different groupings of rhythms and meters used simultaneously. He also uses asymmetrical meters, asymmetrical groupings of notes, and a frequent shifting of meter, particularly in the final section, the *Sacrificial Dance*. The first 10 measures of that section use the following meter signatures: 3/16, 2/16, 3/16, 3/16, 3/16, 2/8, 2/16, 3/16, 3/16, 2/8. The sacrificial virgin dances herself to death; the meter dissociates as does her life.

To a great extent, *The Rite* represents an entire period for Stravinsky: it is significantly different from its predecessors and subsequent works followed different paths. In it, nevertheless, an important idea is established, as significant as Mozart's and Beethoven's assertions that the artist is more than just a servant, but a treasure, one who creates something of value for all time. Just as important to the Revolutionary Age is the assertion that the artist must write what he or she conceives, not simply that which will please the audience.

The premiere of the work is one of the most famous events in 20th-century music: the shock of this new language was so great that an actual riot broke out. Despite 120 rehearsals, the music was still extremely difficult for the musicians and the dancers; all the more so because the uproar of the crowd was so great that the dancers could not hear the orchestra.

The Rite of Spring. © Robbie Jack/Corbis.

American writer Carl van Vechten was present at the premiere and reported on the audience reaction, describing the intense battle between those who were horrified at the shocking sounds and those who felt that the principles of free artistic expression were at stake and bellowed back. At one point, the person sitting behind van Vechten began pounding the rhythms on the reporter's head . . . he was so overcome with the experience that he didn't realize what he was doing.

example

Stravinsky: *The Rite of Spring*, **Part I**

It is perhaps difficult for the modern listener to appreciate completely the reaction that greeted the first performance of *The Rite of Spring*. Since its premiere nearly a century ago, much of the language of this work has entered popular consciousness. The pounding, primitive rhythms no longer shock the listener raised on modern pop music.

But as you listen to this work, try to imagine yourself in that audience of 1913: used to hearing the lush prettiness of impressionist composers such as Debussy or Ravel, or perhaps the music of Brahms for the very conservative. Now, this crazy young Russian starts making sounds like this.

Part I. *The Adoration of the Earth*

Introduction: This passage was played with the curtain down. The first sound is that of a bassoon, playing alone at the highest part of its range. In the ever-shifting palate of sounds, it is virtually impossible to determine key, meter, or any set form. The passage represents the formless chaos of winter, which is about to be overcome by the explosion of life of the springtime. Gradually, a steady meter is suggested, and the curtain rises on the first section of the ballet.

Dance of the Adolescents: Stravinsky immediately shocks the audience by the power of his opening idea: a polychord consisting of the combination an E major triad and an Eb7 chord, pounding steadily with irregular accents. Listen for the brief melodic fragments that occur in this section . . . in another context, these could be primitive folk songs.

Mock Abduction: This scene portrays a ritual of abduction of a member of one tribe by another tribe.

Springtime Rounds: The haunting, ethereal opening of this scene is a rare moment of calmness in this tempestuous work. The music leads into a solemn passage rather like a hymn or a processional, building to a powerful climax before returning to the music of the opening.

Games of the Rival Tribes: Each tribe is represented by its own music, in its own key and meter. The clashes of colors, keys, and meters is at first playful, but ultimately chaotic.

Entry of the Sage: During this scene, the elders of the various tribes gather in a grim procession. The music becomes ferociously intense, with multiple layers of simultaneous rhythms and three separate key centers. Finally, the oldest and wisest of the elders, the sage for all the tribes, comes to the front of the procession.

Adoration of the Earth: Here, in a brief moment of near silence, the sage plants a ceremonial kiss on the face of the earth itself.

Dance of the Earth: During the final section, the people are seized with a mystic sense of terror, as pandemonium breaks loose—and we haven't even gotten to the sacrifice yet!

Despite, or perhaps because of the notoriety of the premiere of the work, *The Rite of Spring* has become one of Stravinsky's most popular pieces. It, along with *The Firebird* and *Petrouchka*, established the young Russian as one of the most important figures of his day—and their continuing popularity helped finance Stravinsky's career through the rest of his life.

Stravinsky's works after 1914 went down a different path. Economic conditions in Europe had deteriorated, and his earlier works for massive orchestras were no longer as practical; later works were often for smaller combinations of instruments and voices. More importantly, Stravinsky's philosophy was changing. He felt that the subjective emotions of Romanticism had led to a dead end. Music needed to be revitalized, and that energy could best be found in the inspiration of the past—in the objective clarity of classicism.

Stravinsky and Neoclassicism (1914–1951)

Neoclassicism is a difficult term to define, though it obviously refers to some revival of classical aesthetic principles rooted in Greco-Roman civilizations. The term has been used throughout history, by various eras. The Renaissance thought of itself as neoclassical, a conscious and intentional rebirth of the classic civilizations of ancient Greece and Rome. The visual arts of the late 18th century were also called neoclassic in their deliberate imitations of Greco-Roman models.

In 20th-century music, *neoclassicism* refers to the revival of classical aesthetic principles of form, order, and restraint; the revival of preromantic forms and idioms (composers began reviving instruments like the harpsichord and forms like the concerto grosso); or even the use of thematic material from preromantic composers. Some writers have even used the term to refer to any 20th-century music that returned to a sense of tonality, as opposed to the more radical experiments in non-tonal music.

Neoclassic composers, according to this last sense, are separate from Postromantic figures such as Strauss, Sibelius, and Rachmaninoff; these composers were firmly rooted in the Romantic era and never abandoned those roots. In fact, both Sibelius and Rachmaninoff were far less popular as composers during their lifetime than they have since become primarily because they were so out-of-touch with the revolutionary innovations in music of the early 20th century.

Stravinsky had come to believe that music was not for the purpose of expression, self- or otherwise, but was solely concerned with the ordering of tones. His works from this period have in common a sense of clarity and objectivity—and little else. He felt, as would any classicist, that any piece had to exist within a structural framework, and the more carefully ordered that framework was, the more successful he could be as a composer.

In the music of the past, that framework had been generally agreed on, in principles of harmonic structure that had been in place since Bach. In our own time, however, those limits had broken down, and anything was possible. Stravinsky believed that he had to establish his own limits and methods, though those could vary from piece to piece. Because of this, the works from his neoclassical period vary widely in their character.

Many of his works from this period make reference, directly or indirectly, to the works of other composers, such as the ballets *Pulcinella* (Pergolesi), *Le baiser de la fée* (Chaikovsky), and the opera *The Rake's Progress* (Mozart). Some, like the *Ebony Concerto*, written for clarinetist Woody Herman, were influenced by American jazz. Other works were inspired by ancient Greece: *Oedipus Rex*, *Apollon Musagète*, *Perséphone*, and *Orpheus*. Still others were based on the classical forms of the concerto or the symphony: the *Violin Concerto* and the *Piano Concerto*, the *Symphony of Psalms*, the *Symphony in C*, and the *Symphony in Three Movements*.

Stravinsky, *Pulcinella: I. Overture*

If you heard this work and were not told its composer, it's doubtful you would guess it was by Stravinsky. Actually, to some extent, it's not by Stravinsky. The work is based on the music of Giovanni Pergolesi (1710–1736), a Baroque composer whose music is an early manifestation of the preclassic movement. The dates are not a misprint; he died at the age of 26. A highly trained listener may be able to notice some aspects of the orchestration that indicate that it is not from that period, but that would be someone who has had more background than just this class.

This, like so much of Stravinsky's music, is a ballet, commissioned by Diaghilev for the *Ballets Russes*. *Pulcinella* is a character in the *Commedia dell'Arte* that originated in Renaissance Italy and featured stock parts, identifiable by types of makeup. *Pulcinella* is the character *Punch* in the *Punch and Judy* puppet shows.

Arnold Schoenberg. © Corbis.

Arnold Schoenberg (1874–1951): Postromanticism and Expressionism

Arnold Schoenberg was born in Vienna, the city that a hundred years earlier had seen the remarkable outpouring of genius from Haydn, Mozart, Beethoven, and Schubert. In fact, Schoenberg, with his pupils Anton Webern and Alban Berg, make up what is known as the **Second Viennese School**; the four earlier composers constitute the First.

Schoenberg was born into a middle-class Jewish family. His father died when he was still in school, and he was forced to drop out and go to work in a bank to help the family survive. His family was not musical, and he was almost entirely self-taught. He began playing violin at the age of eight and began composing almost immediately. His first major influence was Johannes Brahms; later, like virtually every progressive composer from his era, he fell under the spell of Wagner.

Schoenberg's only formal composition instruction came from his friend, and later brother-in-law, Alexander Zemlinsky (1872–1942); the study was done without remuneration to Zemlinsky. The absence of the opportunity for conservatory study plagued Schoenberg throughout his career, mainly because he never made the contacts within the musical community that might have furthered his career. He was always treated as a musical outsider in Vienna.

Schoenberg was a man of immense courage and integrity. He had converted to the Lutheran faith in 1898, but when the Nazis took over Germany in 1933, he was moved to reaffirm his Jewish heritage, in a formal reconversion, at the very time when it would have been advantageous to keep his background hidden. He saw, however, that to stay in Vienna may become dangerous, and the following year immigrated to the United States, where he settled in Los Angeles. In 1936, he became a professor at the University of California, Los Angeles, a post he retained until forced to retire at the age of 70.

Schoenberg's earliest works are in the rich, Postromantic style, discussed briefly in the previous chapter. He was influenced by the music of Wagner and Mahler. Mahler was, in fact, a close friend to the younger composer and was strongly supportive of his work. Schoenberg's music from this era includes his first masterpiece, *Verklärte Nacht* (*Transfigured Night*), written for string sextet, though now most frequently heard in a version for string orchestra. Schoenberg also wrote a symphonic poem after the Maeterlink play *Pelléas et Mélisande*, which had been set previously by Fauré, Sibelius, and Debussy.

Another composition from this period is the massive *Gurrelieder*, a two-hour cantata for huge orchestra, chorus, and seven soloists. This remarkable composition, more expansive even than anything that Mahler had ever conceived, also contains the first use of a technique Schoenberg called **Sprechstimme**. This refers to a sort of vocal delivery midway between speaking and singing—vaguely similar to recitative, but different in that operatic recitative uses specific pitches while pitch is only approximated in the highly inflected *Sprechstimme*. The effect is both eerie and humorous; Schoenberg would return to the technique in other works throughout his life, though he never settled on a specific sort of notation to represent it.

Expressionism: The Emancipation of Dissonance (1909–1916)

Though Schoenberg's early works are still tonal, they each take the free use of dissonance common to the Postromantic language further and further. As Wagner and Mahler had done in their most extreme works, Schoenberg stretches the limits of the tonal language to the breaking point. Wagner and Mahler, however, came to this point at the climax of their creative lives. Schoenberg began his work at that point, and began to feel that it was not only possible, but essential to continue beyond the limits of tonality.

The traditional use of dissonant harmonies was to create a sense of tension and instability, which could then be resolved by some means. As the Romantic period progressed, the use of dissonance became more and more extreme, and the resolutions of those dissonances became more and more ambiguous. All this was designed to extend the use of functional dissonance, to expand the colors, moods, and sensations that harmonic tension could create to its limit. There had long been a tendency in the German and Austrian traditions toward an increasingly greater complexity in music, from Haydn and Mozart through Beethoven, to Wagner and Mahler.

It is important to realize how closely Schoenberg identified with this tradition. Though he is often seen as a revolutionary, as one who overthrew the traditions of tonal composition, he saw himself as the logical continuation of the Austro-German musical heritage. He felt that the next logical step in the development of music was the use of dissonance so freely that it ceased to have any true functional significance. Dissonance was no longer used to create tension that was to be resolved, but it was freed to exist on its own. He referred to this phenomenon as "the emancipation of dissonance," and the works of his next period are his first truly **atonal** works, music without *any* clearly defined tonal center.

A parallel to this process can be seen in the world of the visual arts, as painting rejected the necessity to be representational and became more and more abstract. Schoenberg was himself a painter, part of the **expressionist** school. The work of the expressionists, who were mostly German and Russian, represents a reaction against the pastel prettiness of the impressionist painters. The expressionists sought to express the feelings within the artist, rather than the observed appearance of an object or scene. Their work is characterized by clashing colors, jarring composition, and an obsession with madness, suffering, and death. It was this group that first produced the first truly abstract works, based on no existing model.

$7 + 5 = 12$

A good way for a non-specialist to understand this is by a simple mathematical metaphor: $7 + 5 = 12$. With this image, think of the primary material of tonal music as the diatonic scale, which consists of 7 notes and the repeat of the first, an octave away. But there are 12 possible pitches . . . the extra 5 are those in between the 7 of the scale, whether major or minor.

Now, the composers of the Classical period used the 7 pitches primarily, and only occasionally used the extra 5. But as time progressed, composers explored those extra pitches more and more. By the time of the Postromantics, they were using the 5 almost as often as they used the 7. The next level is simply to combine the two equally; no longer $5 + 7$, but now all 12 are being used equally.

It can seem like a huge leap to the listener hearing atonal expressionism for the first time, but it was, in fact, a fairly short step. When you hear highly chromatic Postromantic music side by side with early expressionism, you will hear that the difference is not pronounced, but rather slight.

Pierrot lunaire, Op. 21

Schoenberg's first truly atonal works are considered part of his **expressionist** period. In these works, he makes a conscious attempt to avoid the use of musical materials that would even hint at traditional tonal music; instead, he constructs his pieces from the development and manipulation of short interval structures. Schoenberg's important expressionist works include several sets of piano pieces; the *Five Orchestral Pieces*, Op. 16; two operas, *Die glücklische Hand* and *Erwartung*; a song cycle, *The Book of the Hanging Gardens*; and a remarkable piece entitled *Pierrot lunaire*, Op. 21.

Pierrot lunaire was composed for a vocalist (using *Sprechstimme*), accompanied by a chamber ensemble of five players who, by doubling, play eight instruments: piano, 'cello, violin doubling viola, flute doubling piccolo, and clarinet doubling bass clarinet. The work is setting of 21 surrealistic poems by a Belgian poet, Albert Giraud; Schoenberg uses a free German translation of the poetry, which was originally in French. The cycle is divided into three sets of seven poems. Each of the three sets has a distinct character: Part I is dreamy and surreal, Part II nightmarish and grotesque, and Part III, ironic and absurd, with an unexpectedly sweet conclusion.

The title is itself enigmatic. It is usually translated "Pierrot of the Moon," or "Moon-struck Pierrot." *Pierrot* refers to a sad-faced clown, a stock character of the *Commedia dell'Arte* we encountered in Stravinsky's *Pulcinella*. The figure is usually made up with a white face with black teardrops. *Lunaire* refers to the moon; the connection here is to the folk legends linking the moon to insanity (*lunar* and *lunatic* have the same linguistic roots). The images of the work are strange, as though from a dream or a nightmare. In some poems, there is an obvious sense of humor, irony, and the absurd. In Schoenberg's music, too, there are occasional references to the popular cabaret music of his time.

example

Pierrot lunaire, Op. 21: Part II, no. 13, *Enthauptung (Decapitation)*

Pierrot looks in deathly anguish at the unsheathed Turkish sword of the crescent moon, imagining himself decapitated by it. It is for vocalist, bass clarinet, viola, 'cello, and piano.

Schoenberg's Atonal Language

One of the striking things about *Pierrot lunaire* is the variety of sounds and textures produced. The combinations of the five instrumentalists playing eight instruments are thoroughly varied, and in only a few of the pieces are all the players utilized. The character of the pieces ranges from the simple and lyrical to passages of daunting complexity. This is indeed one of the qualities that makes Schoenberg's music so difficult: its variety of sound, texture, rhythm, dynamics, form, and of course intervallic structure and harmony. All of this variety is compressed into his music, creating a density of ideas that can be as intimidating to some as it can be rewarding to those with the courage to hear it.

Another quality that makes Schoenberg's, or any composer's, atonal work difficult is the problem of expectation of the listener. For better or worse, few people can experience a work of art, whether music, painting, or poetry, on its own terms, without some sense of what we *expect* the work to be like. Often, this presents a problem: a new work by a familiar composer, painter, or even popular group is likely to be similar to the latest work heard from them.

With atonal music, however, the rules have been changed—or are at least suspended. The effect is similar to an abstract painting or a stream-of-consciousness novel; the standard expectations are no longer in effect. Atonal music no longer presents harmony or melody as we would expect it *because it is atonal*. Traditional harmony and melody are based on traditional tonal practice. Therefore, if a listener expects traditional sounds from a piece that has deliberately rejected those sounds, they will be sorely disappointed.

The accusation is often made against such pieces that they are musical gibberish, lacking comprehensible melody and harmony. This is not the case—it is not gibberish, but music that obeys a *different* set of rules of organization.

As a good analogy, imagine the following situation: you are on a New York City subway, traveling to some destination. On the same car with you are several members of some ethnic group, reading newspapers written in a totally different alphabet and speaking animatedly among themselves in what to you is a totally unrecognizable language. What they are saying, however, is not gibberish, but another language: incomprehensible to you now, but perfectly understandable to someone who knows the vocabulary and grammar of that language.

Atonal music can be thought of in much the same way. It can be appreciated fully once we stop expecting it to sound like what it is *not* and allow it to communicate on its own terms.

Interestingly, Schoenberg was not particularly happy with the music of his expressionist period; not because it sounded too radical but because it did not rest on a secure system of organization. Remember, Schoenberg felt that his music was a continuation of the old Austro-German classical tradition. Just as the music of tonal composers had operated on standards and principles that had been in effect since they were codified in the music of Bach, Schoenberg felt that for his atonal language to function successfully, it had to have a similar sort of framework. After 1916, he stopped publishing his music and began working on the creation of a new method of composing. By 1923, he had developed such a method, dubbed **12-tone composition**, or **serial composition**.

Twelve-Tone or Serial Composition

The 12-tone method of composing (also known as **serial** or **dodecaphonic** composition; or **twelve-note composition** to the British) was based on the equality of importance of all 12 notes of the chromatic scale. In tonal music, one single tone acquires the greatest importance and everything gravitates to that note. The tones of a diatonic scale, major, minor, or modal, on which a tonal piece is based, also have values: each note has a particular function, all leading to the main, tonic note.

In Schoenberg's new method, however, a piece was not based on a hierarchy of notes, but on an equal distribution of *all* possible tones. This is achieved by basing each piece on a set of all 12 notes of the chromatic scale, arranged in a **tone row**: in the row, all notes are used, and each note occurs only once. The row, like any melody, sets up a series of intervals in the spaces between its tones.

The row can be manipulated in a variety of ways. It can be transposed, that is, it can begin on any note; the notes may change, but the intervals will remain the same.

The row can also be manipulated in three other ways. It can be played in reverse order, the **retrograde**. Its intervals can be inverted, or changed in direction; this is called the **inversion**. In this process, if in the original row the interval from the first to the second note goes up by a half-step, in the inversion it will go down by a half step. The third manipulation of the row is to play the notes of the inversion in reverse order, in what is called the **retrograde inversion.**

All of this sounds quite insane, of course. What sense is there in playing a melody backwards, upside down, or upside down *and* backwards. However, *this* part of the method was not new to Schoenberg—in fact, the techniques of retrogrades and inversions had been in use since the Renaissance. Josquin, Palestrina, Bach, Mozart, and Beethoven had all treated melodic material in such a fashion.

What is unique to Schoenberg's method is the distributed use of pitches, in such a fashion that all notes are used equally, and none is more important than any other. In this way, a specific method was created in which it was guaranteed that no single note would assume a central role.

In Schoenberg's method, the row is not simply stated in its original version over and over. The various versions of the row can also be transposed, making 48 different sets of pitches from which a piece can be constructed. Though any note may be repeated as much as is desired, the next note written must be the next note in the row. Each row must be used in its entirety before going on, though two or more rows can be used simultaneously in different instruments.

Any of the notes in the row can be used in any octave, and any rhythms can be used; this gives an immense variety of versions of the row. Chords can be constructed from adjacent notes in the row—a composer can, for instance, make a chord from the fourth, fifth, and sixth notes, as long as the next note to be used is the seventh.

The method is considerably more complicated than can be described to a nonspecialist, but these basics will give some idea as to the mechanics of it. And the method is precisely that: a system of mechanics. Schoenberg was the first to break his own rules where it was necessary for the expression he desired, and he encouraged his students to do the same. As one can imagine, the possibilities for expression using serial composition are vast, limited only by the imagination of the composer, as has always been the case with any system of making music.

Schoenberg once stated that, "I claim the distinction of having written a truly new music, which, based on tradition as it is, is destined to become tradition." In this assessment, he was only partially correct. Virtually every important composer of the 20th century has used the 12-tone method at one point or another—even Stravinsky turned to it after Schoenberg's death. And virtually all of them ultimately abandoned it. Even Schoenberg returned to tonal writing for some of his very late compositions, when that language suited what he wanted to say.

The main contribution of Schoenberg was to take that final leap into the "abyss of freedom," to open the gates to the creation of atonal music. He demonstrated that it was possible to write communicative and passionate music in a completely new language; after Schoenberg, music could never be the same.

The first piece composed entirely with Schoenberg's new method was the fifth of his *Five Piano Pieces*, Op. 23, from 1923. Other significant serial works include the *Suite for Piano*, Op. 25; the *Variations for Orchestra*, Op. 31; the two cantatas *Ode to Napoleon*, Op. 41b and *A Survivor from Warsaw*, Op. 46, both for *sprechstimme* and instrumental accompaniment; the *Violin Concerto*, Op. 36 and the *Piano Concerto*, Op. 42; and the unfinished opera *Moses und Aron*, Op. 50b.

In this last work, the voice of the inarticulate Moses is delivered in *Sprechstimme*, while the music for his eloquent brother Aaron are sung, in some of the most purely lyric 12-tone music ever composed. It is interesting to note that the spelling of *Aaron* was changed to *Aron* in the title of the opera; Schoenberg, for all his brilliance, was terribly superstitious (as were Stravinsky and Mahler), and was triskaidekaphobic—convinced that the number 13 was unlucky. The dropping of the extra *a* changed the number of letters in the title from 13 to 12. The two cantatas, *Ode to Napoleon* and *A Survivor from Warsaw* reflect Schoenberg's more serious reactions to the atrocities of World War II. He was deeply concerned over the fate of the Jews under Hitler and despised any sort of dictatorship.

Suite for Piano, Op. 25: I. Präludium

The Second Viennese School

Schoenberg was not only one of the greatest composers of the age; he was also an important and influential teacher. He had an ability to bring out the best in his students and to help each find his or her own voice. His two most important students, Anton Webern and Alban Berg, could hardly be more unalike and neither sounds like their teacher. The three are commonly known as the **Second Viennese School**.

Anton Webern (1883–1945)

Webern was one of the most important disciples of Schoenberg. Like Schoenberg, his compositional life passed through three periods: Postromanticism, expressionism, and serialism. His musical style is astonishingly different from that of his teacher and from his colleague and fellow Second Viennese School member Alban Berg. Webern's music is sparse, concentrated, and generally quiet. He never wrote a piece longer than 12 minutes—many of his works are less than 30 seconds in length.

His style has the same sort of quiet intensity that can be experienced in Japanese **haiku** poetry, which consists of three lines of respectively five, seven, and five syllables. Within those sparse limits, the poet portrays a single image, with as much power as can be created.

Webern's music is also described as **pointillistic**, in that it consists largely of individual points of sound, separated by range, duration, and timbre from others. In his 12-tone works, for instance, he will only give one or two notes of a row to any given instrument; the next notes will come from some other voice.

Webern, incidentally, followed the 12-tone method more strictly than either Schoenberg or Berg. He also experimented with extending the serial technique (which only deals with pitch) to other aspects of composition, such as duration, tone color, dynamics, and articulation.

Anton Webern. © Bettmann/Corbis.

Alban Berg. © Bettmann/Corbis.

As we will see, it was Webern, in his work with **total serialization**, who was the primary inspiration to the next generation of composers. We will hear the entire set of his *Five Orchestral Pieces*, Op. 10. They were composed in 1913, the year of Stravinsky's *Rite of Spring* and Schoenberg's *Pierrot lunaire*. The five pieces take just over four minutes to perform.

example

Webern: *Five Orchestral Pieces*, Op. 10

Alban Berg (1885–1935)

Berg is the third member of the Second Viennese School; like Schoenberg and Webern, he progressed through Postromantic, expressionist, and serial periods. Unlike his teacher and his colleague, however, he never felt the need to break away from the lush richness of the romantic language. Even his serial works have a sense of a **synthesis of romanticism and atonality**, and it is no accident that his works are the most accessible and popular of the three.

Berg's father died when he was a young teenager. When he began his studies with Schoenberg, he found not just a teacher but a father figure in the older composer, who gave his life a much-needed direction. He served in the Austrian army during World War I. Ill health kept him from combat duty but did not release him from his military obligation. He found the military life a dehumanizing experience, and the ordeal became the source for much of his opera *Wozzeck*.

That opera, Berg's most famous and powerful work, portrays a soldier (the title role) struggling against the degradation of a hostile society and ultimately driven to madness, murder, and suicide. *Wozzeck* is not a pleasant experience, but it is an immensely powerful one. It portrays not a heroic, romantic figure, but an antihero, doomed in his struggle.

His atonal/romantic synthesis can be heard easily in his *Violin Concerto of 1935*.

example

Berg: *Violin Concerto*

IV. *Adagio w/variations (uses Bach chorale, Es ist genug)*

The work was originally written on the death of Manon Gropius, daughter of Alma Mahler Gropius. He interrupted the last act of his opera *Lulu* to write the work and never finished it. The title page is inscribed, "To the memory of an angel." Berg was stung by a bee after the premiere of the work, which ironically functioned as a Requiem for both Berg and Manon.

The concerto does not follow the 12-tone method strictly. The row on which it is based is itself fascinating, because it is constructed of triads, and triads with a traditional relationship at that: g minor, D major, a minor, E major, and then three more whole steps—C#, D#, F to complete the row with all 12 pitches represented. Even when following the strictest version of the 12-tone method, there are always materials found that resemble tonal practice.

Some passages are tonal, some are serial, some are both, and others not tonal but not entirely serial. The combination of the folk song, the Bach Chorale, and a triadic row give the work its ambiguity.

Other Important Composers of the Revolutionary Age

Béla Bartók (1881–1945)

Bartók, born in Hungary, is often considered one of the three most significant figures of the first half of the century, along with Stravinsky and Schoenberg. Like the other two composers, he immigrated to the United States. Bartók came in 1939, in response to Nazi atrocities in Eastern Europe. Unlike those two composers, he came to this country before his music was firmly established, and died, of leukemia, virtually penniless. His contributions were only recognized sometime after his death.

Bartók's significance to music history is in three areas. He was one of the first to do serious work in **ethnomusicology**, the study of folk music. His study of the folk music of Eastern Europe laid the foundations for methods of future study in this discipline and also had a great influence on his own compositions.

Bartók was also a significant educator, though he was known more as a piano teacher than as a composition teacher. He composed a series of pieces collectively called *Mikrokosmos*, a graded set of piano pieces for the beginning to advanced student. These are still used to introduce piano pupils to aspects of the 20th-century style.

Finally, as a composer, Bartók created a long series of uncontested masterpieces. His style, in its frequent use of harsh dissonances and in its powerfully propulsive rhythmic character, is in some ways similar to that of Stravinsky. The influence of Eastern European folk music, however, sets Bartók apart. He refused to use any "new" device unless he could find some precedent for it in folk music. Luckily, there are many strange aspects of those traditions, more than enough to give his music an experimental quality.

Bartók followed a course of life that became typical for composers of the Revolutionary Age: he began as a wildly experimental creator, only to return to a more conservative language as he aged. Among the most popular works of his last period is the *Concerto for Orchestra*, written in 1943. The name comes from the nature of the work: he writes so many demanding solo passages for members of the orchestra that it is effectively just that: a concerto for the entire orchestra.

example

Bartók: *Concerto for Orchestra*

V. Finale: Pesante-Presto

Paul Hindemith (1895–1963)

Though his early works are in the expressionist style, German-born Paul Hindemith came to feel that the revolutionary experiments of many composers were essentially self-indulgent. His mature work is essentially conservative and tonal.

Hindemith also came to believe that composers were making a mistake in concentrating almost exclusively on music for towering virtuosos and giant intellects. He felt that music for skilled amateurs was being neglected and championed a concept he called *Gebrauchsmusik*, loosely translated as "music for use." *Gebrauchsmusik* was written for specific purposes, often for specific performances and performers, and usually within the abilities of a dedicated amateur musician.

Though a conservative, Hindemith's music was too challenging for the leaders of the Third Reich. He left Germany after Goebbels gave him a "leave of absence" and worked for two years in Turkey, at the request of that government, to help revise their music education program. In 1940, he came to the United States, teaching at Yale University for 13 years. In 1953, he returned to Europe, living the final decade of his life in Switzerland.

Hindemith wrote several operas, none of which has become particularly popular. But an orchestral suite from one of them is perhaps his most popular piece. The opera is *Mathis der Maler* (*Matthias the Painter*). It concerns the life of Matthias Grünewald, a Rennaisance artist, and each of the movements relates to a panel in his famous work, the Isenheim Altarpiece.

example

Hindemith: *Mathis der Maler Symphonie*

I. *Concert of Angels*

Benjamin Britten (1913–1976)

The most important 20th-century British composer was Benjamin Britten. Britten was an astonishing child prodigy, composing prolifically since the age of five. His early studies were with Frank Bridge, who gave Britten both a technical and a philosophical foundation from which to develop. Britten, like Hindemith, wass essentially a conservative composer. He was influenced by a wide range of the music of the past and the present, and was constantly changing his approach—he once said, "I do not see why I should lock myself inside a narrow personal idiom."

Britten left England for the United States from 1939 to 1942. He was at odds with his country in many ways: as a pacifist, he was in conflict with the British war effort; as a composer in a conservative country, he was aesthetically isolated; and as a homosexual, he was socially outcast. While he composed some significant works in the United States, his most important work was done after his return to England.

Britten composed some remarkable instrumental works, often for specific virtuoso players (remember his *A Young Person's Guide to the Orchestra*), but his major contribution is in his vocal music. He has an amazing ability to set languages and seems equally comfortable setting modern or old English, Italian, French, or Latin. His operas are perhaps the greatest ever written in the English language, and his song cycles display an acute sensitivity to the text and an astonishing musical inventiveness. His greatest and most powerful choral work, the *War Requiem*, juxtaposes the text of the Catholic Requiem Mass and the World War I antiwar poetry of Wilfred Owen.

Britten was the first great English opera composer since Purcell in the 1600s. His first opera, *Peter Grimes*, written in 1944, is the story of an antihero, a fisherman in a bleak coastal town, who has earned the enmity of his community and who eventually destroys himself. To some degree it resembles Berg's *Wozzeck*, but the beauty of Britten's music, and his ability to humanize even such a figure as Grimes, has made it one of the greatest operas of the Revolutionary Age. He links the acts and scenes with instrumental passages, and these *Sea Interludes*, as they are known, are often played on orchestral concerts.

example

Britten: *Four Sea Interludes from Peter Grimes*

I. *Dawn*
II. *Sunday Morning*
III. *Moonlight*
IV. *Storm*

Olivier Messiaen (1908–1992)

Frenchman Olivier Messiaen was another child prodigy. He studied at the Paris Conservatory from 1919–1929 and excelled in piano, counterpoint, accompaniment, organ, composition, history, and percussion. He was taken prisoner by the Germans during World War II; while in a Prisoner of War camp, he wrote one of his most powerful compositions: the *Quatour pour le fin du temps* (*Quartet for the End of Time*). The unusual instrumentation for the work (piano, violin, 'cello, and clarinet) was chosen because there were prisoners who could play those instruments. He was released in 1941 and sent to teach harmony at the Paris Conservatory, but refused to compose until Paris was no longer an occupied city.

Messiaen's music was influenced by such diverse sources as Stravinsky, Debussy, and Machaut, along with oriental and ancient Greek musical practice. He was a devoutly religious Catholic, drawn particularly to the mystic elements of that religion; he was also affected by Hindu mysticism. His music is in many ways closer to the developments of the latter half of the century than to those of the first. It is indifferent to the standard process of harmonic development and tends to be static, more concerned with statement and decoration than movement.

Messiaen was also an amateur ornithologist. His music often features bird calls, though in quite a different fashion than can be heard in the quick flute trills with which the romantic composers suggested birdsong. Messiaen studied bird calls carefully and transcribed them accurately in all their incredible complexity; he incorporated these intricate lines in his music. You can hear that in the first movement of the quartet.

example

Messiaen: *Quatour pour le fin du temps*

I. *Liturgy of Crystal*

Soviet Composers: Sergei Prokofiev (1891–1953) and Dmitri Shostakovich (1906–1975)

Art always suffers under totalitarian regimes, whether they are right wing or left wing. Many composers, writers, and artists fled Nazi Germany and Soviet Russia, yet some composers elected to stay out of a genuine love of their homeland. The two most important composers from Russia during the Soviet years were Sergei Prokofiev and Dmitri Shostakovich; both had frequent battles with a government that alternately condemned and praised their music.

Because of the totalitarian nature of both the Czarist and Communist regimes, Russian art has long learned to live and even flourish under oppressive circumstances. It is fascinating that even during the tumultuous upheavals during the 1917 Revolution and World War II, the cultivation of art and music was never interrupted.

On the other hand, the chief function of the Russian artist, whether Soviet or Czarist, was seen as twofold: to glorify the state and to amuse or edify one's fellow Russians. All else is decadent. Conformists are richly rewarded. The individualistic artist is ignored or worse.

The label "formalist" came to be dreaded by Russian artists during the Stalin years. It officially referred to the elevation of form over content, though in practice it could refer simply to any work that was in a style which Stalin disliked, and his taste was notoriously limited. He only enjoyed military marches and Ukrainian folk songs. All else was decadent, formalist, and counterrevolutionary.

Prokofiev was an amazing child prodigy. When he entered the St. Petersburg Conservatory at the age of 13, he submitted two piano sonatas, numerous shorter pieces for piano, a symphony, and four operas! He was a rebellious student, but developed into a virtuoso pianist.

In 1914, Prokofiev traveled to Paris. Shortly thereafter, he returned to Russia and left again in 1917, during the revolution, on a world tour as a pianist. He settled in Paris in 1923 and remained there for a decade, only returning to his homeland in 1933. His last two decades were filled with alternating state honors and state reprimands.

Prokofiev's style is essentially conservative. He believed tonality is a function of nature and felt no urge to destroy it. He described three primary aspects of his musical style: **lyricism** (he regards melody as the most important element in music), **motoric rhythm**, and **humorous** or **grotesque** qualities. You can hear all of these in the first movement of his *Piano Concerto no. 3*.

example

Prokofiev: *Piano Concerto no. 3 in C, Op. 26*

I. Andante-Allegro

Shostakovich, by contrast, never left the Soviet Union for any significant length of time. He outlived the oppressive regime of Joseph Stalin (Prokofiev died on the same day as Stalin—commemorations of his death were rather lost in the shuffle); consequently, he lived to experience a period of freer expression. His music, however, is always tinged by a sense of bitter irony, even when it seems superficially heroic.

During the Stalin years, Shostakovich was the target of significant criticism; at that time, that meant significant danger. For some time, he slept in the hallway of his apartment complex, so if he were arrested and "disappeared," he would not wake his family. After one such series of attacks from the press and arts ministry, Shostakovich wrote his *Symphony no. 5*. He accompanied the work with an article in the Soviet press, portraying it as "a Soviet artist's response to just criticism." That was the official stance. He later revealed that his intent was to express, not the triumph of the glorious state, but the horror of unleashing violent power, wielded at will. The last movement could certainly be heard either way.

Shostakovich: *Symphony no. 5 in d minor, Op. 47*
IV. *Allego non troppo*

Prokofiev and Shostakovich are perhaps the most important 20th-century composers whose work continues the traditions of the symphony, concerto, quartet, and sonata. Perhaps this relates to something in the Soviet educational traditions.

"Schoenberg Is Dead!" The Post-1950 Avant-Garde
Total Serialism: The Darmstadt School of Ultra-Rationalists

The battle between Serialism and Neoclassicism was fought through the second quarter of the 20th century. Serialism won. Even Stravinsky, Schoenberg's arch rival, began using serial techniques after 1951. The rallying cry, "Schoenberg is Dead!" was picked up by a new generation of composers—their ire was not a rejection of Schoenberg, but their disappointment that he did not go far enough. Their hero was Webern.

The post-1950 avant-garde is known by several names: the **Darmstadt School**, **Ultra-Rationalists**, or the **Total-Serialists**. Darmstadt was a city in Germany that hosted summer meetings of prominent figures in this movement, of which you should know three: **Milton Babbitt** (1916–2011), **Pierre Boulez** (b. 1925), and **Karlheinz Stockhausen** (1928–2007).

Like Webern, the Darmstadt composers were interested in extending serial techniques to all aspects of music, not only pitch. Their music is characterized by extreme complexity of organization, to the extent that it goes far beyond what can be perceived aurally even by a trained listener.

There is, for example, a polyrhythm in one of the Boulez Piano Sonatas of 11 against 13. To realize this, one has to find a common denominator between the two . . . but 11 and 13 are both prime numbers, so the only common denominator is their multiple, which is 143. Assuming the figure must be played in a second, that second must be divided mentally into 143 sections. Now, audible sound begins at 20 divisions of the second. The figure can neither be executed nor perceived accurately by humans.

The Darmstadt composers were accused of writing music only for other composers, music that was more interesting to look at on paper than to hear. Babbitt responded in his sensitive article, *"Who cares if you listen?"*

Despite the criticism, elements of this school dominated academia for many years, and new composers were trained according to a philosophy that essentially represents classicism gone haywire, a focus on form without any balancing traits of the emotional content of romanticism.

Boulez: *Piano Sonata no. 2*

III. Modere, presque vif

One aspect pioneered by these composers was a fascination with electronic music. This pervades modern popular music, but for the most part, it is used to imitate existing acoustic sounds; only occasionally does an artist use electronic devices to create new sounds unavailable acoustically.

Neither of these aspects interested the Darmstadt composers. They were attracted to the possibilities for total control. The aforementioned polyrhythm may not be humanly possible, but a computer can do it.

The technology for electronic sound synthesis and storage on magnetic tape was only beginning to be available by the early 1950s. The first studios established were the Cologne Electronic Music Studios in Germany, and shortly thereafter in the Columbia University Electronic Music Studios in the United States.

Aleatory: The Antirational School

We've considered all along that Classicism and Romanticism were two complementary opposites, and any work of art cannot exist successfully without some balance between the two. But the Darmstadt School, with its fascination with ultra-complex principles of organization, can be understood as an exploration of the extreme, an attempt to focus on Classical principles of form without the balance of Romantic emotion.

At the same time, in the United States, another composer was exploring the other end of the spectrum and attempting to create a music that was so free of formal restraint that it transcended rationality entirely. That school, known variously as **Aleatory**, **Indeterminacy**, or the **Antirational School** was led by **John Cage** (1912–1992).

Cage believed that the universe exists by chance and that art should reflect that. **Aleatory** from the Latin *alea* (referring to dice: cubes with dots on the side used in games of chance), or chance music, is music that has rejected rational aspects of organization—as it were, romanticism gone haywire, reflecting the passion for freedom to the exclusion of classical organizational principles. It is more anti-Classical than Romantic, in that it has little concern with emotional expression, but it does have the character of an utter rejection of Classicism.

Cage also felt that, "When you get right down to it, a composer is just someone who tells other people what to do. I find this an unattractive way of getting things done." His music is not so much composition as creating a context from which music can emerge, without the involvement of human intention. Among his most famous works is *4'33"*.

This work can be performed by any instrument or voice, or any combination. It is set in three movements (presumably fast, slow, and fast), each of which is blank, except for the word *Tacet* (Latin for silent). If played on piano, the performer lifts and lowers the lid over the keyboard to distinguish the beginnings and ends of the movements.

Cage: *4'33"*

When experiencing a performance of this work, the first thing people notice is that we are not, not ever, truly in silence. We will notice sounds of others in the audience, sounds of the environment such as an air conditioning system. For the right imagination, these sounds can take a musical significance.

Part of the idea came to Cage after being put for some time in an isolation chamber designed to block out all sensory information. He still heard sounds: one high pitched and one low pitched. The researcher controlling the chamber told him that the low pitch was his blood circulating and the high pitch was his nervous system.

One can view *4'33"* as a polemic rather than a composition. The author possesses only one recording of the work and is not anxious to compare competing ones. But the notion that the division between music and not-music is artificial is quite liberating. It takes little imagination to hear morning birdsong or the sounds of the ocean surf as music. It takes some more imagination to hear sounds of rush hour traffic also as musical, but it can be done.

Perhaps, after all the dust has settled and the Revolutionary Age has concluded redefining music, the best answer to "what is music?" comes from Italian composer Luciano Berio: "Music is that which you listen to with the intention of listening to music."

Cage, when not composing, taught a course at the Free University of New York in Mushroom Identification. His music was invariably met with a hostile reception, sometimes extremely so, from music critics. But Cage himself was so charismatic that he brought together a number of followers, and his impact was great. Many works exist that have elements of aleatory without embracing his total aesthetic.

Music in the 1960s

Composers after the battles of the 1950s returned to the idea that music must communicate to an audience and became increasingly accessible. Even Boulez and Stockhausen's work took on a more sensual quality.

This is not to say, however, that there has been a return to tonality—only that new ideas are used for expressiveness, rather than pure cerebration. A few examples follow.

Polish composer **Krzysztof Penderecki** (b. 1933) is not interested in electronic music but in new ways to use acoustic instruments. The *Threnody* (a term borrowed from poetry, meaning a formal song of mourning, a lament) is written for a string orchestra of 52 instruments—violins, violas, 'cellos, double basses—but used in a fashion that creates totally new sounds, more like electronic sounds than acoustic.

The structure is as follows:

1. Opening intense dissonance, almost like white noise;
2. Random blooping/skittering sounds;
3. Sounds ultimately coalescing on single tone, first in the high register, then the middle register, then the low. All sounds eventually join on one pitch, which soon loses stability and moves off in other directions;
4. More random blooping and skittering noises;

Krzysztof Penderecki. © Bettmann/Corbis.

5.   Final tone cluster on all **quarter steps** roughly an octave on either side of middle C.

This final tone cluster seems to represent the collected screams of all the victims of that first atomic blast (the range of pitches is the approximate pitch range of the adult speaking voice). Though the work is not a pleasant one to listen to, it represents something that is not pleasant to contemplate. The horror of nuclear annihilation represents something new to humanity and cannot be represented as powerfully by traditional language.

Penderecki: *Threnody: The Victims of Hiroshima*

Atonality is not only appropriate for depiction of horror. The music of George Crumb (b. 1929) has a remarkable touch for beauty of color and sound. His music is delicate and vibrant, quiet and endlessly changing. Like Penderecki, he is not interested in synthetic sounds, but he often will amplify and alter the sounds of acoustic instruments. His works often use unusual instruments such as a musical saw, a toy piano, Tibetan prayer stones, or the jawbone of an ass.

Ancient Voices of Children won the United Nations Educational, Scientific and Cultural Organization prize for composition in 1970. It features, like many of Crumb's pieces, the poetry of Federico Garcia Lorca, whose imagery has always attracted Crumb. The two instrumental interludes give some idea of his delicate invention. As is typical for Crumb, he uses both unusual instruments (toy piano, musical saw, harmonica, Japanese temple bells, Tibetan prayer stones) and altered standard instruments. In this category, Crumb threads paper through the strings of a harp to get a subtle percussive sound; he tunes the paired strings of a mandolin a quarter-step apart; and he bends the sound of piano notes with a chisel applied to the string.

Crumb: *Ancient Voices of Children*

Interludes: Dances of Ancient Earth, Ghost Dance

Minimalism

Some composers in the 1950s and 1960s were unconvinced of either the extreme complexity of the Darmstadt and the aesthetic anarchy of aleatory. A new music emerged known as **minimalism**, defined as music based on extreme repetition of simple musical materials.

Note that minimalism in music is different from minimalism in other arts, which normally implies extreme miniaturization. As such, Webern's music is closest to that sense. But composers such as **Philip Glass** (b. 1937), **Steve Reich** (b. 1936), and **Terry Riley** (b. 1935) discovered that, by adding subtle changes to the repetitions, it was possible to build a large architecture. Instead of mindless repetition, mature minimalist works can build to a mesmerizing intensity. Indeed, the best minimalist works tend to be on a large scale; shorter works tend to sound trivial because they don't have the time to build.

The leading composer of this movement is **Philip Glass** (b. 1937). During the 1950s, Glass rejected the hyperintellectual emphasis of academia; influenced by Indian music (and Arabic art and architecture), he developed a style emphasizing repetition and gradual development of thematic material.

Glass realized that he was at odds with the entire musical establishment, and that he would have to go to extraordinary means for his music to be heard. Essentially, no one would play it unless he did. So he established his own ensemble, the Philip Glass Ensemble, consisting of singer, three woodwinds, three electronic keyboards, and one person mixing the sounds. His early works were written almost entirely for this ensemble, formed in 1968 and still performing as of the date of this writing.

Philip Glass with performance artist Laurie Anderson. © Lynn Goldsmith/Corbis.

Working with filmmaker Godfrey Reggio, Glass produced a remarkable trilogy of films and soundtracks. Each of the three has no dialogue, only images. The titles are from the Hopi Indian language, and the first, from 1982, is called *Koyaanisqatsi*, meaning a crazy life, a life out of balance—a state of life that calls for another way of living.

The film consists entirely of images of the United States. It begins with images of the land, especially places like Monument Valley and Gooseneck Park in the West, places that resemble the landscape of another planet. Then it shows water and air: clouds, flowing waters, ocean currents. Then we move to man's interaction with the land, in farming and construction. Finally, we see man divorced from the land, living in cities.

Throughout the film, time is altered. Some images are in slow motion, others sped up many times faster than real time. The music is tightly edited to the images, and gives an irresistible intensity that leaves the viewer breathless.

example

Glass: *Koyaanisqatsi*

So . . . what's next?

Glossary

Aleatory: music that rejects rational organization and is created by chance operations; also known as *anti-rational* or *indeterminacy*; John Cage is the most influential member of this group

Atonality: music that lacks a single, central tonal center (called *pantonality* by Aaron Schoenberg)

***Ballets Russes*:** the Russian ballet company, led by Serge Diaghilev, active in Paris at the beginning of the Revolutionary Age; Diaghilev would bring together the finest artists in their specializations—composers, choreographers, dancers, visual artists—to create his vision of a universal work of art

Ethnomusicology: the study of folk music in aesthetic and social contexts

Minimalism: music that is characterized by extreme repetition of simple musical materials; Philip Glass is the most important member of this style

Neoclassicism: a movement during the Revolutionary Age characterized by a return to Classical aesthetic principles, forms, or even source material

Pandiatonicism: the use of traditional diatonic scales in an untraditional fashion, combining harmonies not in triad but in other ways

Polytonality: the use of two or more tonal centers at the same time

Primitivism: an outgrowth of a related movement in the visual arts that portrayed and glorified images of primitive society, characterized by harsh dissonance and a pounding, driving rhythm

Quartal harmony: harmony based on the interval of a fourth, rather than thirds

Quarter tone: half of a half step; found in Middle Eastern music, and in some works of the Revolutionary Age, usually for bowed strings, since piano and most other instruments cannot reliably reproduce quarter tones accurately

***Sprechstimme*:** vocal composition that uses approximate pitch rather than specific; developed by Arnold Schoenberg

Tone cluster: literally, a cluster of tones—all the notes in a given space, sometimes from a chromatic scale, sometimes a diatonic scale, sometimes quarter tones

Total serialism: Composers after Schoenberg, inspired by Webern, whose music features extreme complexity of organization, serializing all aspects of musical composition, not just pitch; also known as *ultra-rational*

Twelve-tone composition: composition based on the equal use of all twelve notes, so that no one dominates and an atonal quality is assured; also called *serial composition* (developed by Arnold Schoenberg

WHAT NEXT?

What next, indeed? The years of the Revolutionary Age were extraordinarily tumultuous, but the last four or so decades have not produced any clearly defined dominating direction. People are still writing tonal, modal, pandiatonic, and atonal music, neoclassic, neoromantic, neobaroque, nationalist, minimalist, postminimalist, holy minimalist, aleatoric, serial (pitch alone or the whole enchilada) music, music influenced by popular music, music influenced by world music, and many variations of those. Can it be that we really have explored all possibilities in music, and thus, is anything possible?

If that is the case, and if such freedom produces a sense of liberation (rather than a sort of artistic paralysis from so many options leading to confusion rather than clarity), then we should be producing a rich tapestry of music, when viewed as a whole.

That is exactly what is happening, though it is occurring across such a broad spectrum that it can be difficult to perceive. Composers since 1970 have taken the view that, indeed, everything is now possible, but that doesn't mean that everything is equally desirable, particularly in such personal choices as artistic expression. While many have chosen to follow one particular approach from those mentioned above, most have taken an eclectic approach. They incorporate ideas they find best fit their creative imagination, and if that means they combine nationalism with aleatory, that's perfectly fine.

This chapter will be brief; we will first discover four works written since 1970, and then we'll end with a brief exploration of American Nationalism.

Four Works since 1970

Henryk Górecki (b. 1933): *Symphony no. 3, Op. 36 "Symphony of Sorrowful Songs"* (1977)

The composer Henryk Górecki was largely unknown outside of his native Poland until his *Symphony no. 3, "Symphony of Sorrowful Songs"* was recorded in 1992, 15 years after it was composed. That recording, and several that followed, was wildly successful, and listeners discovered a work of aching, poignant beauty.

The symphony seemed to have everything against it. It was in three movements, each slower than the others. It was sung in Polish and set deeply sorrowful poems from the Holocaust. The composer was essentially unknown outside of Poland. No one was prepared for the sounds of the opening movement. It is an extended canon, a work that sets the same melody in a series of voices. It starts in the double basses, slowly emerging as if from a distance, and so quiet as to almost be inaudible. The slowly trudging canon builds to the central section where the soprano enters. Her line is as simple as can be imagined, a rising scale over a halo of sustained strings. After the poem is sung, the canon begins again, but this time with all the instruments, now gradually dropping out until we end as we began, with only the double basses.

The music uses the modes of the medieval Catholic Church, music still used in that country's religious liturgy, and the text is a traditional Polish lament of the Virgin Mary. The effect is archaic, but the music is that of our time.

chapter twelve

Górecki: *Symphony no. 3, Op. 36 "Symphony of Sorrowful Songs"*

I. Lento—sostenuto tranquilo ma cantabile

Postminimalism: John Adams (b. 1947): *Harmonielehre* (1985)

The term Postminimalism is widely used, if not finally standardized. When does minimalism cease to be minimalism? When does a composer who uses the repetitions of minimalism make enough changes to the lines that the music ceases to be minimalism?

The question is probably not important; music is important not based on how it is described or labeled, but how it affects the listener. The music of **John Adams** is clearly founded in minimalism, but he has quickly grown to have a much richer and more varied palate of sounds, so the description of his work as minimalist doesn't do it justice.

Adams was born in Massachusetts and began his series of important compositions around 1977. His work *Shaker Loops* from 1978 was clearly minimalist, related to similar works by early Philip Glass and Terry Riley. But by 1985, his music began to expand in its range of sounds and its frequency of changes. He has made a particular mark on opera, starting with a modern masterpiece, *Nixon in China* from 1987.

That year saw his composition for orchestra *Harmonielehre*. The title means "Harmony Textbook" and was an homage to Arnold Schoenberg's book on composition by that name. It is in three movements, with long, expressive melodies and shifting, beautiful harmonies. The work has joined the orchestral repertory and is likely to stay there.

The third movement has a puckish title: *"Meister Eckhardt and Quackie."* It is an image of a dream Adams had, in which he saw his little daughter Emily (whose family nickname is "Quackie") riding through space with a 14th-century theologian Ekhart von Hochheim, known as Meister Eckhardt.

example

Adams: *Harmonielehre*

III. *Meister Eckhardt and Quackie*

Women Composers

We've seen, throughout this course, only a few women who have left a histori-cally important body of work. And we've discussed the barriers and prejudices that women have fought over centuries. Those in power were mostly men and most took the attitude that it was only appropriate for women to create small persons, not works of art. Those men in power deprived the world of half of its creative potential with that misconception.

Once in a while, a woman composer did surface. Usually, this was from some sort of accidental circumstance—particularly if the woman were the daughter or wife of a musician. That was the only way they could acquire the training necessary for the field. Past figures like Barbara Strozzi, Elizabeth-Jacquet de la Guerre, Fanny Mendelssohn Hensel, and Clara Schumann all got their opportunities in this way.

Between the late 19th and early 20th centuries, several prominent figures arose, who by the force of their own personalities made their mark as composers and performers. These included such women as Amy Beach, Ethel Smyth, and Cecile Chaminade (each of whom died the same year, 1944). These were con-servative voices, firmly fixed in the language of Romanticism, but remarkable nonetheless. Each fought prevailing prejudices, but just as women were gaining the right to vote, they began to have an increasingly equal access to higher edu-cation. And those trends to increase access and opportunity have continued.

It would be presumptuous for a man to write that society has finally pro-gressed to the point that women now have equal access to training and pro-fessional opportunities as composers and performers. Nonetheless, since the 1960s, we have seen more than one generation of women who have estab-lished themselves as leading composers. They are composing in all styles—se-rial works from Elizabeth Lutyens; experimental music from Pauline Oliveros, Sophia Gubaidulina, or Meredith Monk; modern eclectic composers such as Joan Tower, Libby Larsen, and Janika Vandervelde, even those influenced by popular styles such as Laurie Anderson—and it would not be a stretch to say that of the top 10 composers currently active in the United States, half are women. This section includes works by two of those figures.

Jennifer Higdon (b. 1962): *CityScapes* (2002)

Jennifer Higdon is currently at the peak of her career. She is firmly established as a serious and successful composer. She has had commissioned works (a contract for a composition, usually by a performing group or a foundation) from the Philadelphia Orchestra, Chicago Symphony, Atlanta Symphony, National Symphony Orchestra, Minnesota Orchestra, Brooklyn Philhar-monic, Pittsburgh Symphony, Indianapolis Symphony, Dallas Symphony, Oregon Symphony, St. Paul Chamber Orchestra, pianist Gary Graffman, Tokyo String Quartet, eighth blackbird (a contemporary music chamber ensemble), and the San Francisco Opera.

Rather than work from an academic appointment, she has chosen to serve several terms with various organizations as "Composer-in-Residence." She has been the featured composer at several prestigious festivals, including Vail, Norfolk, Winnipeg, and Cabrillo. She was Composer-in-Residence for the Pittsburgh Symphony Orchestra (2005–06 season), the Green Bay Symphony Orchestra (2006–07 season), the Philadelphia Orchestra (2007–08 season), and the Fort Worth Symphony (2009–10 season). As this was being written, news came in that she was awarded the 2010 Pulitzer Prize in Music for her Violin Concerto.

This pattern for a composer is increasingly common. A position with a major orchestra guarantees a high quality and immediate performance of one's work by a great orchestra and often includes recording opportunities. Recordings are the most important venue to gain recognition, and they are easier to get and distribute through a professional orchestra.

Higdon writes with a bold, colorful style. Her music is, like much of the post-1970 era, recognizably modern yet mostly tonal. As you might suspect from the description of her career to date, much of her works are for orchestra; she has composed equally prolifically for chamber ensembles, chorus, song, and even wind ensemble.

---

example

Higdon: *CityScapes*

III. Peachtree Street

CityScapes is a set of three symphonic poems that celebrate Higdon's childhood home in Atlanta, Georgia. It is a rich, virtuosic work, demanding for the players but exhilarating in its energy. Higdon has a clearly individual voice, but there are also influences from other composers, notably Aaron Copland, who will be discussed below.

Ellen Zwilich (b. 1939): *Septet* (2009)

Ellen Zwilich was born in Miami and educated at Florida State University and the Juilliard Conservatory. She received the first Doctor of Musical Arts in composition Juilliard ever awarded to a woman. She is a fine violinist who played for seven years with the American Symphony Orchestra under its founder, Leopold Stokowski.

Her break came in 1983, when she received the Pulitzer Prize for composition for *Symphony no. 1*, which had been composed and performed by the American Composers Orchestra under Gunther Schuller the previous year. She was the first woman to win the Pulitzer in composition. The publicity from that award, and subsequent commissions and successful works, has enabled her to live, like Philip Glass, entirely from the income from her compositions—a rare state for a composer.

Her early work tends to feature heavy dissonance, angular melodies, and harsh timbral combinations. However, Zwilich has taken a path similar to many 20th-century composers, moving from dissonant and complex to simpler and more accessible (a path seen in Bartok, Hindemith, Penderecki, and others).

She has attributed this, at least partially to a personal tragedy: the death of her husband in 1979. She married Joseph Zwilich, a violinist in the Metropolitan Opera Orchestra, in the late 1960s, before entering Juilliard in 1970. He died suddenly of a heart attack during an opera performance. Her response was a reassessment of her priorities. She accedes that there has been considerable pain in the past century, but came to feel that music should also aspire to express the more beautiful, noble, and creative aspects of life.

She is thus described frequently as neoromantic. Like Shostakovich and Prokofiev (and drawing from Mahler, as had those two, along with most of the rest of 20th-century composers), Zwilich is frequently concerned with classical multimovement forms. She has written symphonies, concertos, sonatas, string quartets . . . all just like Haydn and Mozart had done (as had Prokofiev and Shostakovich). She is among America's most popular and successful composers. With Ellen Zwilich, one needs to no longer add the description "women" composers.

You have learned in this course that two kinds of chamber music ensembles are sufficiently common that their instrumentation has been standardized: the string quartet and the piano trio. Zwilich's *Septet* was written as a combination of the two. She had written for two such ensembles before (the Kalichstein-Laredo-Robinson Piano Trio and the Miami String Quartet) and had the idea to create a work that combined the two.

example

Zwilich: *Septet*

II. *Quasi una Passacaglia*

The author reviewed the Palm Beach premiere of the work for the *Palm Beach Daily News* in January of 2010:

Zwilich's style is immediately identifiable. Her music is bold, passionate, intense. She is fascinated with sound, as are these musicians, and they produce some of the most beautiful and moving combinations of sound this reviewer has heard.

The opening, Introductions, quotes earlier works for each ensemble; then gradually integrates them all into a whole. Frankly, it is never fully clear whether the work is for piano trio and string quartet or for a septet for piano and strings—every time the two ensembles start to work separately, she finds a way to integrate them in endlessly variable combinations.

The heart of the piece is in the second movement, Quasi una Passacaglia. *This was profoundly moving music; dark, suffering sounds, full of longing and pain—yet so very beautiful. It brought to mind Dmitri Shostakovich's deepest pages, if without his utter hopelessness. Games, in the spot for the scherzo, recalled the literal meaning of the term: joke. The concluding movement, Au revoir, was to convey the sense that the two groups were departing, not forever, but only for a time. Yet this parting was deeply sad, full of nostalgic recollections of their shared experiences, as earlier moments were quoted or alluded to.*

From *Palm Beach Daily News*, January 2010 by Jan Sjostrom, Staff Writer. Copyright © 2010 by Palm Beach Daily News. Reprinted by permission.

The Musical Canon

French composer Arthur Honegger once commented that the public does not really want new music. The only thing it demands of a composer is that he be dead.

One of the dilemmas of the Revolutionary Age was that, while composers fought about what direction music needed to take, many did not consult the listening public. And the result has been a disconnection between modern audiences and modern music. But people continue to make music, and once in a while, something emerges that promises to join the ranks of the musical canon.

Marcia Citron, in *Gender and the Musical Canon* (University of Illinois Press, 2000), proposed a four step process:

1. Creativity: one possesses talent and has the opportunity to develop it
2. Professionalism: one has access to the profession and gets hired in some professional position

3. Creation: one composes music
4. Reception: people listen to one's music; it gets performed, recorded, published, anthologized, and studied; not just once, but repeatedly

These two examples by Higdon and Zwilich are products of the 21st century. Zwilich's *Septet* only came out in 2009. Can either of these works be considered "classical music"? Only time will tell. But chances seem good that they will join that canon; and sooner, rather than later.

American Nationalism

"American," here, is in the restricted sense of the United States of America. There are two large American continents, the inhabitants of which are all Americans. There is a rich tapestry of music coming from Latin America, much with varying elements of nationalism (though certainly not all), and Canada has several important composers that will repay your explorations. But we will close with four figures who, to some degree, can be linked to American Nationalism.

This country took many years to establish a musical style that was not a pale imitation of European models. Apart from Gottschalk, who can hardly be accused of writing great music, no one emerged with a truly individual, and at the same time, identifiably American voice before Charles Edward Ives.

Charles Edward Ives (1874–1954): *The Fourth of July*

Charles Edward Ives was America's first great musical genius. He studied at Yale University under Horatio Parker, but his real influence was his father, George Ives. George, himself influenced by the New England Transcendentalist philosophers (figures such as Emerson and Thoreau), taught young Charles that the **substance** of music was more important than its **manner**—we would say style or technique. He also taught his son the conviction that everything in the universe is related, "from a rock to a star."

Because of this belief, Ives' music often consists of a complex interweaving of seemingly unrelated materials, which for Ives reflected the wonderful diversity of life itself. This might include quotations of folk songs and hymn tunes with which Ives had grown up—often with intentional "wrong notes," as though played by an amateur town band—against backgrounds ranging from the simplest consonance to the most intense dissonance.

George also taught his son that he "could keep his music interest stronger, cleaner, bigger, and freer if he didn't try to make a living at it." So Ives was not a professional composer, but worked (with considerable success) in the insurance business. Indeed, he was a pioneer in the life insurance industry, which he saw as an outgrowth of transcendentalist philosophy. The idea was that a community would contribute to a central pool, and individuals who got into some financial trouble, particularly a family whose primary earner had died, could draw on that pool for support.

Ives had a deep belief in the idea of "the average man." As the head of Ives & Myrick, he became a millionaire several times over, but would only keep what he felt was an average salary, after he had invested enough insurance to cover his family's needs. The rest of his earnings were either reinvested in his company or used to help finance the spread of new music: his own or that of other composers.

Charles Edward Ives. © Bettmann/Corbis.

Ives is one of the most remarkable geniuses in the history of music. His business activity prevented him from any exposure to the musical revolution that was happening in Europe and left him composing intensely during his only free time, over nights and weekends. Working in that isolation, however, Ives managed to anticipate virtually all the innovations of the first half of the 20th century (and a few of the second half), often years before they were done by anyone else.

Ives stopped composing after 1920 because of a heart attack and spent his time arranging his music into some publishable shape. It was years before he had any substantial following because his music can be quite challenging to the listener. Ives himself, however, had only contempt for those who would only listen to "nice" music, which he described as "weak, lily-livered, an armchair for the ears." He once barked at a concertgoer who was walking out of a performance of dissonant music, "Can't you take a good dissonance like a man?"

Ives received the Pulitzer Prize in 1947 for his second symphony, almost 40 years after it had been written. In typical fashion, he refused the prize, claiming, "Prizes are for boys; I'm grown up."

Ives' music is filled with references to the America in which he grew up. No matter how challenging the sounds can be—and much of his greatest music is certainly challenging—there are always recognizable tunes, whether popular songs, patriotic melodies, or hymns that were part of his New England world.

Ives composed four symphonies. The first was a project from his school days, written as a graduation project; it contains some lovely music, but no real hint of what he was to become. The second and third see his voice emerging, and the fourth is perhaps his greatest work. It is immensely complex and requires two separate conductors to keep it together.

The *Holidays Symphony* is not actually a symphony, but four symphonic poems on specifically American holidays: *Thanksgiving*, *Washington's Birthday*, *Decoration Day*, and *The Fourth of July*. It was written over a period of four years, between 1909 and 1913. In *Memos*, he describes the work:

"

It's a boy's '4th—no historical orations—no patriotic grandiloquences by "grown-ups"—no program in this yard! But he knows what he is celebrating—better than most of the county politicians. And he goes at it in his own way, with a patriotism nearer kin to nature than jingoism. His festivities start in quiet of the midnight before, and grow raucous with the sun. Everybody knows what it's like—if everybody doesn't—cornets, strings around big toes, torpedoes, church bells, lost finger, fifes, clam chowder, a prize-fight, drum-corps, burnt shins, parades (in and out of step), saloons all closed (more drunks than usual), baseball game (Danbury All-Stars vs. Beaver Brook Boys), the sky-rocket over the Church steeple, just after the annual explosion sets the Town Hall on fire. All this is not music—not now.

"

example

Ives: *Holidays Symphony*

III. *The Fourth of July*

Aaron Copland (1900–1990)

Ives wouldn't approve, but we'll now move to some "nice" music. Aaron Copland was born to Russian Jewish immigrant parents in Brooklyn, New York. He studied in Paris from 1921 to 1923 with one of the century's most remarkable composition teachers, **Nadia Boulanger**, a woman who would become mentor to a long series of American composers.

Nadia Boulanger (1887–1979) was a French professor of music theory who came to believe that her mission was to teach aspiring American composers how to master their craft. Her sister, **Lili Boulanger** (1893–1914), had immense gifts as a composer, but her life was cut tragically short by Chron's disease, and only a few works survive.

Nadia adored her younger sister, and never felt that her compositional efforts could compare, but she was gifted as a teacher—among the greatest of her or any time. A list of her students who have appeared in *Grove's Dictionary of Music and Musicians*, the most important English-language reference work in music, runs to almost 150 names. Included in that list are Copland, Philip Glass, Eliot Carter, and Quincy Jones, among many others.

What immediately stands out about Boulanger's list of students is how different they all are. She did not believe in teaching her students all to compose the same way, but could bring out each student's individual genius and allow it to reach its full potential. She shares this quality with another great composition teacher, Arnold Schoenberg.

Like Hindemith, Copland's early work was strongly dissonant. After the first performance of his *Symphony for Organ and Orchestra*, the conductor turned to the audience and announced that "if a young man at the age of 23 can write a symphony like that, in five years he will be ready to commit murder." Copland took the comment as a compliment.

As time went on, however, Copland came to the belief that his music needed to appeal to a broader spectrum of audience, to become more accessible to the common man. Like many Russian Jewish immigrants, he was a strong Marxist—the Tsars had made persecution of the Jews something of a national sport for centuries, and that community initially was delighted to see the Soviet Revolution topple their reign. Copland's change of style was not intended to make his music more profitable, but to make it more relevant to the proletariat.

During the 1930s and early 1940s, Copland infused his music with the essence of American folk styles. Not surprisingly, his most popular work comes from this period, including a remarkable series of ballets for the Martha Graham Dance Company: *Rodeo*, *Billy the Kid*, and *Appalachian Spring*.

Appalachian Spring was written in 1944. It dances the story of a young couple moving into a community in western Pennsylvania in the 19th century. As the scene opens, to music that will recur at the end of the ballet, the sun is rising, and the various players are revealed, motionless. Once all is lit, the first dance bursts to life. The loose tale includes dances between the newlyweds, square dancing, and a sermon by a revivalist preacher.

Copland: *Appalachian Spring*

The original score was for a chamber ensemble of 13 instruments, but Copland later excerpted the most interesting music in a suite, arranged for full orchestra. The closing number is a set of variations on an old Shaker hymn, "Simple Gifts," followed by a return of the opening music for a blissfully serene close.

George Gershwin (1898–1937)

With George Gershwin, we confront the increasingly evident divide between "classical" and "popular" music: it is not a product of the years of Rock 'n' Roll, but predates that to the early part of the century. Gershwin was not trained as a classical musician. He initially thought classical music was just for sissies, obviously never having met Charles Ives. He made his living on Tin Pan Alley, home to a number of composers of popular songs and musicals. Those figures ranged from marginally skilled hacks to near geniuses, and Gershwin was certainly close to their finest.

figure 12.2

But as he matured, he gained new respect for the western artistic heritage and developed his dream for which he is now best known. In his own words, he wanted to "make a lady out of jazz," to synthesize aspects of American popular music (which at this time was jazz) and classical styles and forms. His finest works are in this vein: *Rhapsody in Blue*, *Piano Concerto in F*, and *Porgy and Bess*.

Gershwin called *Porgy* a "folk opera," a distinction that doesn't exist. Some think it is a musical comedy; but if so, it is on a much higher plane artistically than nearly any such work at that time. Others believe it is a full opera, one of the greatest and most moving ever produced by an American at that point in history.

George Gershwin. Library of Congress, Prints and Photographs Division, Bain Collection, Reproduction Number: LC-USZ62-60866.

The story is set in Charleston, South Carolina, and the African-American community there. It emerges from an era of deep prejudice and stands out in that it is one of the earliest works to focus on that community and to set it sympathetically and seriously. White characters exist, but are almost irrelevant. The crippled Porgy loves Bess and is attempting to get her away from her destructive, drug-dealing boyfriend, Sportin' Life.

example

Gershwin: *Porgy and Bess*

Overture; Summertime

Leonard Bernstein (1918–1990)

Bernstein is one of the century's most important musicians. He was not only a composer, but a conductor, teacher, writer, philosopher, and pianist. He is perhaps best known for his conducting: he took over the New York Philharmonic in 1943, and he has been a frequent guest conductor for nearly all the world's greatest orchestras.

As a teacher/philosopher, his impact has been immense. He is both highly articulate and charismatic, and his public presentations are legendary. These range from the series of Young People's Concerts, that were responsible for introducing a generation to classical music, to the Norton Lectures at Harvard, where he presented a linguistic analysis of the musical experience based on the work of Noam Chomsky.

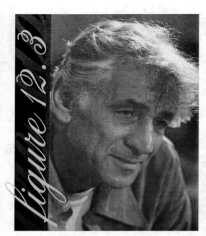

Leonard Bernstein. Library of Congress, Prints and Photographs Division, U.S. News and World Report Magazine Collection, Reproduction Number: LC-DIG-PPMSC-0325.

Then there are his compositions. His works range from serial compositions to Broadway musicals, from solo piano works and songs to operas, symphonies, and sacred choral works. Perhaps his most famous work is *West Side Story*. Even more so than Gershwin's *Porgy and Bess*, this musical transcends the limits of Broadway-style entertainment. It presents a story of deep pathos.

West Side Story was conceived as a modern retelling of Shakespeare's *Romeo and Juliet*. Less widely known is the fact that when Bernstein and librettist Steven Sondheim originally discussed the work, it was to be the story of a doomed romance between an Italian Catholic boy and a Jewish girl, to be called *East Side Story*. Both men's careers took them in different directions, and when they returned to the project, New York City had seen the arrival of a large number of people from Puerto Rico. The tension between the newly arrived Hispanics and the older residents was considered more timely, so they moved the setting across town, and *West Side Story* was born.

In 1970, Bernstein wrote a setting of the Roman Catholic Mass. The question may arise, what's a nice Jewish boy doing writing a Mass?

The short answer is that he was paid to do so: it was written for the opening of the Kennedy Center in Washington in 1970, commissioned by the late president's widow (Bernstein had been friends with the Kennedy family). But this was not just a project for payment. It touched on something deeply meaningful to Bernstein: the struggle and the need to believe in God.

The full title may offer more explanation: *A theater piece for singers, players, and dancers. Text from the liturgy of the Roman Church with additional texts by Steven Schwartz and Leonard Bernstein.* That "additional text" is the key. Just as he had argued with God in his earlier *Symphony no. 3, Kaddish*, he continues his questioning here. But ultimately, he finds hope and redemption. Along the way, Bernstein mixes musical styles ranging from the classical avant-garde to romanticism, to folk music, to jazz, blues, and rock, to traditional liturgical styles. The journey is harrowing and exhilarating.

Mass opens as do all Masses, with the *Kyrie eleison, Christe eleison*. The music begins with quadrophonic (the precursor to surround sound) tape of percussion sounds, run from speakers in the four corners of the auditorium. In each of the four corners are singers: in one a bass, then a soprano, then a tenor and mezzo soprano, and a mezzo soprano and alto in the final corner. Each individual or pair of singers is in a different key, meter, and tempo, as they all intone the Greek text.

The music reaches a chaotic level, at which point the dissonance is wiped out by a major chord on an electric guitar, played by the celebrant. The celebrant, played by a young man in his early 20s, dressed in blue jeans and a simple shirt, then sings the opening hymn, *A Simple Song*.

example

Bernstein, *Mass: Kyrie and Hymn*

Conclusion

It's been quite a journey. If you came to this course with no formal musical knowledge, you have now acquired a strong foundation and have lots more to discover. Even if you had a strong background, you probably discovered some things of value along the way . . . and, likewise, have found much more that you can explore further.

And it is the music itself that is the prize. You may well have already forgotten the different parts that make up a Baroque *concerto grosso* . . . but if you remember Bach's *Brandenburg Concertos* or Vivaldi's *The Four Seasons*, you will have earned something worthwhile from this course.

One final observation—civilizations make their mark in history by two things: what they create and what they destroy. That which lives after a culture has passed from dominance is their artistic heritage: paintings, sculpture, architecture, literature, and music. The story of their military conquests, both whom they conquer and who conquers them, also outlives the culture. What was bought and sold is lost to the ages.

You have just completed a course devoted to understanding, studying, and celebrating that which is creative in human culture. You are richer for that.

Glossary

Canon: in the context of the arts, the set of works that have stood the test of time, outgrowing the audience for which they were initially intended, and continue to interest and enrich future audiences

Jazz: American popular music of the earlier part of the 20th century; characterized by syncopated rhythms, swing time, blue notes, and a particular importance to the saxophone; George Gershwin achieved a synthesis of jazz and classical compositional techniques

Nadia Boulanger: French composition teacher of the Revolutionary Age, who taught scores of influential American composers

Postminimalism: used to describe music that is clearly influenced by minimalist compositional practices, but uses material too well developed and complex for the simplicity inherent in pure minimalism

Transcendentalism: American philosophical school, with Emerson and Thoreau as prominent members, that emphasized both self-reliance and the interdependence of all of existence; very influential on Charles Ives

Reference

Kirkpatrick, John, ed. *Charles E. Ives: Memos*. New York: W.W. Norton; 1991, 104.

Tear-Out No. 4

Identify the following musical examples as music of the Renaissance, the Baroque, the Classical Period, the Romantic Period, or the Revolutionary Age.

1. _____

2. _____

3. _____

4. _____

5. _____

The information in these tables may help you:

	RENAISSANCE	BAROQUE
Rhythm	Gentle, often asymmetrical	Driving, powerful
Major solo instrument	Lute	Harpsichord or organ
Vocal music	Mostly *a cappella*, or unaccompanied	Usually with contrasting instrumental accompaniment
Instrumental music	Mostly dance music, without *basso continuo*	Fugue, *concerto grosso*, *solo concerto*, always with *basso continuo*
Aesthetic ideal	A homogenous blend of equal sounds	A celebration of contrasting sound, intensity of emotion

	CLASSICAL	ROMANTIC	REVOLUTIONARY
Harmony	Simple, clear, and balanced	More intentionally dissonant, varied	Can be highly dissonant or even silent
Orchestra	Smaller, lighter	Expands, adds extra instruments like trombones and harps	Often small, with unusual instruments
Melodies	Regular phrases, tuneful and simple	Longer, more complex phrases, richer harmony	Intentionally *not* lyric, wide and angular leaps
Instrumental music	Sonata cycle works: symphony, string quartet, sonata	Program music, form determined by program rather than preexisting outline	Increasing use of unusual combinations of instruments
Aesthetic ideal	Balance, clarity, emotion contained in form	Individuality, creativity, emotion, freedom	A challenge to traditionally accepted notions of what is desirable in music